T0197357

GOD
—AND THE—
SYSTEM

GOD
—AND THE—
SYSTEM

Anthology of Thoughts

DR. FERIDOUN SHAWN SHAHMORADIAN

iUniverse®

GOD AND THE SYSTEM
ANTHOLOGY OF THOUGHTS

THE HOLY BIBLE, NEW INTERNATIONAL VERSION®, NIV® Copyright © 1973, 1978, 1984, 2011 by Biblica, Inc.® Used by permission. All rights reserved worldwide.

iUniverse books may be ordered through booksellers or by contacting:

iUniverse
1663 Liberty Drive
Bloomington, IN 47403
www.iuniverse.com
1-800-Authors (1-800-288-4677)

Because of the dynamic nature of the Internet, any web addresses or links contained in this book may have changed since publication and may no longer be valid. The views expressed in this work are solely those of the author and do not necessarily reflect the views of the publisher, and the publisher hereby disclaims any responsibility for them.

Any people depicted in stock imagery provided by Thinkstock are models, and such images are being used for illustrative purposes only.
Certain stock imagery © Thinkstock.

ISBN: 978-1-5320-2793-2 (sc)
ISBN: 978-1-5320-2794-9 (e)

Library of Congress Control Number: 2017910885

Print information available on the last page.

iUniverse rev. date: 07/12/2017

In the name of the Omni potent, Omni present, Omni temporal, and the Omniscient God.
The most merciful, the most gracious, and the most compassionate.
The proprietor of patience, time, space and beyond.
The fiduciary of all there is and the nonexistence
In the name of the almighty God.

A SYSTEM CAN BE COMPRISED OF an array of orderly groups with detailed methods, structures, and actions intended to cause a specific activity, perform a task, or solve a problem. A system can be organized consisting of certain links and correlated elements (ordinances, parts, entities, agents, members, etc.). These basic units, with which the system is methodically built, continually influence one another (directly or indirectly), driven to keep their activities and the existence of the system intact to achieve its objectives.

Many different parts applicable to a system should work in concert coherently to attain the particular system's overall objective. For example, the human body is a biological system composed of different parts that work uniformly; other examples include bee colonies, ant colonies, nature, galaxies, or the solar system. Speaking on the solar system and how gravity should indicate an ultimate system, Sir Isaac Newton once said, "gravity may put the planets into motion, it could never put them into such a circulating motion as they have about the sun; and therefore, for this as well as other reasons, I am compelled to ascribe the frame of this system to an intelligent agent."

At present, certain government systems are currently acting in conjunction with powerful transnational corporation empires (aristocratic and political division); however, their union causes harm for the sake of maximizing profit and power, where political corruption and the underlying dark heart of greed is evident in so many mishaps. Instead, democratic governments should effectively serve the citizens who helped put them in power, rather than to mislead and become complicit in the afflictions of the mighty rich, dealing in connivance with misdeeds for the wealthy elites against the people. These actions give meaning to the proverb "no good deed goes unpunished" or "eaten bread is soon forgotten."

The ruling system is obligated to mandate positive plans and induce productive programs to make the entire governing body run smoothly and to meet the inhabitants' needs to the best of system's ability. No one should be discriminated against, pushed aside, or left behind, as hope for surpassing standards of living ought to become contagious and truly practical. since the care of human life and welfare, and not their demise, is the primary and only object of good government.

The global systems of governing should act in collaboration and maintain responsible actions to nourish planet Earth and foster its inhabitants. Any governing system should definitely encourage the prevalence of an enlightening culture and constructively permeate the environmental and socioeconomic atmosphere through wise operations to procure (obtain) eminency (notoriety, renown) through concerted effort to create an educational system with quality skills and worthy training agendas and to modulate (attune, harmonize) positive programs in elevating knowledge conducive to human nature for the common good and better living standards.

The system is well aware that people are influenced by their surroundings and conform to what they are taught, which makes sense and should relate to the natural world. After all, aren't we all relatively the products of our habitat? Hence, it is imperative for any reliable and trustworthy system of government to manifest an awakening cultural revolution and to integrally introduce a pleasant learning atmosphere vehicle fortified with dynamic schooling and robust tutelage programs to save people from the clutches of ignorance.

We should not refute that humans are relatively selfish and undeniably social; any progressive culture needs to tilt toward

2

behaving socially and identifying with collective activities, rather than emphatically portraying individual success at the expense of others, where financial icons are glamorized and rewarded for self-interest quirks (mannerism, idiosyncrasy) to further isolate people and polarize classes. This type of division has resulted in extreme income inequality; people should not have to die to live, struggling for employment, food, and shelter, fighting for the basic necessities of life to keep them afloat. Billions face devastating conditions just to survive. This is not how living should be. There are serious flaws in the allocation of resources and grave wrongdoings in how humanity needs to be treated. It seems that justice is managed by force and by the power of guns. I wonder if God has anything to do with it?

Human beings are an intelligence species. We are capable of wisdom and compassion. We irrefutably can become emotionally attached with love and by devotion. We are curious, hopeful, and imaginative. We seek truth, knowledge, and justice. We are thoughtful, with ideas and dreams. We are also affected by good and unpleasant memories and much more. But this does not mean we cannot become mentally overpowered by others. Some in positions of power have greater access to educational resources and can render us into submission to do as we are told, as if we are in a trance. The world becomes ugly when people are manipulated to comply with agendas against their self-interests. We often accept irrational plans masterfully designed to exploit us as commodities, aiming at empowering the rich elites into master-slave relations as they undermine and yoke the populace. They have financially dominated the rest of society; instead, we should opt out of schemes and programs intended to enslave and demoralize us as a proud society.

The rich elites have the means to hire the most intelligent individuals, employ experienced advisors and planners, including adept psychologists, psychiatrists, neurologists, anthropologists, sociologists, economists, statisticians, talented executive procurators (i.e., agents), masters of public affairs, philosophers, professional business-minded men and women, biologists, chemists, physicists, and geologists. They buy off legal political advisors, politicians, lobbyists, judges, attorneys, counselors, skillful negotiators, experienced mediators, law enforcement authorities, prosecutors, detectives, spies, military and combative advisors, journalists, and news broadcasters. They pay off conglomerate commercially driven social medias with lucrative salaries rendered to thousands and thousands of contemporary social scientists, surgeons, doctors, pathologists, pharmacists, pharmaceutical sales representatives, meteorologists, and so forth. Many would not hesitate to vote contrary to the truth and in opposition to what is right, so that they might uphold the interest of the influential elites and further preserve the status quo. This has leveraged a plutocracy government to desensitize masses of people to what should matter in socioeconomic and geopolitical discourse.

We should know that social and economic dynamics will not change when we are apt (prone) to act in a perfunctory (mechanical, lacking interest) manner and in doing business as usual, which unless the oppositions become as mentally competitive to challenge the mind of global capitalists that are well rounded in tactics and strategy and often with oozing intelligence to stick together, despite their showy disagreement on radical issues. Moreover, the corporate capitalists are backed by the state, which is empowered through military, police force, and its affiliated agencies in making a just society impossible. And unless the reactionary forces stick together and become equipped with equal, if not better, might, they will not overcome. It is like games of chess, and like superb poker players, the winners must rely on mind-power and experience to win and reach their goals. And let's not forget that since the inception of capitalism, workers have frequently resisted against the wage system, either by sporadic efforts or through unionized face-offs, demanding part of the profits and even, to some extent, making publically owned business enterprises a reality.

It is also important to reject outdated thoughts and credences (assents, beliefs, credibility) that are in disharmony with today's time parameter and contrary to modern lifestyle because they stoke (stir up, spur to action) them to protect the interest of those in power, which regrettably inflict much harm on the entire nation and sometimes threaten to annihilate the whole world. But then, has it crossed your mind why we think the way we do? Do the standards of how to behave, the way we learn to comply with life, the culture we follow, where we are born and raised have anything to do with our fate?

Do we pay any attention to who sets and influences our ethos, criteria, social norms, and the modi operandi, customs, agendas, modes, rules and regulations, and the overall concepts of the sociocultural yardstick, and social welfare? By the way, who are those inconspicuous elements behind powerful propaganda machines that are untouchable because they are not in the public eye and impossible to reach? Ironically, we relate to them as we subconsciously follow up with daily agendas in which the norms are constituted as they are reiterated. Because they set the standards and lay out the entire sociocultural foundations and institute economic rules of engagement, which significantly affect consumers and the way people think. Are the social norms, cultural stigmas, taboos, and tenets that we follow or the forbidden doctrines we reject correctly disapprove or are they justifiably accepted? Are the issues we cherish or those we avoid conduit to make any sense? Most dogmas are probably the reason for our declivities.

Should we not think that some traditional matters are bombastic (pompous, overblown) and backward? Which, if not practiced, they couldn't have left much dire and apprehensive effects on our lives? Or do we not care whose interest is really served when most of us blindly accept and follow so much nonsense that I am afraid is safeguarded and preached as fact, as the financial elites and colonial powers control and render public opinion obsolete, and in making sure the victims give up believing in themselves, while many corporations keep up with the octopus of bigotry, lying, cheating, stealing, deceiving, fraud, bribery, killings, and in executing every other prohibited biblical injunctions as the good book advises against corruption and as it instructs against any wrongdoing and prohibits misdeeds.

Why should wise and civilized people with so much experience and plenty of information fall trap into jarring (out of harmony) and manufactured methodology with myth-driven maneuvers that are structurally designed against ramshackle (ropey, vicious, rundown) people and irrationally mold them into submissive behaviors through azoic (not animated, deaden) logic, making them careless and irrelevant to the harsh reality they endure.

Where the system gradually purges people from their true identities, contaminating their spirit with premeditated toxic agendas tailored to make them complacent and passive, this often results in so many seeing themselves as incompetent and unworthy of reaching their dreams and even ashamed of who they are, regarding themselves as failures. The system misleads and psychologically entraps people, where the victims misconstrue the real reason behind the actual causes of socioeconomic problems, which globally impacts billions for worse. Citizens are discouraged from unitedly raising their voice and expressing their grievances, as the system manipulates them into submissive behavior and permeates the culture structured to render people incompetent, and in making them unconcerned or to break those that are not in compliance with the system, they are adamant to nullify reactionaries and deliver chivalrous critics despondent or choke-off any legit uprising directed at the system.

Here is what Henry Wallace said about fascism in America: "The dangerous American fascist is the man who wants to do in the United States in an American way what Hitler did in Germany in a Prussian way. The American fascist would prefer not to use violence. His method is to poison the channels of public information. With a fascist the problem is never how best to present the truth to the public but how best to use the news to deceive the public into giving the fascist and his group more money or more power

If we define an American fascist as one who in case of conflict puts money and power ahead of human beings, then there are undoubtedly several million fascists in the United States. There are probably several hundred thousand if we narrow the definition to include only those who in their search for money and power are ruthless and deceitful. Most American fascists are enthusiastically supporting the war effort."

"The Danger of American Fascism," in The New York Times, April 9, 1944, quoted in Democracy Reborn (New York, 1944) p. 259. He then went on to say that the American fascists are most easily recognized by their deliberate perversion of truth and fact. Their newspapers and propaganda carefully cultivate every fissure (narrow opening) of disunity, every crack in the common front against fascism.

What I am alluding to is that societies must not give in to dull and cluttering ideas, which often are purposefully designed to stop open-mindedness and meant to impede enlightenment. Where cognitive abilities and mentally progressive notions are derailed from potentiating a merit based lifestyle and can create a dictatorial environment in any society and make fascism alive to present a recipe for cultural and socioeconomic disaster. Therefore, citizens ought be vigilant in noticing autocratic steps that might initially start as quiet as cat steps, but eventually turn into a rowdy beast devouring its victims, without empathy and with no control.

Where the populace must further be awakened to systematized main stream media outlets that simply brush aside the truth and rig information brainwashing its victims. The corporate media has relied on lies and embarked on formidable techniques to violate the sanctity of what is decent and continue with trickery to misinform its prey.

It is imperative that we do not fall trape into cognative dissonancy (disharmony, cacophony, discordanance) which can sometime manifest irraprable damages, since what we do not know, it can capture our thought process, and subtly creep into our mind as facts, and be perceived as reality, which can hurt us, and might radically change the course of our life for worse. We are emotional beings, and sometimes what we think makes sense, and perhaps is rendered as fact, cannot be further from the truth, as it can play us wrong. Our feelings and emotions can play a bias role, and influence our sense of reasoning and logic, especially if our critical thinking is not honed and sharpened.

We are not born with wisdom to readily access inference, and instinctually exhibit ratiocination (reasoning power) this must be challenged, and learned throughout our life. We become fairly equipped with right thinking leveraged by education, and sweet and sour experiences, and through many trial and errors; which will eventually help us to become relatively insightful, and perhaps able to distinguish datum (given, verity, truth) from fiction.

Remember what you perceive to be as fact, it might been distorted in your subconscious mind, and already out of shape, infected by grudge holding feelings, and bitter emotions, exaggerated with what you are inclined and like to believe.

It is not an over statement to say human brain occasionally does foible (minor flaws, quirk) and our perception could often be incorrect. Our sensory processing unit can cause optical illusion, and attention- blindness, with erratic assumptions and many other scientifically known ailment which make attention deficit disorder possible, making our comprehension wrong. Hence distancing, and depriving us further away from the reality.

We should not deny our brain shortcomings that could lead us to miscalculation, and in making it difficult to reach appropriate result, also it is wise to notice that: Misinformation, not enough facts, fabricated news, skewed judgments, emotions and biased feelings, dubious source relinquishing humbugs (phony, nonsense) and lies, hasty judiciousness and execution, and perhaps not enlightened enough about the reality, along with so many other decisive factors, which can make our decision depleted of a proper judgment; lacking sensible argument forcing many people to behave irrational, and not able to retain a correct and feasible conclusion.

Remember, the system, the ruling parties, and business elites are the ones with power because they hold the entire resources; it is at their discretion to either allocate funds to edify (furnish knowledge, illuminate) people or deny distributing money toward educating the public. They know awakened societies are not easily fooled, which makes it difficult for the magnates (tycoons) to sell their troubling plans devised to torpedo people's social and economic status. The imperial capitalists know it will take an epic battle to deceive knowledgeable citizens into submission; they realize when faced with an awakened society it demands cat-like moves to gradually creep and materialize insane plans and strategies for coup d'etat to manifest a catastrophic idea, often through bloodshed, which sometimes is too late to embark on an abiding (incorruptible) solution to overcome a frenzy situation facing people. The ultra-rich often sacrifice values and undermine their principals for aspiration to maximize wealth and prestige.

For instance, legal authorities interrupting the rule of law will not move the illiterate citizens to challenge the menacing governors or ombudsman(government official.) Since the rich 1% label any nonconformity with treachery, they can target individuals as quislings (apostates, defectors, deserters, and malediction.) They control the media and influence the press to accordingly befit and benefit them as they wish. In many cases, they manufacture lies and make treble images of dissidents, which then makes the opposition easy prey, open to trumped-up charges, arbitrary indictment, making them vulnerable to imprisonment, torturing, and long sentencing without due process of the law.

They enhance credibility where they see fit and discredit justice when it is not favoring them. They fable history, as they conjure (solicit, invoke, mention) terrifying images of internal and external enemies to make fear rule the day and mar whomever is not aligned with their vicious policies. They establish mobsters and thugs to harass citizens and eventually aim at instituting a gulag fascism (labor camp) system, like in Russia, to make certain that democracy gives in to apprehension, where freedom is mocked and questions of human rights are answered by the power of gun; then of course truth offends the hypocrites.

Think of how it all started. As George Carlin says, "America was founded by slave owners who informed us, 'All men are created equal.' All men, except Indians, niggers, and women. Remember, the founders were a small group of unelected, white, male, land-holding slave owners who also, by the way, suggested their class be the only one allowed to vote. To my mind, that is what's known as being stunningly—and embarrassingly—full of shit."

People are not even safe in many faith gatherings and worship assemblies, as believers are bombarded with a hodgepodge of lectures, which are often stupefying and irrationally sermonized, giving the impression that troubles facing humankind are all metaphysical and must be resolved through praying, as if we have a demonic God fired up for vengeance against humanity. And millions blindly follow forged blueprints on how they should pay homage to God, without thinking twice, like blinds leading blinds. And most of what is delivered has no reasoning power and in truth discredits God, religion, and humanity with no remorse. Professing that other religions, other races and nationalities are the actual culprits and the real troublemakers is meant to divide billions of retainers and to cause trouble and harm.

Many followers sightlessly act sacrilege and behave prejudice against others, claiming their faith is superior, as if they see and hear God praise certain denominations or value particular creeds designated as being comparably prominent, and hence should be preferred. Is it not charlatanism to claim such? They con people, like the faithful are unconscious or dazed.

> Difference of opinion is advantageous in religion. The several sects perform the office of a censor morum over each other. Is uniformity attainable? Millions of innocent men, women, and children, since the introduction of Christianity, have been burnt, tortured, fined, imprisoned; yet we have not advanced one inch toward uniformity. What has been the effect of coercion? To make one half the world fools, and the other half hypocrites. To support roguery and error all over the earth. Let us reflect that it is inhabited by a thousand millions of people. That these profess probably a thousand different systems of religion. That ours is but one of that thousand. That if there be but one right, and ours that one, we should wish to see the 999 wandering sects gathered into the fold of truth. But against such a majority we cannot effect this by force. Reason and persuasion are the only practicable instruments. To make way for these, free enquiry must be indulged; and how can we wish others to indulge it while we refuse it ourselves. — Thomas Jefferson, Notes on the State of Virginia

The problem worsens when deceivers push to convince followers that unless they do what is preached, they have sinned and are peccant (sinful) and will end up in hell, burning through eternity and devoured by several-headed firing dragons, but if they comply, the heaven above will await them with enormous rewards beyond anyone's imagination.

They refuse that good prophets of God symbolized hell and heaven, denoting punishments and rewards to mandate accountability and enlighten people that no good deed goes unnoticed. Those with empathy and mercy will be rewarded and those who do evil will justly be punished in one way or another, and one's kindness and humanity will vibrate back to them and vice-versa, reiterating the expression that "what comes around goes around." It is the 21st century and oddly to our astonishment there are those who still say God's revelation was for them to collect funds and to follow instructions on gathering money, or when religious quacks (fake, fraud) claim they can heal chronically ill worshipers as they touch them—not only a ridiculous claim, but doubtful and infuriating beyond belief.

They are naïve enough not to understand how vast and infinite the creator of universe and the almighty God really is in dimensions unimaginable to man and utterly indecipherable to our human minds. And when they are questioned on the validity of their irrational acts, they either deny the truth or simply brush the questioner off, by saying it is the "placebo effect" that can probably cure the patients and the victims of their fraudulent behaviors. Placebo effect is the beneficial effect generated by a placebo medicine or cure that cannot be explained to the properties of the placebo itself and must therefore occur because of the patient's belief in the treatment. They take advantage of believers when they are weak and most vulnerable to their pseudo-religious conduct. I wonder if God has anything to do with it.

We need not be duped into believing a God with an address, where the creator of the heavens and earth is beyond time and space, and our God is not spatiotemporal. The omnipresent God is ubiquitous and past what we can imagine. We should seek God in our heart, in our mind, in our soul and spirit; we should search for God in what is just and divine, rather than listening to deep pocket phonies preaching a material God.

God is the silent voice within you, behind every nuance of existence. God is beyond the infinite universe. God is not matter, as "positivism doctrine" and other beliefs so naively utter: "I must see God to believe it." God is the silence pulsation and the rhythmic throbbing that you experience, making you feel alive. God is the unseen thoughts and invisible memories, in which one can experience the effects, literally impossible to live without. God is in your well-founded courage to protect the innocent and defend the helpless. God is when telling the truth sets you free, when you long for peace and tranquility, and eminence against injustice, where you do everything in your power to set others free.

God is the oxygen circulating through your veins. God is your faith. God is your good conscious, your kind behavior. God is the cosmic energy that permeates all beings and percolates everything in existence. If God could be seen, then God would have descended to our physical level. God is the infinite spirit beyond the mind of the universe, and we are so lucky to be the proprietor of a single drop of this holy soul. Bear in mind that no manufacturer can be seen in what one created and has manufactured, but one's marvel can be noticed from what is the essence of one's artifact.

One feels God when being enlightened, considered, compassionate, and when in love; you sense God when you empathize and feel for others in need. It is when one is strengthened with faith and acts hopeful despite difficulties, as one sacrifices, forgives, and believes in piety and patience. One feels the presence of God when one is philanthropically active, as one notices God, when one passionately tries to save lives.

Your ingenuity, intelligence, and talent, your dreams and desires, seeking truth, fighting for freedom, democracy, equity, justice, and peace are all reflections of God within you. Only then will you feel God, as one sees no choice but to practice one's higher self, where the spirit of goodness directs you to do no evil and become pleasantly righteous in all that you do. It is then, when you are in a realm engulfed with the spirit of the almighty God, the omnipotent, omniscient, and omnipresent father, so accorded with infinite silence of the almighty God within you.

Do not fall trap to the world of the blind leading the blind, as some people stand their dogmatic ground like an "empty walnut shell with no kernel" and claim, why believe in something that one cannot see? Which pushes them to the brink of being delusional in their belief and deprived of any adequate reasoning. It makes them obscure and despondent. They do not realize that "ideas are the origin and cause to all matters, since thought are energy driven, and because matter disappears, as matter is never stable to rely on."

Some unduly try to mimic and build an artificial human brain in laboratories, practically an attempt in vain, not knowing their effort would be futile. Since our human brain comes with a super complex software called the "mind" that is inseparable from the cosmic

12

programming, potentiated to conquer the universe, and is linked to cosmic energy, which has rendered sanctuary to humankind and enabled humanity to reach the heaven above.

Unfathomable. It is an EXTRATERRESTRIAL and metaphysical domain that rejects making brain hardware manufactured by mortals beyond our limited senses. It is the world of unseen that surreptitiously maneuvers the quantum world, the world of string theory, and the world of subatomic particles, where even the most complex telescopes and advanced magnifiers are not as efficient as they need to be to reveal the magic that lies in the heavens above, as its magnanimity should be appreciated.

It is about the prevalent sacred energy, the electromagnetic forces, the gravity, and the small and big atomic forces that are so potent, and not visible, which we take for granted. it is the work of the unseen energy that fuels everything that we do via the internet, cellphones, digital gadgets, PS, computers, TVs and satellite, radars, and so many other things, such as x-rays, scans, MRIs, medical technology influenced by the undetected energy, making our lives healthier and much easier.

It is all about the unperceived world that orchestrates and rules the world we see; it is all about the supernatural and metaphysical world that God permits and reveals incrementally through the might of man. It is all about the almighty God, which some credulously choose not to see; it is all about our prevalent God, a God that does not wait in hell to punish us or expect to reward us in heaven. It is all about our creator with no address, as everything and everywhere and all that we can ever see, feel, or imagine should acknowledge the presence of God.

> Astronomers now find they have painted themselves into a corner because they have proven, by their own methods, that the world began abruptly in an act of creation to which you can trace the seeds of every star, every planet, every living thing in this cosmos and on the earth. And they have found that all this happened as a product of forces they cannot hope to discover. ... That there are what I or anyone would call supernatural forces at work is now, I think, a scientifically proven

fact." — Robert Jastrow, astronomer, physicist, and founder of NASA's Goddard Institute of Space Studies

Confucius said, "Real knowledge is to know the extent of one's ignorance." There is much truth in what Confucius said, which can probably help many not to be conceited—at least as it evolves around our actions and in what we credence as truth. For one, we have become lopsided believing in the self so much, and I might add unreasonably emphatic in self-adequacy, that we have forgotten about who actually is in command.

We must stop this sham, this counterfeit claim to humanity. We need to simply overcome our silly pride in praising and glorifying such noble titles. It simply does not befit us because, when acting beastly, which so many often do, they simply shouldn't be adjudicated with being called human and honored with such grace because humanity is scared. It is a right made in the image of God. Where ground for prejudices should apply to unduly conducts and inhumane behaviors.

"Rejoice with those who rejoice" is paired with "mourn with those who mourn" in Rom. 12:15. Even more interesting is what follows: "Live in harmony with one another. Do not be proud. Do not be conceited." (v.16) "Be careful to do what is right in the eyes of everyone." (v.17) "If it is possible, as far as it depends on you, live at peace with everyone" (v.18.)

I do not mean to be sarcastic or to make a mockery of our human spirit or denounce that we all are potentiated to act virtuously, but it perplexes me that we do not make the all-out effort to explore one's heavenly attributes from a young age and not leave anyone's fate to chance or leave them unattended without expert guidance and professional help. Why should we expose newborns to the ill will of harsh and undesirable environments, which would impact one's character for the worse and most vulnerable to ugly traits, since it can manifest ambiguity in who is who, where so many lack human qualities, as they fictitiously carry the name human because they look like one.

We should not need expert sociologists, professional anthropologists, psychologists, or require psychiatrists or neurologists, and experienced statisticians, or skillful economists to tell us we are overpopulated, and divided into a world of private opulence, and they have—not public, since the majority of the global population simply lacks the means in upbringing their children right and to properly educate and train them to become productive members of society, not to exclude requiring necessary funds, compounded with deficiencies in skills, and the expertise for correctly managing their children's welfares. Billions of parents are deprived of talents to adequately raise their kids and are incompetent to meet the adequate requirements and huge responsibilities to guide and to properly support them because having kids is an exponentially great task, which should not be toyed with. New generations are those who must carry the torch of living for reaching its destiny. Then of course there are other tragic and harsh realities to humans, like when so many unexpectedly lose their parents because of accidents, illness, divorce, and hundreds of other maladies, and trouble-oriented situations, leaving millions of children unprotected, which denies them decent lives and often, at a young age, where they become orphans and vulnerable to fall into the wrong hands and at the mercy of child predators or trapped in dealing with hardcore criminals, and so forth.

We need to be reminded that the system's creativity and the system's professional planning and assistance is most definitely required to appropriately deal with the intricacies of children's apprenticeship (instruction, tutelage, pedagogy) since so many couples should themselves become abecedarian (one learning the rudimentary of) productive livings and be enlightened with managing their own lives first before they should respectively learn about planned parenthood and taking on having babies. So many children are not in any way safe to stay with their biological parents. I am afraid that the family environment has become unsuitable and more perilous for kids, as national news and global statistics in child abuse, murder, and even incest testify to despicable facts stemming out of family violence.

We are dealing with decisive human issues, in which we need to constructively challenge the benchmarks open-mindedly for the next generation, and without categorizing such imperative duty into private and public endeavors, where first-, second-, and third-class mindsets should privilege some to excel and desert the majority of children. They are left behind, entangled with mediocrity, as they are obsolete in their blinded efforts for literacy and in hoping for a better future. The system must start paying attention to the reasons behind mushrooming crimes and worsening violence, as millions of troubled juveniles are integrated into already malfunctioned and ill cultural atmospheres, struggling to survive through corrupted sociocultural and abusive socioeconomic environments.

Let's bear in mind that we are "trainable animals" with thinking and learning abilities. We can relatively adapt to different circumstances. If we are denied education and lack discipline, as we should professionally be instructed to learn and grow as potentially possible, to wise up, and know the difference between right and wrong, then we can become aberrant (deviate from what is right) and gravitate toward self-destruction and most likely end up harming society.

People do not start out insane at birth. In people's first few years of living and growing up, they determine if the world around them is a safe place or not. At young ages, perspectives are practically formed and their lenses are shaped, in which they utilize those learnings and experiences in their life. While growing up, they memorize how to function within their environment. If early on, and at the young ages, they have positive interactions with others and experience happy and safe atmospheres in their preliminary stages of living, they will feel safe and build healthy relationships, where they most probably become productive members of society. If otherwise and they see the world bitter and unsafe, they constitute destructible and unsafe skills to overcome the difficulties and the land mines of life, which significantly affects them and society for worse.

This should make one wonder, who is really at fault? A helpless born orphan, who has already lost their father and mother at birth? Or is the system at fault that so cruelly gives a blind eye to millions of tragedies and millions of other mishaps, leaving so many families with perils of poverty, with no reliable social programs, that irrefutably exposes society to crimes and criminals. Since most of those desperate souls are definitely going to malfunction and behave evilly because they were victims of wicked cultural and bad environmental learnings, as devastating situations overcomes them, they do not know any better to properly challenge life and constructively deal with the dangerous and inhumane world created around them by an unreasonably stratified society, maneuvered by a crazy system.

These kids have no academic opportunities, entrenched in poverty, most are physically, sexually and psychologically abused, ignored and abandoned wandering place to place, desperately struggling to find their next meal, with no housing, education, or medical opportunity. They certainly comprise millions of victims, among others caught in the midst of corporate ravaging economic and societal malevolencies (vicious ill will, spite or hatred.)

The rich elites and their goons have made a mockery out of the judicial and juvenile justice system beyond any sane mind or any rightful decision making. What is satirical? They ironically call death trap prisons and mental torture entities correctional facilities where they often sentence 13- and 14-year-old boys to life in prison without the possibility of parole, where older inmate predators perpetrate rape and violently abuse these kids sexually with no remorse. This should alert good people with conscious that something is horrifyingly wrong. These atrocities among a thousand others occur under a system that claims God and disclaims moral turpitude and supposedly strives for justice beyond a reasonable doubt. Bear in mind when a system is troubled with irresolvable economic riddles and is constantly faced with sociocultural problems beyond its capacity to fundamentally correct them, they refuge to force, as they implement the cultural of fear, as the only way out of the plight (a perplexing situation). And I wonder if God has anything to do with it?

According to many expert neurologists, well-known psychologists, and prominent psychiatrists, people's prefrontal cortex which mostly has to do with thinking abilities, does not completely mature until 20-30 years of age. I gather those who are engaged in disciplinary practices, including judges, prosecutors, attorneys, and other experts in this rather sad situation, should have a clue of this biological fact and other related issues when they render decisions in sensitive matters. These rudimentary problems cannot just coincidently happen where millions are jailed and punished under prehistoric laws purposely planned to cause fear and irrationally frighten societies. As Niccolò Machiavelli said in the book *The Prince*: "It is better to be feared than loved, if you cannot be both." Which in reality has sent many kings, princes, and queens to their death by firing squads, guillotine, exile, or imprisonment, since people eventually woke up to know who is really at fault.

And, yes, we are homo sapiens who can become malleable, as our brain plasticity can adapt to harsh conditions for staying alive, as it can be molded into accepting irrational thoughts and behaviors as norms. We are comparatively the products of our environment because manifesting proper atmosphere can potentially dictate our success in life or substantiate our failure when we are held back in disadvantaged positions. I am afraid the system's social settings have conceptually placed people under siege, where implicit discriminatory behaviors and undermining public opinions is not questioned, and preferential treatment of the rich elites is praised. Sociocultural structures and capitalism's socioeconomic pillars are meant to differentiate, as they are classified and delivered as models to be measured with.

We ought to remember that the enemy's mindset toward unity, peace, and tranquility is not genuine; they strategize to further "divide and conquer." People with a conscience should be vigilant of the culprit's schemes and be wary of perpetrators meant to be booby traps, as they can bring demise to the victims of such deadly gambits and those propagating staged outrage among people. I am not daunting (disheartening) theodicy, but I want to make it clear that we have reached an age in our spirituality and wisdom which need not let insensible views linger against anyone with different belief and value system, or deity, as billions worship and praise the omnipotent God in their own ways.

But, then again, any faith, ideology, or religiously based school of thought, not in accord with time parameters will gradually subside and eventually disappear. Many supposedly logic-oriented subjects were accepted by millions and as applicable to the past era and are now frivolous and even futile. Most inhumane dogmas are presently punishable under civil and criminal laws, and as human consciousness further rises, it proportionally expels irrelevant religious beliefs and discards cult-like activities that often are toxic and demonic. Thanks to Amnesty International and other affiliated human rights agencies, many superstitious beliefs are presently illegal in most parts of the world and unlawful to exercise.

It perplexes one's mind how far we have travelled away from myth driven credences and uncivilized behaviors and thank God are still improving. Who would have believed that man could go to the moon and Mars, to urinate and pick up samples and return safely to Earth, or to certain other planets for that matter? Who could have believed that the planet Earth was not really flat before Galileo? Who would have believed that "clitoridectomy" was actually practiced in the West before declared a transgression and a huge sin, which then was gratefully stopped for good? But unfortunately it is still exercised in some African countries. And what about the insidious act of honor killings, which disfranchise and forbid females to express their love in many parts of the world or face death if they do? According to an Amnesty International report, there is hunting for humans; many "albinos" live in fear since they are murdered for their limbs and bones in Malawi, Tanzania, and many other African nations. Some of them superstitiously believe an albino's bodily parts bring prosperity, wealth, good luck, and charm.

Bride burning is when men incinerate (burn) wives to death if they are unable to give them money and materials, "demanding dowry" common to stupefied traditions. Or, in this era of supposedly empowering and focusing on equality and human rights, it is hard to equate with the Hindu practice of sati, the burning to death of a widow on her husband's funeral pyre. Undeniably the practice is outlawed and illegal in today's India, yet it does sporadically happen and is still considered by some Hindus as the ultimate form of womanly faithfulness and sacrifice.

The most outrageous and inhumane form of widow killings is practiced in sati (also called suttee) among some Hindu communities by which a recently widowed woman either voluntarily or is coerced into killing herself as a result of her husband's death. The best known form of sati is when a woman burns to death on her husband's funeral pyre. Although other forms of sati are exercised, not to exclude incineration and being buried alive with the husband's corpse and drowning. The term sati is derived from the original name of the goddess Sati, also known as Dakshayani, who self-immolated (to kill as a sacrificed victim often by fire) since she was unable to take her father Daksha's humiliation

19

of her (living) husband Shiva. The custom of ritual suicides by widowed women is still respected in certain communities of India, and despite long ago being prohibited, such cases unfortunately are still carried out occasionally and continue to occur.

It is noteworthy to mention the negative roles the British Empire actively played in allowing this horrifying action to take place with no impunity to them, since practicing sati was initially legalized by the colonial British officials specifying conditions when widow suicide was allowed. The tradition of sati was dominant among some Hindu communities and was witnessed in aristocratic Sikh families, also observed outside South Asia in a number of localities in Southeast Asia, such as in Indonesia and Champa. Then the practice was outlawed in 1829 in territories in India (collected statistics suggesting an estimated 500-600 instances of sati per year), followed up by laws as authorities in the princely states of India in ensuing decades helped put a general ban for all of India, issued by Queen Victoria in 1861. In Nepal, sati was banned in 1920. The Indian Sati Prevention Act of 1988 further criminalized any type of accomplice, aiding, abetting, and glorifying of sati.

Rage against women can happen in many shapes and forms, from perturbing (bothering, disturbing), harassment, and exploitation, to rape, torture, and killings. One of the most abominable (despicable) and shocking forms of violence against women is bride burning. It is exercised in Pakistan, India, and Bangladesh. Men drench their wives in kerosene and set them on fire. The reason men burn brides, instead of shooting, stabbing, strangling, or poisoning them, is because they can later play innocent and say the woman killed herself.

The inconceivable act of bride burning is connected to the habit of dowry, the funds, goods, or estate that a woman brings to her husband in marriage. Thousands of young married women in India, Pakistan, and Bangladesh are routinely tortured and murdered by husbands and in-laws who want more money from the bride's parents. After burning the bride to death, the husband is free to remarry and receive a new dowry from a new bride's family. In India, every hour and 40 minutes, a woman is killed by her husband or in-laws consumed by greed. More than 5,000 women are murdered for dowry and lack of material belongings each year.

In 1995, *Time* magazine reported that dowry murders in India increased from around 400 a year in the early 1980s to around 5,800 a year by the middle of the 1990s. One year later, CNN published a story saying that every year authorities receive about 2,500 to 3,000 reports of bride burnings. The Indian National Crime Records Bureau said that there were about 8,172 dowry death cases registered in India in 2008.

In 2004, Amnesty International said, "at least 15,000 women are slaughtered in dowry oriented cases annually in India." Some women's organizations in India believe the actual number is much higher. Of course, all cases are not reported. The Ahmadabad Women's Action group has announced that because of dowry related cases, at least 1,000 women are murdered each year in Gujarat alone. In Pakistan, 300 women are burned to death each year by husbands or in-laws. Women organizations in Pakistan would presumably say, the actual number is much higher than 300. Or forcing girls as young as five years old to marry despicable 60- even 70-year-old men, who happen to be rich and financially competent to hold many young girls hostage in the name of marriage and holy matrimonial ceremonies. I wonder if God has anything to do with it?

Do we not exhibit bitter smiles when hearing about rituals, ghost detecting maneuvers, and tactics that remind us of nothing but cult behaviors and weird conventicles (assemblies)? So many moronic credences have entangled humankind in a web of uncertainties and have cluttered billions of people with absolute nonsense and mischief. I marvel if God has anything to do with any of these bizarre and inhumane behaviors.

It is crucial to know about the formations of these misdeeds and to reject those who deny the cusp (turning points) and positive changes taking place in the history of humankind, since they stubbornly promote evil path for their own interests and ambitions at the expense of others. They employ devious conduct which does not make any sense except harm and purposely plan to dissuade people from acting civilized since they deny people the truth. These travesties and ape-like functions must be halted, but we ought to also know that cynical actions will not deactivate unless we collectively grow and become part of the solution. No matter where we are or what position we hold, people need to collectively respond when they hear a cry for help. We ought to reply and defy bullying because atrocities imposed on one is not justice done to all.

The rich elites make no commitments to stop flagrant conduct; hence, it becomes crucial that people fight vile situations from the bottom up and not rely on the mercy of powerful elites. We need to realize the average human intelligent is still unripe since our compassion and caring is exhibited only to scratch the surface for other's pain and suffering; they are desperately in need of help. Societies are entangled with widespread crimes and rampant violations of people's rights beyond belief. Our pride for progressive thoughts, civility, human rights, freedom, democracy, liberty, and the pursuit of happiness are yet to be sought and diligently strived for, as these endeavors are immature because they are still raw to express any satisfaction.

Our attempts to assist the needy keeps failing since there is no structurally designed program viable enough to alter the broken public sector networks and truly revolutionize the concept of a socialized system of governing. Lack of proper education and questionable wisdom, the absence of progressive thoughts and skillful training has misdirected so many to lose priorities for rescuing societies from malaise driven cultures and dysfunctional socioeconomic conditions, which has crippled billions. We should resolve difficult criteria with antidotes of knowledge and information and encourage redistribution of wealth to establish a more equitable society where everyone can grow—not only the privileged few.

Lack of knowledge and information potentiate a fertile ground for those who benefit from people's ignorance to stir up troubles and eventually start a war of some sort, killing and maiming millions of innocent people, which frequently are based on lies and fabrications. They succeed in their wrongdoings because the essence of a culprit's success lies in sequestering (withdraw, segregate) the truth and quarantining the facts, making ugly images from the so-called enemy. As merciless financial elites foment psychological techniques applicable to all sorts of rabble rousing, lies, hubbub, demagoguery, falsehood, and misrepresentation to eventually reach objectives for maximizing profits and to congeal (coagulate, solidify) their bogus position.

Josh McDowell said, "We've had a major shift in what truth is and where it comes from. We've gone from being God-centered to self-centered, from being objective to being subjective, and from being internal to external."

Many in the field of social sciences, psychology and psychiatric studies, anthropology, investigative neuroscience, and humanism agree that people are social animals. When they are stranded and singled out, they suffer many anxiety-related issues and they also become hostile. People with different backgrounds, no matter how culturally apart, manage to get along fine when they live in melting pot societies that encourage adversity.

This should reaffirm the fact that human beings prefer peace and blithe in lieu of violence and wars. People care about maximizing their happiness and minimizing pain. Having access to modern technology, such as computers, the internet, TVs and satellite, cellphones, fax machines, and social media can help mitigate loneliness, as many aver (assert, avow, say, affirm) that technological intermediaries globally bring people closer and more attuned with each other way of life.

One of the most important factors that divides nations, and if given a chance it could prevent many atrocities against humanity, is being estranged from each other. People are basically afraid of the unknown, especially if the unknown is rumored as harmful and deliberately blown out of proportion, where information is hyped and contrary to facts. When societies are apart and not familiar with each other's customs and way of life, that can create vacuums through lies and misconceptions that can baselessly stir trouble and develop hatred toward others.

What about the system of global plutocracy paying no attention to nurturing planet Earth, in which so sadly no viable commitment is made by the imperial governments to save Mother Nature, since no funds are dispensed to rejuvenate the soil that we all crucially depend on, except for multinational corporations to exponentially deplete global habitats from its critical nutrients, minerals and natural resources, as they so ruthlessly are destroying the entire ecological system and ruining that which sustains humanity. It should not be a matter of deep philosophical debate or complicated arguments deducing a narrative as clear as our dependency on nature—that is literally at grave risk of destruction.

To better understand this, let's imagine that our water and waterways were polluted and extremely unpurified, the soil is perilous, and the air we breathe is unsafe. Envisage the food we eat is so contaminated with harsh chemicals and bacteria that would make it impossible to carry on living anymore. Or, let's imagine that we become deprived of any source of water and devoid of food because a widespread famine is taking over and has caused extreme scarcity of our natural resources, extreme shortage of food we consume, and created energy depletion compounded with difficulty to breathe toxic air, leaving billions in a state of emergency, making it impossible for humanity to survive.

The reality is that we do not have to imagine the above pessimistic scenarios or to conceptualize any other catastrophe when trouble faces the planet, our life supporting system, which surely jeopardizes our position and puts human survival at grave risk. To contemplate this, all one needs to do is listen to news and everyday reports on the grotesque effects of climate change and notice that many ecologists are screaming their lungs out because of global warming and worsening ecological atmosphere.

Agrarian societies, awakened people of industrialized nations, concerned meteorologists, and news broadcasters, environmentalists, farmers, botanists, biologists, and agriculturists plead for help, as they are desperate without any solution as demonic activities of multinational agrochemical, agricultural and bio-technology corporations, and their affiliates fabricate and purport lies about the safety issues on the GMO (genetically modified organism) producing products which retrograde (worsen, degenerate) and endanger people's lives, as menacing authorities from these problematic corporations are utterly impervious to reason and common sense. Their inhumane approach to toxic macro food production of livestock, vegetables, fruits, corn, seeds, and other edibles with disease-carrying agents is beyond comprehension. The populace has no choice but to consume poisonous food because multinational corporations have monopolized the food industries, generating venomous based ingredients and products that have created an extremely hazardous atmosphere and ill criteria that are not easy to deal with. I wonder if the culprits are some type of anthropoid (ape-like) characters who act caitiff (cowardly) in not telling consumers the truth about so many killing agents concentrated in the food they produce for human consumption. Or have they simply gone mad with being greedy? Either way, such inhumane and cruel deeds should worry anyone conveying an inch of goodness in them because the plutocratic regimes deliberately ignore the enormity of damaging problems facing humankind as they relentlessly pulsate irrational conduct.

The incredulously ruthless and rancorous corporations have turned into a malignant cancer adamant to harm humanity despite many scientific findings that clearly testify that the food we eat, the water we drink, and the air we breathe are contaminated since. They afflict, mar (harm) it due to the illegal activities of the multinational food corporations and other menacing wealth-producing giant companies with no regard for Mother Nature and its inhabitants, ignoring that, "curses are like young chicken: they always come home to roost." I am also sure they have heard phrases such as, "what comes around, goes around" or "do onto others, what you would have them do to you."

Then again, unless we raise our cognitive faculty for making wise decisions which can become a positive turning point in our private and social life, it will be business as usual. We need to elevate our consciousness, and thinking facility to excel our status, and also for other generations to pick up the fruits of our labors, and ingenious actions. But when we flinch and draw back from resolute and vastly important issues, they can become curse-like billet (work) to disappoint and often break us. Our incompetency may correlate with lack of knowledge and not having enough experience to overcome difficult tasks or perhaps deficient in courage denoting a dearth (scarcity) in maturity of mind and spirit. Disturbingly enough, many keep silent to protect their interests and doting (coddling, excessive attention) their position to guaranty how high they stand in the ladder of life. Because of their cynic and despondent behaviors, progressive movements lose support and have to bear confluences of negative outcomes with dire ripple effects, resulting in roguish (vicious) situations that would take years to correct and heal.

It is not riddling (perplexing) to unravel the rationale behind what holds many societies back from grasping success, which obviates (prevents) so many from ascending to decisive and gratifying positions. It is in our DNA to cultivate and search for a better life, but unless people's talent and might is unlocked by giving them a chance, an opportunity to exploit their full potential, billions would be denied to make the right choice and to play the music of living as they could orchestrate what would often be as heavenly and beautiful. To hold infinite resources in a few individual's hands with no clemency toward the financially deprived is not healthy because it makes the atmosphere vulnerable to outburst and bound to violence from masses of impoverished inhabitants and unhappy comparisons since they are without any protection against the storms of life, as their uprising could perhaps set a milestone for better living in the course of human history and be remembered as challenging one.

It is vitally important that people call for a new practical and dynamic system to replace the obsolete imperial governing. The current system cannot by nature correct and overcome its serious shortcomings because it has become a destructive force and, hence, a huge liability facing the populace. Let's reiterate, the capitalist system inherently has two major flaws: the system is quite unstable and when it spirals down into UN employment, inflation, recession, stagnation, extreme income disparity, and economic depression, it takes millions down, as their lives become damned and, in many cases, suicidal. The system also produces growth inequalities because a tiny portion of the world population own 99% of the wealth, while the rest have to survive at the powerful elite's mercy. It is simply not in the system's nature to accommodate decent livings for the entire population; it will indisputably have collateral damages, where loss of lives will immaturely happen since there are no viable social programs available to protect the fallen victims of the capitalist system.

I am not saying we should act lazy and expect life's goodness on a silver platter, as it sure makes a huge difference in how committed we are to accomplishing our goals, to persevere for prosperity, to believe in work ethic, determination, and must have driven, to believe in oneself. Our resiliency in trying and how eager and willingly we should struggle to succeed depends on tillable (fertile, arable) grounds to spread potentiated seeds. Our success rate is contingent on the right education, the right skill and training, the right tools, the right people, and of course, the right atmosphere.

Since everyone has a belief system and unless one's environment is constructively altered, one will be stuck to the same motto and the way of life will prove one futile. In a world where integrity, dignity, and truth are commoditized, love of money and self-image has formed public amnesia into believing there is room for everyone at the rendezvous for success. Some talented individuals are occasionally revered and decorated, as they are exhibited as paragons (symbols) because they shine as the hallmarks of eminency and true happiness to set an example and to show that we all can overcome and excel on ultra-difficult positions before reaching the pinnacle of victory, which is not practical, but is rather a childish positivism

They tactically make few icons from millions of disenfranchised people to gravitate many into believing they are simply not good enough to reach success or perhaps they are not blessed with the grace of God, as if the cross has turned into a lynching tree, where the innocent should be victimized. The system is inundated (overwhelm, overflow, flood) with institutionalizing separation and encouraging disunity as the system colludes with big overlord corporations and powerful elites to further exploit billions of ordinary folks as they mold them into believing "it is what it is," implying that the poor are predestined to accept their sometimes horrific fate, where they often question if the merits are truly justified.

Creating idols can motivate many and perhaps bring jubilancy and hope for millions of eager souls, but the fallacy behind such tactics are plenty since the actual winning numbers are one in millions, as real statistics sing much gloomier songs, as so many fall into booby traps of false hope and insane positivism—just like pumped up cowboys in rodeo shows with their hands wrapped, caught under the tight rope while riding the bull, falling and being dragged on the ground into dirt trying to win the ram of success. Hence, it is imperative for a democratic system of governing to encourage and provide golden opportunities for all of its citizen, not only the chosen ones. It makes sense to cultivate general talent and let everyone enjoy the fruits of one's prowess (ability) and not behave haphazardly in selecting candidates for showing off occasional success. The corporate elites should avoid acting tacitly bias and prevent prejudice, to shun from operating delusional with disregard for reality and to defy common sense.

In the meantime, we should be insightful and depend on what makes sense rather than becoming exposed to the malice of often surgical conditioning and ought not to precipitate in accepting what we see and hear because our perception is not always genuine. Rushed decisions frequently victimize and shackle millions, which often occurs when damage is done and is already too late to stop the problems. The financial elites spend billions to deceive us into seeing the surface of things because they capitalize on propaganda and advertising machines to lure people into the quicksand of accepting the wrong sociocultural, socioeconomic policies, and dreadful political agendas, without victims even noticing what is actually taking place as they are being brainwashed, as if hypnotized.

The key is to homogenize us because, when they do, they can control billions of avid consumers, as they gradually acquaint people with superb advertising tactics and via expertly manufactured set points, in which so many become addicted to an artificial lifestyle, as anything outside their comfort zone is difficult to bear. Multinational corporations operate in a clandestine manner, as they surreptitiously brainwash people into branding culture and through a buying spree, where designated thought consumption, product consumption, and selected information, and related technologies has become an obsession, which without people, they are not cool enough, or even worthy of connecting to those who are big spenders, or behave in certain conditional patterns. People work so hard to catch up with the microwave lifestyle, racing in the fast lane, as so many societies gone mad spending their savings, just to catch up with the new products off the assembly lines, to either show off, compete with peers, or quench their thirst of addiction for buying things, as millions become annually indebted and are fettered since they financially behave irresponsibly, as they often are delirious enough to go beyond their purchasing power to meet their insane cravings and to own and hoard hundreds of unnecessary items rarely used.

Adyashanti, the American-born spiritual teacher, offers a theory as to why the acquisition of new possessions provides only a temporal feeling of happiness. He explains it this way: When we make a purchase and/or get what we want, we are temporarily happy and fulfilled. However, the reason for happiness is not because we got what we wanted, but because for a brief period of time, we stopped wanting, and thus, we experience peace and happiness.

Market oriented mechanisms require that supply and demand fluently operate, where maximizing profit depends on the restless consumption of goods and services, making it necessary for the corporate capitalist economy to mastermind the human psyche and making sure how human consumption behaviors are patterned. They have succeeded in linking our temporary good feeling with buying stuff, in which neuropsychology, neurologists, psychologists, and many other related fields agree that our brain exudes good hormones, like endorphins, serotonin, dopamine, and oxytocin, which can last for a couple of days after exercising what we craved for, which often gets us hooked and addicted to shopping for new things to experience that mood and for perhaps running away from our trouble with no avail.

It is imperative not to hastily grasp what seems apparent in the outside world, often skillfully carried out under false pretenses because accepting hypes can irreparably damage our social and private life, including our family affair, marriage. It can also hurt our finances and health-related issues; it can malfunction in legal matters and render us misjudgment with disappointing outcomes. We need to drill beneath headlines and meditate on troubleshooting what is visible, act thoughtfully on vital matters, and must not be distracted and not rush into dialogues on vital issues or act hasty to deliver an answer, and rendering prudence.

"Nothing can be done quickly and prudently at the same time." — Publilius Syrus (1st Century BC-?), Roman writer and poet.

The real truth is often laid under what is visible. After all, no physician can correctly diagnose illnesses without blood tests, urine tests, saliva, or without x-rays and MRI scans, cardiograms, etc., since internal tests can reveal the cause of diseases or detect any injury, and in most cases helps doctors and surgeons remedy the problems. Legal authorities should also have access to DNA technology in the analysis of criminals, where the world of forensic laboratory testing plays a huge role in identifying criminals. I believe our intelligence and savviness of mind, or naïveté, are inversely proportional to how abruptly we approve and fall into traps believing what is apparent, which we sometimes pay a heavy price to learn otherwise because in most cases, we become gullible to the exterior of things and are misled by glamorized issues.

There is a saying: "Do not believe everything you hear and believe half of what you see." The real truth is: "the visible things are made of things that are not visible" so contemplate on what you do not see. What I am saying is not to take the bait and fall trap into premeditated false news, deceptive practices, and devious propaganda designed in bad faith to suppress people; resist becoming molded into safeguarding the status quo, where the super-rich enjoy a bountiful life, and billions have to pray for survival, since the indigents are subjugated by ceaseless emphasis on self-actualization, and pressing on believing in oneself, but plutocrats do not lift a finger to help the needy out of their gruesome and grievous (ominous) position.

The system strategies to manipulate public opinion through outbursts in stubborn individuals, which often makes them do the unthinkable, not to exclude ignorance, hatred anger, and fear, which are truly challenging issues for all to overcome. We become prone to our animal instinct when angry, and we feel nervous and worried when fearful. It is not easy for many people to control these very damaging emotions because they can gradually build up wrath. If things do not go our way or behave dogmatically with one-track-mindedness to avoid compromise, as some show no flexibility in what they believe is the right way. There are many reasons behind stirring up outbursts in stubborn individuals, which often make them do the unthinkable, not to exclude ignorance, hatred, chronic insecurity, jealousy, greed, acting selfish, resentment toward others, or perhaps not socially belonging.

This, in turn, can load people with an inferiority complex that is sadly felt when victims of misfortune are denigrated and see others experiencing the life of luxury, and often with superiority complex syndrome because they are having good times and showing jubilancy for ruling the day, as they also exhibit signs of discord toward the less fortunate. This certainly can, in turn, manifest as animosity and create clashes among people, making it easier for financial elites to take advantage of common man by worsening people's ugly behaviors by triggering nationalism, race, color, gender-based dislike and misogyny, faith-related differences, and xenophobia. They push it as scientific through "Darwinism natural selection" and other tyrannical social philosophies like "eugenics," which advocate the improvement of hereditary qualities through selective breeding, which was also done by Hitler's pseudo-scientists to create the best Arian race, intending to comprise a racist nation that would be superior to other ethnicities.

But before finding answers to the above malaise and millions of other cultural and social, economic disorders, we need to change the way we think, so that we can change the way we live. Hence, we should not question the super-structure and cultural orientation of things, but rather, we need to understand fundamental architects and the actual forces behind the way we function in imperative matters that ironically impede our progress and, in many cases divide us. The system often takes advantage of that.

For instance, it is not easy for millions to put up with a selfless image and feelings of being nobody in a world where image sizes success and importance, as prestige and so-called class status distinguish who is who in a world of fame and prominence, where money rules. Many try their hardest for financial glory and notoriety, but they often fail despite the hard work and extreme effort made. An economic noose is now much tighter than it used to be, as probabilities are higher for one to arrive at one's financial merits and to substantiate upper mobility, which would have made it more practical, then, for living in the land of milk and honey.

Let's not forget that it is much harder for one to arrive at one's success, which is often accompanied with so much distress. A stressful life can ruin our health, our social welfare, where negative emotions can deny us relative happiness, with no spiritual well-being, which sometimes can be so destructive, needing immediate medical and psychological attention, making it unworthy for the price we must pay to live in glamour and arrive at financial glory. Since, it has forced millions not to pay attention to sacred moderate living and not to respect balance, which is the essence of life and our human existence. We need to break loose from temptation and exercise control over vain desires, to halt stress-related issues and not endure ill feelings toward others, which can sometimes trap us into our death if not stopped. We need to realize the best gift one can give to others is one's time, which if dedicated to pay attention to. It can relish the self and integrate people, rather than individualizing and segregating them by constantly reciting that "time is money."

Other issues in need of our attention should start with seeing the ugly ramifications of too much power in anyone's hand, with having absolute authority in any network, group, government entity, organization, party, corporation, and so on. It always brings awful results to deal with, which affects people in the worst ways, even debilitating so many globally. We are becoming like a small village, which enables us to have access to dynamic communications and as fast as lightening too. And thank God for some sincere independent media that are not commercially driven and as vigil as eagles, which report decisive news via marvelous technology leveraged by honest, brilliant journalists.

With information and knowledge comes power, which needs to blend in with intelligence, understanding, and compassion to bear tolerance and give diversity in human concept a chance to grow and bind people's healthy relationship impermeable to any prejudice. This is not only exclusive to certain ethnicity or nationality but uniting the entire human race leaving no one behind. We should not have moral depravity and turpitude toward each other, and ought to act in righteous ways as building blocks in every society. Look, it is the tendency of human nature to become arrogant, psyched up and pompous when having too much power, spurring one to go over one's head and play God. But then can you imagine an unwise, rube, and unjust beast of a person with absolute power or with having an utterly powerful network of financial tyrants colluding against ordinary folks. The problem can become so colossally wicked that sometimes seems impossible to confront or manage to control, as populations are forced to live below a normal and hegemonic power structure.

The rich elites behave as caudillos (conquistadors, Spanish military dictators) that are not frugal in ravaging human lives and do not hesitate to kill, maim, and destroy anyone standing in their mighty path since no opinion should be contrary to despot's ruling or tolerated against their absolute command. They bulldoze unfavorable plans and destroy constructive programs, if the ideas are not meant for strengthening their position as they wipe out any archetype (model) believed to oppose their reigns, which may endanger dictator's ruthless status or activate any thought against the conglomerate allies and powerful network of fascist's regimes. The problem worsens when many decipher to evoke a socialist system as an alternative, which glorifies "dictatorial of proletariat" as its focal point, believing the socialist system could set us free and render the proper solution to our abstract sociocultural and socioeconomic dilemmas. But then again, it does not make a difference if either the corporate fascists have us by the throat or dictatorial of proletariat tyranny is ugly—no matter who is executing it.

Forgetting that too much power is in anyone's hand, any party or assembly, group, organization will most definitely spell tragedy of paramount size because they can grow beyond rules and regulations, where the laws are then too anemic to control them. God forbid if the ruling party lacks knowledge and empathy to comprehend intricate human nature. We are perhaps exhausted with wisdom, not able to understand the veracity and the complexity of our human soul that is undeniably a part of cosmic energy where no socialist or communist ideology can fathom. Any system worthy of ruling ought to identify with God and realize the prevalence of sacred cosmic energy, which without life, is never possible. The system needs to know that not only our individualistic efforts, but our social enthusiasm and collective culture of thinking, our emotions and spiritual longings are as part of divine intervention, as they are not aimless, and should not assess them as without having meaning, since no being lacks having a purpose.

The situation exacerbates when an unbridled central government run by a central party system called "central bank" or federal reserve bank plays as bad as dictatorial of proletariat, when it financially strangled the daylight out of ordinary folks, as they keep bailing out the bankers and resuscitate huge financial entities without taxpayer's consent. People have to pick up the tab and bear the ugly consequences of a wicked economy that has gone bankrupt, which burdens the entire society with trillions of dollars in deficit. We should activate a depth of wisdom within all of us and encourage to awaken each and every one to the bitter reality of what is happening before it is too late.

The bottom line is that no system can survive without "humanism" and no humanity can survive without compassion and if depleted of moral conduct where no faith in God is venerated but replaced by becoming infatuated with accumulating wealth and striving for power. I am afraid this has become the hallmark of many transnational corporations in serious delinquency of ethical codes and inhumane conduct.

Either through individual efforts or by collective urges and cooperation, we need to find meaning for so many unanswered questions and unravel solutions to millions of mysterious questions, to quench our thirst in finding the unknowns, to serve human curiosity, to exercise our intuition, to patent innovative and inspiring thoughts, to marvel and create groundbreaking ideas, to search for happiness and the aesthetic, to look for truth and beauty. Our craving for divinity and piety, poetry, art, and music, our human longing for freedom, democracy, and human rights, and millions of other crucial human devotions, which cannot flourish in a despotic and dictatorial environment, where social calamities and unjustifiable rule of law can become a rudimentary and fundamental part of cultural and social norms.

Remember, no imperial hegemony has ever lasted for the same reason of bullying citizens and expanding their autocratic power since no human being wants to be yoked and deprived of one's freedom. It is just part of man's nature to rebel against injustice and to emancipate oneself from enslavement. This gives meaning to preserving people's freedom and not to lapse in respecting human rights and democracy, to encourage wisdom and knowing one's rights, to know moderation not only is virtuous, but plays an essential role in holding power, the secret to survival. Having too much of anything means bad business, which should not exclude power and wealth.

It is not that the empires of wealth and power do not have the means or cannot identify with the criteria of an adequate system of governing, which if the government of powerful elites choose to saintly operate, it could give meaning to the word hope and make a better world possible.

They just choose not to operate in a dignified manner, since withering away an ecosystem, draconian lifestyle of the poor, and continuously wasting human lives in crime-ridden societies, the absurd inequality gaps, wars of aggression, terrorism, and threat of nuclear and atomic war hangs on our shoulder, which has no impact on the elites, since it leaves no ill repercussions to the wrongdoing of the mighty rich and the agents of horror.

In the meanwhile, the intrusive and bullying empires are flagrantly (shamelessly) proud to cuddle and call the most despicable puppet regimes of terror allies, which they operate mercilessly against what humanity stands for. The whole world witnesses these incriminating fascist regimes and religious extremist states behave cowardly lynching the opposition and their continuous rancorous beheadings and public display of headless bodies, demonic stoning, slashing, wicked torturing, and rape, to scare off the public. Many wretched regimes steadfastly support honor killings, encourage misogyny, gay bashing, xenophobia, cruel and inhumane treatment of political inmates, and illegal imprisonment of dissidents without any due process.

The totalitarian regime of terror scoops very low and acts so condescendingly to breed fear and expect utter obedience to impose savage and prehistoric rules of conducts on their subjects. It seems the culprits are numb to extremely robust and active international communication, where the newsworthy items spreads fast like a wildfire, exposing the procurators of violence and crime against humankind; brave and talented journalists and nimble whistleblowers are still available, but neither are engulfed with glamour nor lost in the atmosphere of greed that are adamantly decisive to let the vital information out and let the entire international community hear the good news and travesties of the world. The empires of misdeed and corruption have forgotten that in the contemporary world even the farthest dwellers of the planet earth are unquestionably affected by global political, cultural, and financial interactivities, where conglomerate (cartel, trust, consortium) news media is leveraged to influence so many through modern telecommunication and technological innovations.

Today's generation possesses advance industries that can unfold superb thoughts and brilliant activities. We are able to disclose helpful breakthroughs and information via dynamic ways of communication. Since technology has made the globe much smaller, billions of people can share and enjoy an exchange of ideas, access plenty of information, and become enlightened on vital issues, and learn about other cultures. As pedagogy (education) can certainly play a key role in differentiating facts from fictions and to identify with progressive ways of life and to speed up taking part with those who truly value freedom and human rights.

It is a blessing where none commercially driven social and news media empower people to discern lethal ideologies from constructive outlooks and enable us to distinguish antiquated thoughts from revolutionary concepts that are potentiated with robust plans and animated programs to make a better world possible. This further gives meaning to the expression that "knowledge is power" because related sociocultural cognizance should certainly make us aware of taking sides with those who value humanity and what it stands for, rather than blindly aligning with static beliefs and backward traditions in which they literally squander so many lives as we speak.

With astonishing headways in science and great technological novelties (inventions), unrivaled logistics, enormous military, and puissant (powerful) policing, along with massive accumulation of wealth and influence beyond anyone's imagination, the wealthy empires can positively resolve many prolonged iniquitous (sinister) sagas beholding humanity. Imperial corporations can halt consolidated attacks from fiendish (perversely diabolical) jihads and put an end to the prolonged purgatory state of mind that has disturbed world peace and tranquility, where so many diversified groups and guilds have yielded to subtle fear from small scale business meetings to large enterprise assemblies.

People worry in important gatherings and affluent communities, in government entities, even at places of worship, in national and international airports, as millions of innocent travelers become nervous, not knowing where terrorists have designated their next targets and when or how terrorists are going to strike again and again, blasting themselves off and exploding other harmless human beings to pieces.

They can stop religious extremists' sporadic attacks and their fragmented inhumane terrorist behaviors at will. But they do not. The mighty powerful are an illusion. Unlike ordinary people, who have no protection against sinful terrorism and other wicked misconduct, the wealthy can live in a bubble impervious from harm. The powerful elite act so indifferently to people's sufferings and the fragile situations they endure. Many empires believe that wars give birth to advance civilizations, which fools them into spreading their wings too far, where they do not belong and the very reason for losing it all.

Albert Einstein said, "The pioneers of a warless world are the [youth] who refuse military service." Charles Sumner said, "Give me the money that has been spent in war and I will clothe every man, woman, and child in an attire of which kings and queens will be proud. I will build a schoolhouse in every valley over the whole earth. I will crown every hillside with a place of worship consecrated to peace." And Eve Merria so eloquently said, "I dream of giving birth to a child who will ask, mother, what war was."

Former President Thomas Jefferson said, "I recoil with horror at the ferociousness of man. Will nations never devise a more rational umpire of? Differences than force? Are there no means of coercing? Injustice more gratifying to our nature? Than a waste of the blood? Of thousands and of the labor of millions of our fellow creatures?"

The oligopolistic governments choose to kill people who kill people, to show that killing and maiming is barbaric, and since they do not concoct realistic plans for constructive peace and productive investments to improve people's lives, they rather steadfastly plan for wars and are antsy (fidgety, impatient, restless) to spend billions in bombing campaign against common people and leave irreparable traces of hatred behind. It shouldn't take a genius to ask why thousands of young wannabe martyrs attach suicide vests, detonate explosives to end their own lives and take innocent lives. The recruiters of hell swarm naïve and vulnerable individuals' poisoning their minds, seducing them into believing that life is much happier on the other side, and the act of suicide will put them in paradise where the angels of heaven can't wait to embrace them, and I wonder should female martyrs expect handsome males as well to greet them in the heaven above.

They are quite successful in enchanting many into fools and deranging young cadets' minds to create time bombs since they literally facilitate and remind their prey of the primordial lifestyle and the bitter experiences that are structurally designed by the foreign corporate intruders backed by government hegemonies to colonies, and exploit them into agonizingly poor condition, where there is no way out but to commit suicide and to kill innocent others in an act of revenge. Recruiters of hell radicalize potential suicidal cells by luring them into cul-de-sacs (blind alley, dead end) and making them understand the cause to their despicable poverty; the ruling despotic regimes are pumping oil and gas out of their backyards and extracting minerals and valuable stones from poor people's mines and territories without giving a damn about them, while forcing natives, who are the real proprietors of wealth, to live in subhuman condition.

Leaving the victims with no choice out of their financial tumult, pushing them into abysmal pain and suffering since they rob ordinary people from what belongs to them and with impunity to those responsible for their misery? Human traffickers are successful because they capitalize on the exploitation of the poor and those desperately vulnerable individuals, as the poor do not have the means to higher professional help, as they are unable to financially litigate their mortifying situation. Basically, the victims of capitalist societies are not empowered enough to fight back against the social, criminal, and economic injustice facing them.

They become prey into the hands of merciless profiteers exploiting them without fair compensation, except for the so-called next martyr terrorists to be remunerated (pay) in their next lives. Natives' anger and hatred is coalesced (compounded) when seeing the loss of loved ones and family members, friends, countrymen, and noticing death of so many innocent human beings as well, asking why? As they witness firsthand the harsh ramifications of an ugly war of aggression imposed on them as they are being bombed with no mercy and for no apparent reason, and I wonder if God has anything to do with it. We should be reminded of what Socrates said, "It is better to suffer wrong than to do wrong."

In the meanwhile, we should know that every time we are pushed to the limit, which sometimes forces one to kill oneself for one reason or another or become the victim of homicide, we have infringed on the sovereignty of God, which common sense should tell us that if killing was relegated to oneself, then one is bound to repeat the same living, if not worse, as we immaturely end our own life or perhaps murdered by other soulless beasts which will endure God's punishment through awful means, as no one is ever believed to have given life to oneself, as all and everything created is due to the wisdom of our creator and belongs to God. One can act spiritually careless and as morally deprived as one wants, since this materialistically glamorous world has made so many impervious to the real picture and blinded them to the reasoning power of what is just and human. Paramahansa Yogananda says, "The spine is the highway to the infinite, your own body is the temple of God, and it is within your own self that God must be realized."

Globalization has also marked its pervasively (ubiquitous, universal) irresponsible effects on millions of immature characters, where images of sex, glamor, and violence made by movie industries and news agencies exhibited through TV, satellites, the internet, and shown by thousands of internationally known social media channels have left a jagged view, skewed with narrow-mindedness, and misinterpreted outcomes, bewitching millions of youth into hallucination and leading them to perdition (hell, eternal damnation.) Since they are apart from the real happenings, obscure from the reality, and unfamiliar with what actually takes place in the business world because they are also strange to the shark-like entertainment environment and the cutthroat venture societies, compounded with crude-mindedness, they are longing so naively for a piece of the action, as they thrive to become part of the powerful images. In making a name for themselves, so many of them are already looking for a cause to rebel. They wrongfully fall into the hands of demagogues and religious extremists with no way out of their decadent position, in which the predators evolve them into sublime madness to do the unthinkable.

Let's not forget that there is a dark and callow side to human nature that can become flammable and vulnerable to deception, since no one figuratively speaking is perfect. Charlatans and traders of evil know how to ignite others for reaching their sadistic objectives and beastly goals. The question is why should such a cruel apparatus and such demonic missions materialize in the 21st century. It really is an enigma—perhaps part of human genome. But then again, history has witnessed that literacy and education, wisdom, building knowledge, and gaining constructive information along with civility of mind and manner, professional therapeutic approaches, effective psychological trainings, and positive people around you, also the presence of decent role models and competent mentors can make a huge difference in dwindling violence and lessening vicious behaviors in human pathology and deviated conduct.

Sadly, the resources that are essentially needed to correct human maladies, to treat and improve byzantine (complex, convoluted) mental and psychological shortcomings, to further literate and enlighten the populace are held by corporate oligarchy and plutocratic governments for arriving at their inhumane objectives. This should leave no doubt that those running the global system have premeditated to eradicate us, as if they have found suitable ways to control population growth. The aggregate illusionism and deranged positivism have held so many hostage to metastatic (cancerous, wicked in nature) conditions, where dire reality is not an obstruction to our suckling dream-like desires and our insane ambitions, which since has infected our minds with autoimmune diseases and venom-like substances, forcing us toward self-cannibalism aimed at the very destruction of humankind.

It does not take an oracle to know the reason behind so many destructible forces that vortex billions collectively to the bottom of the abyss, where enormous atrocities and rapacious behaviors by the powerful elites are covertly planned against ordinary masses of people without any self-reproach. They are untouchable as they are well-guarded by furtive (sneaky, stealthy) intelligent agencies and secret services, vast police forces, national guards, and the mighty military machines, which by the way, consume a colossal chunk of national budget. But financial elites are incompetent in self-restraining and extremely weak against craving greed, as the accumulation of wealth by a tiny population has caused a financial fiasco and created a huge gap between the haves and the have-nots. Since, this has manifested immense poverty turning billions into some type of subhuman creatures. The ultra-rich understand they cannot live a day without police protection because they are shielded by privilege and power, versus justice and truth.

If not greed, why the rich should lack moral imperative to act with such indifference toward people's pain and suffering, making citizens exposed to insensible socioeconomic malfeasance and undignified rule of conduct, intimidating the poor to rise and retaliate against the elites' unduly actions and prepare for a bloodied class war. Mahatma Gandhi so justly said, "Earth provides enough to satisfy everyman's need, but not every man's greed."

It is urgently required for corporate autocracy and the powerful elites to unplug their myopic and cultic behavior to show funambulism (mental agility) and exit this deteriorating and deadened state of mind to comply with humanly virtues, to ameliorate (improve) the harsh, and unbearable situation that masses of ordinary people are sadly experiencing. And as Emmanuel Kant said, "In law, a man is guilty when he violates the rights of others. In ethics, he is guilty if he only thinks of doing so." The conglomerate capitalists, ingratiated with global government empires, are too powerful, as their military industrial complex is so advanced that it should not let a Rwanda-like genocide occur or a Bosnian massacre to happen, and can prevent, and not permit, ISIS cleansing of innocent ethnics and murdering other religious factions and denominations to substantiate and where no holocaust situation can take place without a green light from the imperial powers.

Transnational corporations are the very cause in preventing many of under-developing nations from progressing since they rub them from their natural resources, annually sums up to billions of dollars if not trillions. Native's national wealth is taken without people's consent, since revenues as such can verily (certainly) create miracles in countries that are in urgent need of socioeconomic and sociocultural literacy, education and in need of immediate infrastructural agendas, especially places such as Liberia, Rwanda, Congo, Afghanistan, Iraq, and other crime-stricken societies that have to deal with fascist regimes and genocide, and so many other beastly atrocities beyond anyone's imagination.

When people are kept illiterate by design, they easily succumb to fallacies of the ruling system, as they acquiesce (submit, give in) to dishonest politicians who are in cahoots with business elites deemed to preserve the status quo. The prerogative gentry are entitled to receive the best, while the underprivileged and financially repressed are restlessly engaged in an unbearable lifestyle, worrying about their next meal and a roof over their head and how to deal with irreparable health problems.

That is exactly why no weight is put on the miracle of learning for the deprived, coupled with keeping people busy with a difficult life, which results in ill conditioning for the poor and jeopardizes their position, making it impossible for them to grow, despite so much insane positivism and obsolete affirmations, which supposedly is meant to motivate the hopeless and help the destitute.

It should remind one of Pacific salmon, which are motivated to lay their eggs and determined to breed after an arduous journey struggling upstream and sometimes amid a ferocious storm, which makes them exhausted, and that is the very reason for their death. And if they are not caught by fishermen and other predators, like bears and eagles, or not trapped behind dams and large waterfalls before breeding, they are very lucky since so many do not make it to fulfill their mission and what they are destined to do.

The suppressors are well aware that literacy, knowledge, and information awakens people to question more and ask why. All answers should apparently lead to bizarre sociocultural and socioeconomic plans meant to cultivate the worst in people and to bind them to the psychology of work while facilitating millions with the conditional techniques to make them one-track-minded in maximizing productions for the rich elites and to act docile (amenable, obedient) and robot-like in taking orders.

You, the corporations, turn nations into beggary status with your unbridled and heedless behaviors. You take what does not belong to you when obviously they are not able to stop your mighty military paving the way for you to pillage (looting); they turn against each other, murdering over bones and what garbage that is left behind. When mentally disturbed soldiers return from the war of aggression and kill themselves or other innocent people or lose their lives because of post-traumatic stress disorder, it is your fault. When pregnant women are snatched in Liberia by child soldiers, gang-raped, and cut open to pull out babies from their womb, it is your doing. When, because of genocide, one million innocent people are wiped out in Rwanda, it is your fault. When young boys and girls are imprisoned, raped, and turned into killer machines, you are at fault.

When an insidious (treacherous) crime rate skyrockets in so-called civilized nations, you are at fault; when prisons are over populated, and so many young people are condemned to death or being incarcerated for life, as you have waged war on millions of inmates and degraded them as they are inhumanely treated, you are accountable. You ought to elucidate on your hubris and inhumane conduct. When people are forced into bankruptcy and default on their loans, losing their homes, their means of transportation, and are forced to sell personal valuables to survive because you fired or laid them off, which then, I am sure you expect escalating violence and higher crime rates, it should be in your conscious. Every time veterans of belligerent wars return home and end up panhandling and are homeless, it is your fault.

And when democratically elected governments are overthrown or a president elect is assassinated, you are engaged, and of course, no coup d'etat can take place anywhere, without your invisible hand executing the event or acknowledging it.

Citizens should call to ostracize your transnational corporations and renounce your board of trustees since they do not hesitate to destroy human beings for their corporate interests. And it is you who fuels violence and keeps people from growing up intelligently and becoming consciously competent individuals, since you take away their precious resources that can otherwise play a decisive role in enlightening millions and helping them form cultivated societies to reach prosperity and to institute better standards of living. But I am afraid they cannot fulfill such vital tasks since their national wealth is so viciously extorted by the corporate bullies of the world, which in most of the so-called "free" world, corporations have grown more powerful than the state, doing as they wish, where there are no checks and balances left for people to depend on, as the system only works for the tyrannical few.

The odd thing about the whole picture is when the powerful elite lie, rob people of their wealth, wage pugnacious (belligerent) wars, rape, mass murder, violate citizens' rights, force people into unemployment and bankruptcy, extort billions of taxpayers' money under the "bailout" laws, and are the cause of so many despicable crimes, they are called "heroes." They operate behind the iron curtains and are able to cover up misdeeds and can hide their malignant actions, where they "do not let the cat out of the bag," but when one commits a single wrong, one is labeled as a "felon."

And for fairness' sake, no one ought to be free of any responsibility when one commits a crime, including the privileged few. This is not rocket science. When you expropriate (usurp, annex, seize) people of their natural resources, you then so egregiously (shamelessly) force them into bleak poverty that consequently kills any opportunity to help them grow; it boycotts them from developing into civilized and knowledgeable societies, and when they are not, then we should naturally expect all hell break loose.

We ought to know that economic inequality that has led to inexorable (unswerving, relentless, steady) poverty is the mother of all terrorism. It is a curse imposed on humanity, the real cause to all manmade ills, and the root cause of all evils. If correctly ratified, the hell that we are forced to experience will transform mankind to taste the power of heavens and acknowledge what blissful life is meant to be. I wonder if God has anything to do with it.

We should bear in mind that once one detects evil, then it becomes one's moral responsibility to divest from demonic sources that are bereft of any conscious or empathy, as transnational corporations are. They are blind as bats and choose not to see their irresponsible warmongering behaviors for monopolizing global resources and masterminding tons of other wicked actions, which displaces millions and leaves thousands dead and maimed, which should ardently call for global wake-up calls to defend what is just and humane. John 10:10 says: "The thief cometh not, but to steal, and to kill, and to destroy, I am come that they might have life, and that might have it more abundantly." John Steinbeck puts it this way: "War is a symptom of man's failure as thinking animal." And George Washington said, "My first wish is to see this plague of mankind, war, banish from the earth." And Albert Einstein said, "I know not with what weapons World War III will be fought, but World War IV will be fought with sticks and stone."

And George Orwell said, "All the war propaganda, all the screaming and lies and hatred, comes invariably from people who are not fighting." They globally keep people in poverty, knowing the rich do not have to fight to survive, but the deprived millions will run to the frontlines, risk dying to make a living for themselves and their loved ones, if they are lucky enough to make it out alive, not maimed or permanently disabled.

But, then again, since there are powerful international forces in denial of ugly historical events, atrocities are to be expected redundantly without remorse, and the superpowers are very afraid of the word peace. They are skillfully able to brain wash people into systematic doubt and literally make citizens skeptics of their predatory and insane actions against humanity. The system of corporate capitalists convey "sociopath behaviors" defined as "having antisocial personality disorder. The syndrome further is characterized by a disregard for the feelings of others, a lack of remorse or shame, manipulative behavior, unchecked egocentricity, and the ability to lie in order to achieve one's goals."

This ought to legitimatize social rage against the system of corporate culture and necessitate people's defiance facing bureaucratic governments, to emancipate citizens through rebellions and sublime madness to frighten menacing powerful elites by the might of justice and truth. Where moral imperative of revolt should call for, to manifest the power of the powerless, and unveil the ill will of corporate ideology and cultural hegemonies, which have undeniably ossified sociopolitical and socioeconomic agendas, through which they have shackled masses of people and haunted billions for worse. It is imperative to further investigate the nature of the beast, which literally operates as a sociopath that behaves absentmindedly toward people's unbearable suffrage.

Profiling a sociopath with narcissistic attitude:

Narcissistic personality disorder, also known as NPD, is a personality disorder in which the individual has a distorted self-image, unstable and intense emotions, is overly preoccupied with vanity, prestige, power, and personal adequacy, lacks empathy, and has an exaggerated sense of superiority, acting nonchalant with smooth charm, controlling, and conning. They do not acknowledge the rights of others and see their self-serving conduct as admissible. They appear to be entrancing (delightful), yet are furtively malicious and bossy, seeing their victims as merely agents to be taken advantage of. In a bold sense, they see what does not belong to them as their right. They are pathological fabricators, since they lie and act in falsehood. They have no difficulty lying easily and it is almost impossible for them to be factually coherent. No feeling of regret, abashment, or guilt—none. With rooted rage, which is cleaved off and restrained, they are roiled (disturbed) and do not see others around them as people, but only regard them as dupes (fools) and possibilities. Instead of friends or colleagues, they have targets and accomplices who end up as victims; at the end, they justify the means and allow no obstacle in their way. Superficial feelings and emotions. When they present what appears to be friendly, warmth, happiness, love, and empathy, it is more fake than experienced and serves an ulterior(further, future) reason. Violent by insignificant stuff, yet linger to be unshakable and cool by what would fumble (upset) a normal person. Since they are neither genuine, nor are their commitments. They lack the ability for love and cannot truly belong. Desensitize with having no compassion, unable to sympathize with the suffering of others. They have only disdain for people's feelings of trouble and are ready to take advantage of them and lack concern with their ill impact on others and are morally insane, paranoid of the word revolution.

Other connected merits are:

Hateful to those who try to understand them. Do not believe anything is wrong with them. Covert, but try to keep conventional appearance. Has an emotional need to justify their crimes and therefore needs their victim's affirmation (respect, gratitude and love). Incapable of real human attachment to another. Not able to feel remorse or guilt; they have a malignant personality and are radically narcissistic and ambitious. They may say readily that their objective is to conquer and rule the world, since only wealth, power, and influence can palliate their relentlessly zealous inhumane behaviors. Substantial (genuine, meaningful) religious agendas, virtuosity, morality or other human values play no part in their lives.

The overlord rich elites have no feeling of mercy for others and are capable of violence. Under psychological terms, they fall into the breed of sociopath or psychopath, but unlike the typical psychopath, their behavior is masked by a shallow social façade; they are habitual liars. The point is that such malfunctioning characters often hold extremely important posts that can put humanity at grave risk of total annihilation, if not dealt with sensibly.

They have created hideous situations and a chaotic environment impregnated with fatal flaws and despair, but it can improve and change for the better, if only the money spent on genocidal weaponries could be allocated to assist the victims of wretched poverty, rather than dropping bombs to kill unarmed men, innocent women, elderly and children, which definitely manifests seeking vengeance in return—that also leaves behind contempt, plague, and despair among so many victims. We can instead, and in all honesty, call for educating people in good faith to implement peace and show the world we mean business not in killing, but in saving lives.

And notice that billions of funds will not be wasted to keep the powerful elites safe, and their so-called global enterprises immune from harm, money inefficiently spent to manage security for the super-rich, and to protect their universal investments, which should instead be put in good use to educate and train young generations and show them we care, to give young minds hope, making them feel exhilarated and thrilled to join the massive international workers, and help them become productive members of society, and not violators of law and order or suicidal murderers.

Let people have something to live for. Do not ceaselessly take all of people's possessions, which they have toiled for; avoid annexing everything from the poor under legal premises and through wrongful reasoning, as if God has anointed you to plunder and subjugate the weak, or just because you can. Immanuel Kant said, "May you live your life as if your maxim of your actions were to become universal law."

The mighty elites need to generate constructive programs to bring deprived masses of people hope and prosperity, to stop alliance with oppressive regimes, and to make weapon embargo against dictatorial regimes. Fascist governments are in the business of mass murdering, mass incarceration, and horrific tortures and abuse, and ironically and quite chillingly are antipathetic toward freedom, liberty, democracy, human rights, economic opportunity, and they stringently campaign against sacred humanistic values.

We ought to be reminded that the west has come too far in preserving some precious and certain enlightening values, as many so-called allies and friends are not in favor of these progressive ideas, as they are the very reason behind many cases of ill will and terrorism against the west, and in which the so-called allies play "wolves in sheep clothing."

It is noteworthy to know many wars of transgression are induced by transnational corporations to control weak nations, beating them into submission as they outsource jobs to designated parts of the world to gain access for cheap labor and free natural resources, to excavate inexpensive raw materials, aim at maximizing profit. And also have the luxury of not paying taxes, while bribing the authoritarian regime to suppress and keep the poor natives silent, which is the main reason for many illegitimate wars that the weapon industry is thrilled to have and who said "you cannot have your cake and eat it too."

The tyrannical regime have learned how to oppress citizens and keep them poor, where they incapacitate them by force not to fight back. Mark Twain once said, "Lack of money is the roots of all evil." And if not turning neighboring nations into rival enemies to purchase billions of dollars for armaments and sophisticated weaponries; how else the ordnance industries are to sell their warmongering products to profit trillions annually and not giving a damn about millions of innocent lives taken and maimed, as unjustified wars break loose.

President Dwight Eisenhower said, "Every gun that is made, every warship launched, every rocket fired signifies in the final sense, a theft from those who hunger and are not fed, those who are cold and are not clothed. This world in arms is not spending money alone. It is spending the sweat of it laborers, the genius of its scientists, the hope of its children, this is not a way of life at all in any true sense. Under the clouds of war, it is humanity hanging on a cross of iron."

Corporations are financially so powerful and potently influentially that they can manifest better living condition for billions of victims. They can economically leverage the natives with indigenous own resources and national wealth to improve their infrastructures and lifestyle, so that no one would most likely care to be summoned for terrorism, keeping so many deprived, and without any economic opportunity to improve their lives, as poverty is what puts them in trouble, as it has a lot to do with their insane conducts. Do not extort and take all of the pie and confiscate what inherently belongs to the indigenous inhabitants; give them some of the pie. Let the impoverished majority share a bit of the liberty and the prosperity you abundantly afford to enjoy—after all, it is their money for God's sake and not yours. Try to earn your share of the pie by doing some good for humanity's sake and not in pirating people's wealth.

Allow people's standard of living to change for the better; let their ways of life positively alter and ascend. Give them a chance to rebel against the recruiters of hate and monstrosities, to deter them from entering the gates of hell and avoid becoming sitting ducks, victims, so vulnerable to be hunted and perished. Help them to abstain from their inhumane terrorist's mindset, and divert them from cruel behaviors and gruesome actions. If you, the mighty elites, illustrate the power of compassion and mercy that real human beings are blessed with, it will certainly bring them peace and happiness; show them that God exists.

The imperial elites should start constituting universal economic relief and manifest programs toward globalization, so that boundaries can gradually collapse and mobilize billions with education, skill, training, and realistic hope, and not just in rhetoric. Call for true culture of humanism, rather than the petty nationalism you crave—where no animosity toward any race, gender, or creed can be tolerated, and where the global natural resources, and the international wealth and productivity are fairly allocated, and for the right reasons too.

The global government and the powerful elites should cooperatively challenge nature for the best outcome, as climate injustice has undermined human rights all over the globe, since no practical effort is ever taken by plutocracy of the corporate governments to mend the worst global warming ever experienced by humankind. And to rescue humanity from the clutches of hatred and warmongering actions, to discourage and halt sadistic conduct toward Mother Nature. It is time to ease off on international boundaries, to cut down the legal barriers, and let humanity mature to one government, one nation under God.

It is time to let diversities in racial, cultural, and religious differences become a blessing rather than a menace, which should help us have access to collective brotherhood. Let's lessen national debt, balance the budget, control population growth, and have a global system competent enough to structurally create full employment, mollify income inequality, and control inflation, recession, depression, stagnation, and other socioeconomic maladies. Here is what Alan Greenspan, former chairman of the U.S. federal reserve, said about income inequality: "I consider income inequality the most dangerous part of what's going on in the United States."

Furthermore, let's socialize health coverage, subsidize housing, free public transportations, and above all, let's have a free educational system accessible to everyone, and let's have progressive retirement plans where social security and networks of financial and professional assistance can efficiently help retiree and protect the elderly, the seniors, and those unable to work. You might ask where the funds should come from to orient and constitute grave and humanly deeds as above possible, and I say rest assured with the wealth and the infinite resources that the rich 1% hold; the entire planet earth can be refurbished, and its population can epitomize in good living 100 times over than what we are presently experiencing, and for many generations to come, and still have plenty of funds left to deal with municipalities' concern for attending to imperative matters if professionally managed, prioritized, and suitably allocated. In the meanwhile, the rich elites should choose to see that imperative issues, such as housing, education, health-related concepts, retirement plan, disability programs, social security, free transportation, and so on, as theses are rights, as they are not commodities to make money off at the expense of people being wasted. They are urgent necessities that must be dealt with intelligently and socially, but not based on business perspectives and for maximizing corporate profit.

And finally, let's be civilized, and not act hypocritical in bullying the weak into silence and submission, while catapulting their natural and human resources for minimal compensation and halt policing and destroying the world. And, yes, God has blessed and strengthened some nations with the stupendous (awesome) technology and amazing instrumental power, but it does not mean they should wipe out the entire planet. Let's give meaning to "in God we trust" and earnestly practice true democracy because you cannot choke off discourse and defend freedom.

In order to keep peace, it takes wisdom, as societies should thrive to establish law and order and practice civility of thinking and manner; otherwise, it leaves authorities with no choice, except refuge and force to quell violence. If the average reasoning power has not yet matured, then it leaves no option but to implement harsh rules to prevent chaos, and as Emmanuel Kant said, "If man makes himself a worm, he must not complain when he is trodden on." And of course, it is most appropriate if the ruling class and the powerful elites commit to people's education and invest in a constructive mental and intelligence makeover, to bring positive changes that can resonate with the entire nation.

It takes information, and knowledge to ascend consciousness, to awaken the masses with prudency, but it seems the financial elites are afraid to push for a global cultural revolution in higher education and for acquiring insight and wisdom. This, in turn, can raise a collective understanding of how the system is so unfairly operated, as people would notice the very reason behind their misery. Billions can then realize the real cause to their problems is not fate-related, but rather, game plans meant to oppress them, which awakened masses can, in turn, endanger the plutocrat's position, putting the entire governing system at grave risk of falling. If laws are the cause to people's insecurity and desolation, then it is the laws that must be changed since this literally ineffective socio political and dull socioeconomic situations begs for enlightening the masses and awakening them with honest geopolitical agendas, and letting people know the real reasons behind so much financial disparity and curses like poverty, making citizens aware of their rights, where justice can be served. As Emmanuel Kant said, "A categorical imperative would be one which represented an action as objectively necessary in itself without referencing to any other purpose."

They rely on brainwashing billions of people, intoxicating their minds for so long through dubious propaganda, luring them with insane positivism into collective delusional behaviors, which has shrouded the populace with uncertainty, and in acting complacent, no meaningful changes ever constitute, and they further linger in maintaining the status quo. The powerful elite want to make sure the economic chokehold is not loosened on the rest of the world since they have to be reassured with exploiting the globe and by enslaving the planet's inhabitant with no remorse, which in response the people must fight back incessantly to deliver sagacity (wisdom, reasoning power) potent enough to permeate and even change the most hardened of irrational minds and souls. English poet John Milton (1608-1674) said, "Prudence is the virtue by which we discern what is proper to do under various circumstances in time and place."

The oligopolistic behavior of the rich elites has pushed people into anomie (social instability resulting from a breakdown of standards and values; also personal unrest, alienation, and uncertainty that comes from a lack of purpose or ideals, also with dearth of connection to society), which can become a blessing in disguise since present situations are critical and potentiated to explode into revolutionizing the entire social and cultural norms and values that have kept society's ugly status active, as billions of ordinary people are economically struggling to survive, which should call for peaceful rebellions and make sense upheaval against the abusive situation. Dr. Martin Luther King's speech at Western Michigan University (December 18, 1963) is excerpted in which King addresses modern psychology and introduces the idea of creative maladjustment.

There is a word that is probably used more than any other word in modern psychology: It is the word "maladjusted." This word is the ringing cry to modern child psychology. Certainly, we all want to avoid the maladjusted life. In order to have real adjustment within our personalities, we all want the well-adjusted life in order to avoid neurosis, schizophrenic personalities.

But I say to you, my friends, as I move to my conclusion, there are certain things in our nation and in the world in which I am proud to be maladjusted and which I hope all men of goodwill also will be maladjusted until the good societies realize. I say very honestly that I never intend to become adjusted to segregation and discrimination. I never intend to become adjusted to religious bigotry. I never intend to adjust myself to economic conditions that will take necessities from the many to give luxuries to the few. I never intend to adjust myself to the madness of militarism, to self-defeating effects of physical violence.

In other words, I'm convinced now that there is need for a new organization in our world. The International Association for the Advancement of Creative Maladjustment—men and women who will be as maladjusted as the prophet Amos. Who in the midst of the injustices of his day could cry out in words that echo across the centuries, "Let justice roll down like waters and righteousness like a mighty"?

I believe globalization will progress to induce a world in which the boundaries collapse, and humanity should then inaugurate one system of government with one nation under God, where people could unanimously call themselves citizens of the world. Murray Gell-Mann in complexity, science, system, said, "Today the network of relationships linking the human race to itself and to the rest of the biosphere is so complex that all aspects affect all others to an extraordinary degree. Someone should be studying the whole system, however crudely that has to be done, because no gluing together of partial studies of a complex nonlinear system can give a good idea of the behavior of the whole."

We ought to persist on an effective system of ruling that digs into a host of vital issues indigenous to people's existence. It should plow into human activities and discourage immoral temperament and not malfunctions with misdeeds and other ill characteristics, such as vile personality makeups infused and fortified with avarice for accumulating material wealth and power, which makes an environment of grotesque inequalities forcing many to believe in the "survival of fittest" attitude and a cut-throat society, where human lives and dignity are neglected, as atmosphere of crime, violence, corruption, and insatiable bodily joy becomes the norm and accepted as a natural way of life.

Individual quenchless thirst for money has alienated us from our values, from each other, and has distracted so many from God and nature, as the culture of hoarding money has taken over not as a medium of exchange, but rather a measure of wealth, influence, prestige, prosperity and power. We are infatuated with money and are so tempted to produce huge wealth, which since it has undermined human veneration and because billions act herd-like, where they are distracted and cannot prioritize, making people lost in how they should objectify imperative issues in their lives and the world around them. We need to be inspired to constructively challenge life and to act collectively within balance, to accomplish quality living for all. Unfortunately, the entire monetary system—not to exclude financers, bankers, which are known as the high priests of finance, the corporate executives, and the so-called board of trustees—control our lives just like the Middle Ages, where religious tyranny was a curse upon humanity.

The invisible hand of the tyrannical financiers has replaced the invisible hand of the market and controls and influences our lives like in medieval era, where Pope Innocent III declared, "Anyone who attempts to construe a personal view of God which conflicts with church must be burned without pity." So does poverty, which can burn us without pity as well; wretched poverty induces all sorts of crimes and vices, as did the word inquisition, where financially bankrupt people become so desperate that many could potentially do much wrong to survive, as the Roman Church was associated with murder, torture, robbery, treachery, lies, arson, deceit, rape, lust, hypocrisy, cupidity (avarice), holiness, which no other word in all languages is so abhorrent and owes its notoriety to its link with the inquisition's infamously hideous reputation, as the "financial terrorists" of our times, which should remind us of medieval religious atrocities.

The capitalist economy and its supporting political system is constantly faced with systematic failure, with no hope of actual recovery expected, we need to realistically find a viable option that can sustain humanity financially. The current economic system has become deadlocked, stuck, and dilapidating (decay, ruination), and policing is what keeps it from falling, where systematic brutality is contrary to what George Washington did remind us of: "The basis of our political system is the right of the people to make and alter the constitution of government."

The capitalist system relates to capital and objectifies money as a mean to justify the end, which prioritizes making profit at any cost, but often defaults because of its serious deficiencies, making it very difficult for such a monetary system to resolve its problems and to overcome the innate shortcomings as it faces a stream of ill ripple effects that sometimes paralyzes the whole nation and even troubles the entire globe. When an economic system becomes incompetent and ridden with irresolvable problems, it delivers the system stagnant and in ruination, and because the system discourages better alternatives, it leaves no choice but to make loss of human lives inevitable. The system enters into a game of Russian roulette that in every second looks for the next victim. But then we smile like nothing is wrong and pretend that everything is all right, although inside it truly hurts, referencing Rumi the Persian poet who said "These pains you feel are the messengers, listen to them."

The corporate capitalists make democracy demeaning, which should spare us time to delve into the word democracy and see if democratic sovereignty is truly exercised or is just a hype that is overblown into publicity, as people are disillusioned with how democracy hypocritically works to further serve the interest of the few against the world population. Since we dispatch powerful armies and unrivaled military forces to police the globe to export democracy and ironically under the banner of human rights. Let's keep our ducks in a row at home first before messing with others' questionable liberty. The idea to discern is why any democratic nation that would advocate diversities in products and push for availability of hundreds and hundreds of brand items, which believes in multiculturalism and integration, drive people into accepting two political parties that have grown blunt and are morally coward to admit their inefficacies in action.

And why corporate empires do not let democracy flourish at work where twelve to fifteen board of directors, who each owns millions of shares, as they can decide what to produce, how to produce, where to produce, and what to do with the profits, as they rule over thousands of workers who work their rear-ends off to make and manufacture the products, but absolutely have no rights to cast any vote or have any say in what should be assembled. By the way, the products generated are often not what should have been planned for satisfying consumer's demand and their consumption's need. It is solely done to maximize profit, which is why we either face glutton or shortage of commodities, and occasionally within a global scale. The system cannot assimilate democracy by nature because the system is implicitly incompetent to accommodate everyone with even the most basic necessities for survival. When millions are longing to work because their living and the life of their loved ones depends on working, but cannot find employment, it sure proves democracy futile.

Democracy should provide everyone with equal economic opportunity and assist people to surpass their capacity in becoming the best they can be and not push for meritocracy and only leverage those rich elites who already possess billions of dollars and consecutively win millions of lottery tickets, as they are positioned for insider trading, as being counterfeit. But they are portrayed smart and believed to be intelligent investors, with no penalty or any concession of guilt—that is not democracy. When millions graduate despite overcoming so many hurdles manufactured through draconian tests and arduous examinations, and they surmount state requirement this, or pass state implementing that. But they end up with thousands of dollars in student loans and with high interest shoved down their throats. When they graduate but are unable to find jobs, that is not democracy. Of course not being able to find jobs for meeting their financial responsibilities, yokes and petrifies them since it ruins their credit, as if they are repeated felons.

Most graduates under pressure succeed despite facing tough conditions, but simply cannot do anything productive without good credit, which makes it their fault, labeling them with ineptitude or unfit for hiring. The system simply replaces its inability to create adequate work for millions of student graduates and passes the buck of guilt to the apprentices who are now qualified for good positions in the job market, but find it impossible, which then one should bear in mind that is not democracy. When corporations decide to outsource jobs to other parts of the world to benefit from raw materials and plenty of natural resources and abundance of cheap labor and capitalize on paying no taxes, as they close their doors on millions of workers at home, leaving them stranded and unemployed without a future, positioning them in a life-threatening situation—that is not democracy.

Democracy is a sacred word that should not be trampled on. Democracy unfetters hopes for people to maneuver freely and spurs big dreams, and it pushes humanity into achieving kinghood. Democracy is as implicit with our human spirit as roses are with gorgeous fragrant bloom and smashing vigorous red and enchanting pink color. Without freedom, we just wither away. Democracy is what God has consecrated every human being with; no one with an inch of propriety should dare to seize what is anointed to humankind by our creator. Let democracy show its miraculous essence and manifest hope to billions. Let's give democracy the transcended values it deserves and honor its heavenly attributes.

And I say, "Isn't it amazing that we are all made in God's image, and yet there's so much adversities among us. Those who do not deny God, but tell us God is a lie with their actions as they oppress and take people's freedom away, and those who lose their very breath and die to keep humankind free and to uphold democracy, to tell the rest of humanity that there is a God." In the meanwhile, we need to keep pounding on the question of financial terrorism of our time, which has since kept a malignant position facing humanity. We should incessantly ask if not tyranny, then what is it that keeps societies from transforming to positive changes and better living conditions. We are not exhausted without options; there are sensible alternatives, such as cooperative (co-op) economic systems, which if given a chance, can play a quintessential role in our lives and significantly flourish and improve everyone's life.

In co-op systems, local communities and the actual wealth-creators, the workers, can start bottom-up companies, and since they own the means of production, it enables them to assess the actual need of the market, where supply and demand can truly meet. And because the allocation of natural and human resources is properly designated to where it is most needed, rather than for sole profit, it will help to maximize the efficiency of the market productivity, sales, distributions, and in avoiding enormous waste, as so sadly is experienced within the present capitalist system.

In co-op systems, profits are decently shared, which can incentivize laborers to work harder and trigger collective geniuses to cultivate true innovation, ingenuity, resourcefulness, motivation, imagination, democracy at work, and give meaning to honest cooperation. Collective ownership of the means of production will replace a futile privatization enterprise system that must constantly be resuscitated (revive) at the expense of workers themselves and all taxpayers. If so, and it should be the taxpayers' obligation to bail out these "too big to fail" institutional bankers and other humongous financial corporations with no rewards and without any monetary return for the actual people who keep saving the fat cats—then why not let public ownership replace these monstrously big financially institutionalized entities owned by few individuals that so narrow-mindedly see only their own interest.

It is sad that we are entering 21st century, and the era of the solar system, but yet some people behave so naïvely toward the inalienable rights of others. They support private opulence and negate public squalor as they act so indifferently toward the suffering of billions of ordinary masses. This should call for a radical change in the landscape of the entire financial system peacefully; in the meanwhile, we should make the idea of having a socialist and dictatorial party system remote and detour from any perceived hostile revolutionary attitude. We must not take the infinite silence of God for granted, as patience is God's virtue; it will indiscriminately deal with cruel hearts, no matter which side one is on.

The system of capitalists' coercion and monetary domination is not ordained by God, hence the modern life parameters clearly indicate the fallacies and wrongdoings of the system. By nature, the system has become stalemated and in decay, which is no longer fair play, and a dynamic force to reckon with. The capitalist system indoctrinates people to identify with its political and economic way of life that has institutionalized class differentiation, where extreme income disparity absolutely thwarts (contravene, to oppose successfully, defeat the hopes, or aspiration) collective bargaining and social movements, which should be the essence of human interactivities. Human beings by nature gravitate toward collectivism and generally dislike to be isolated and reluctant in fairing alone; it is the essence of humankind to be cooperative. It is in our DNA; otherwise humanity would have not pulled through for billions of years from prehistoric times to the current civilization era.

We should not fall trap into believing that human species are some type of abstract beings, money-driven by nature that resonate with greed and self-centeredness. These types of analogies are nothing but shams, which since have created cosmetic pretext and intoxicating environments to direct and encourage the individualism school of thought that is the pillar of the capitalists' philosophy and its belief on how societies ought to run. The fact is that people are divided between having extreme wealth and being entrenched with extreme poverty—in which no positive marginal change can possibly resolve the systematic problems facing the capitalist system.

We should manifest revolutionary ideas and utilize dynamic plans, where intelligently refined products are generated to constructively improve people's living standards. We should not inhibit our thoughts or limit our actions to preserve the status quo; it is time to conceptualize big dreams and enter new horizons, where refreshing ways of life can set us all free. We should not hold on to what only benefits a tiny portion and leave billions of inhabitants with no option, but to perish like autumn leaves. Martin Luther King Jr. put it this way: "The ultimate measure of man is not where he stands in moments of comfort and convenience, but where he stands at times of challenge and controversy." It has become necessary to rescue people from the power of greed and a malfunctioning system. Since there are other decent and efficient economic systems that can gradually work their way up democratically and make the actual evolutionary process a dream come true for billions of people without bloodshed and institutionalize the co-op system in a global scale from the very bottom up locals and communities. Prosperity and saving precious human lives can become mandatory and a must priority and not optional and just another rhetoric. It is importantly vital to replace this system by peaceful means, since we definitely have the resources and the techniques to do so.

Look, animals must resolve their animosities through violence as they can only resort to hostile behavior to settle their differences. They are unable to think; they cannot talk and dialogue. Animals are not open to constructive criticism, and they do not possess the will, the technology to behave amicably. The beasts are not endowed with consciousness, they are deprived of knowledge and information, they lack decisive intelligence, and they do not have the power to dream and to imagine. They are exhausted of spiritual endeavors, and it is difficult to say if one can detect any emotion or feeling that any beast might own. They cannot resonate with having hope and persevere for a better future. To deny those very sacred, essential human attributes would mean we have lowered ourselves to animal level, which otherwise would make it necessary for solving our conflicts through common sense and diplomacy, to collectively reach our objectives solely by counseling and effective colloquy (talks, confabulation, conversation) where everyone can win. Our goal must gravitate toward minimizing harm, not violence, and maximizing cooperation in orienting goodness and prosperity for all.

I consider it a mark of great prudence in a man to abstain from threats or any contemptuous expressions, for neither of these weaken the enemy. Threats make them more cautious, and the other excites their hatred and a desire to avenge themselves.

Niccolò Machiavelli (1469-1527) Italian political philosopher and statesman.

The system should aim to correct those who illegally hoard billions of dollars at the top with devious intent and disgraceful conduct, which has replaced God in their lives. They have accumulated so much wealth beyond comprehension and call it economic thriving for the blessed ones, as if deprived others are born from behind and have arrived from sub-terrains and are perhaps the citizens of inferior planets.

The system needs to mollify (appease, reconcile, soften, assuage, placate, conciliate) the concept of "everyone to his own philosophy" and avoid extreme individualism culture, where survival of the wisest can lead to collective moral intelligence and prosperities, rather than promoting self-centeredness through mischievous and cynical behaviors with irrational conduct. Financial predators, loan sharks, and economic hit men devour their victims as they exhibit the most unrestrained and inhumane actions in the name of business and self-interest. They have implemented a toxic atmosphere of "not what you know, but who you know," which counts and makes upward mobility possible.

It is who you know that moves you up in treacherous zigzagging of life's walk ways, making a mockery of fair play, since they so unjustly appreciate designated individuals, that either rank them high (elevating many in the socioeconomic hierarchy) through nepotism or via bribery, and other immoral favoritism and misconduct. An effective economic system with full employment leveraged by genuine democracy at work and a justified socioeconomic relationship among people would most likely remedy many irreparable problems facing the capitalist system and not to exclude correcting briberies, sexual cronyism (partiality) and also mending nepotism.

Many scientists acknowledge the fact that the human mind is not detached and that our mind is in tune with social interconnectivity rather than being individually isolated. The mind is more than just the brain, say scientists. Our mind is not constricted to our brain or even our body, so free your mind. Occasionally one might marvel what is happening in other people's minds, may admire someone's great mind, or perhaps say one is out of one's mind and try to unfold and free one's own mind. But the question should be what is a mind? Identifying the concept is an amazingly slippery job. The mind is the place of consciousness, the extract of your being. Without a mind, one cannot significantly be regarded alive. Therefore, what exactly, and where precisely, is the mind? Inherently scientists have managed to define the mind as the product of brain activity. The brain is the physical matter and the mind is the awakened product of those firing neurons, according to the classic argument. But deepening evidence shows that the mind travels far beyond the physical workings of our brain.

No question the brain maneuvers a remarkably vital role. But our mind cannot be cramped to what's inside our skull or even our body, according to a definition initially addressed by Dan Siegel, a professor of psychiatry at UCLA School of Medicine and the author of a the book *Mind: A Journey to the Heart of Being Human*. He first came up with the definition more than two decades ago, at a meeting of 40 scientists across disciplines, not to exclude neuroscientists, physicists, psychologists, psychiatrists, sociologists, and anthropologists. The objective was to grasp an understanding of the mind that would implore for common ground and gratify many challenging the inquiries across these fields.

After thorough investigation they concluded that a key component of the mind is: "the emergent self-organizing process, both embodied and relational, that regulates energy and information flow within and among us." It's not catchy. But it is interesting and with meaningful implications. The most surprisingly shocking part of definition is that our mind expands beyond our physical body. They decided that our mind is not just our perception of experiences, but those experiences themselves. Siegel argues that it's not possible to absolutely unravel our subjective view of the world from our interactions. He adds, "I realized if someone asked me to define the shoreline but insisted, is it the water or the sand, I would have to say the shore is both sand and sea. You can't limit our understanding of the coastline to insist it's one or the other. I started thinking, maybe the mind is like the coastline—some inner and inter process. Mental life for an anthropologist or sociologist is profoundly social. Your thoughts, feelings, memories, attention, what you experience in this subjective world is part of mind."

The definition has since been advocated by research across the sciences, but they admit that much of the archetype (a perfect example, prototype) idea came from mathematics. Siegel realized the mind meets the mathematical definition of an intricate system in that it's open (can influence things outside itself), chaos capable (which simply means it's roughly randomly distributed), and nonlinear (which means a small input leads to large and difficult to predict result) which he denotes. In mathematics, byzantine (complicated) systems are self-organizing, and Siegel says this idea is the foundation to mental health. Again borrowing from math, optimal self-organization is flexible, adaptive, coherent, energized, and stable. This means that without optimal self-organization, you arrive at either chaos or rigidity—a notion that, Siegel says, fits the range of symptoms of mental health disorders. Finally, self-organization demands linking together differentiated ideas or, essentially, integration. And Siegel believes integration—whether that's within the brain or within society—is the foundation of a healthy mind.

Siegel "wrote his book now because he sees so much misery in society, and he believes this is partly shaped by how we perceive our own minds. He talks of doing research in Namibia, where people he spoke to attributed their happiness to a sense of belonging. When Siegel was asked in return whether he belonged in America, his answer was less upbeat." He further articulates: "I thought how isolated we all are and how disconnected we feel. In our modern society we have this belief that mind is brain activity and this means the self, which comes from the mind, is separate and we don't really belong. But we're all part of each other's lives. The mind is not just brain activity. When we realize it's this relational process, there's this huge shift in this sense of belonging."

In other words, even understanding our mind as simply a product of our brain, rather than social relations, can make us feel more apart. And to value the benefits of interrelations, we simply have to open our mind.

But then, overwhelming evidence that indicates human beings are socially oriented, rather than being individually cultivated, which has financially deepened the gap between the haves and the have-nots, forming extreme classified societies. It has produced so many inhumane consequences, with traumatic events beyond remedy instigated by powerful corporations, as they incessantly keep pushing for even more cultural aberration (divergence, abnormality, deviation) designed to ingratiate "every man to his own philosophy" into people's thought process, making them believe this is how life is meant to be.

Capitalism is dangling people's face where billions do not have the buying power to participate in the activities of the so-called free market because so many are demonized with poverty and deprived of the very basic necessities of living. They are exhausted of daily sustenance, as if a refutable curse has befallen the indignant indigents. This urgently calls for the mind and the heart of justice to assuage (soften, mollify, placate) this stupidly cemented class gap and to alleviate horrifying income inequality between the rich and the poor that should not be solely dismissed as greed, but rather needs to be recognized as utter discriminatory economic and socially malignant criteria turning into financial endogamy (inbreeding, incest) among the rich elites.

The business empires subversively act against "the have-nots," where financial perverts are addicted with self-pollination and stricken with heresy (eccentricity, dissents, nonconformist) since the sadistically super-rich undermine commoners with multifaceted forms of economic deformity and social oppression, plunging the poor into incompetency to fight back. The power of the people has been radically diminished, and the military industrial complex and the police state have denied citizens dignified social and political insurgency against the tyrannical corporate elites and associates. And hence rational discourse has eventually proved futile, leaving no option but to nonviolently dare the system into aligning with good, against what is wretchedly inhumane.

The populace must further be awakened to systematized mainstream media outlets that simply brush aside the truth and rig information brainwashing its victims, since the corporate media has relied on lies and embarked on formidable techniques to violate the sanctity of what is decent and continue with trickery to misinform its prey.

The powerful elites hunt their prey with impunity since no repercussion faces them, as if their barbarically unconstitutional practices, ferocious manhunt, and civil disobedience should be rewarded. The corporate plutocracy somehow believes no better living is ever possible without their incredulous and incriminating ways of dealing with society in the name of the free market economy, which unleashes its predatory behavior repressing the middle class, the working class, and the poor, exploiting nature that has already caused so much damage to the entire globe beyond repair. What should be awakening is the blatant atrocities and explicit violation of global human rights, global warming, war of aggression, terrorism, jihadism and radicalism, extreme income inequality, sexism, human trafficking, implicit racism, and other inhumane and ugly traits that to stop, and if not, they sure can become antecedents to a catastrophic nuclear war ending life as we know it, which can surely exacerbate the already explosive sociopolitical and socioeconomic situation by unduly, disturbing actions of governing plutocracy, and through destructive corporate conducts and their goons.

Multibillion-dollar platforms (political parties) are steadfastly mobilized to prominent corporate oligopolies for manifesting a horrific world as we are experiencing, where truth-tellers are made ineffective, but the corporate bootlickers in cahoots with conglomerate media corporations are premiered at the frontline of our democracy as they present the interest of the plutocrats, where they have delivered a coup de grâce (a decisive finishing blow) against the republic and what it stands for. In which the oligopolistic government has made days of destruction inevitable, bringing us closer to days of revolt, since the corporate machine has lynched billions with poverty and utter insecurity, telling them they do not matter as they are forced into disdain and hopeless positions.

The global casino capitalists mock and strip people of their rights where so many are pushed to the edge and left with no choice but to try to take all the levels of power against the financial tyranny of our time that has rendered citizens impotent and paraplegic in their efforts for subsistence. Let's dig a bit into the root causes of our problems, since it seems the further we struggle, the further we sink into the quicksand of life, which if not wisely attended to and resolved can drown billions into the abyss.

We access our brain and strive to act mindful for making sense of things from the simplest to most puzzling tasks, where the outcome should accordingly differ because some are blessed with higher IQs, since they possess relatively potent intelligence than others. It is not facetious (joking, waggish) when scientists say we are basically utilizing about 10% of our brain capacity, which should mean 90% still constitutes gray matter bound to become explored. Yes, the human brain is a very complex entity because it performs millions of elegant and magnificent sublunary (worldly) acts, but then if we could tap into the remaining 90%, perhaps it would enable us to have telekinetic (mind over matter, paranormal mental effects on the physical, faith heeling, psychokinesis) and novel (space age) powers, which I am certain would positively rub on our civility and decent conducts too.

The 10% notion has been linked to the American psychologist and author William James, who argued in *The Energies of Men* that "We are making use of only a small part of our possible mental and physical resources." It's also been associated with Albert Einstein for explaining his cosmic towering intellect. The myth's durability, Gordon says "stems from people's conceptions about their own brains: they see their own shortcomings as evidence of the existence of untapped gray matter, this is a false assumption, what is correct, however, is that at certain moments in anyone's life, such as when we are simply at rest and thinking, we may be using only 10% of our brains. Evidence would show over a day you use 100% of the brain."

Says John Henley, a neurologist at the Mayo Clinic in Rochester, Minnesota. Even in sleep areas, such as the frontal cortex, which controls things like higher level thinking and self-awareness, or the somatosensory area (being sensory activity having its origin elsewhere than in the special sense organs as eyes and ears), which helps people sense their surroundings, are active. He said, "What's not understood is how clusters of neurons from the diverse regions of the brain collaborate to form consciousness. So far, there's no evidence that there is one site for consciousness, which leads experts to believe that it is truly a collective neural effort. Another mystery hidden within our crinkled cortices is that out of all the brains cells, only 10% are neurons; the other 90% are glial cells, which encapsulate and support neurons, but whose function remains largely unknown. Ultimately, it's not that we use 10% of our brains merely that we only understand about 10% of how it functions."

I believe when Henley refers to using our 100% of brain usage, he should indicate 100% usage of the 10% available, which Einstein was able to manifest when he discovered his famous relativity equation; otherwise it is odd to relatively utilize 100% of our brain and only understand 10% of how it does actually function. And referencing historical evolution it makes sense to adequately perceive and acknowledge that no caveman from Stone Age times and prehistorical era could have had access to 10% of their brain, which is presently available to modern man, and if so, then billion years of evolutionary time span, which has molded a complex cerebral cortex (part of the nervous system, the thinking brain) should render futile; rather than accepting its tremendous progress in cognitive ability since the prehistoric era. Or perhaps we should accept that our modern and relatively civilized world is just an illusion, and we have not advanced and progressed a bit in our evolutionary concept of understanding the human brain. Besides, I also believe much of the gray area not in use is not just going to forever lay there idle; it is eventually going to be pushed to its limit.

I am only investigating statistics and numbers; no disrespect or impropriety is directed at anyone at all. But then, the provocative question should be, Why do we behave the way we do? Let's accredit animals with using 1% of their brain, and since not everyone is gifted to utterly manifest 10% of their brain, then in relative terms some people proportionally can manage their lives respective of how far each and everyone's mind is potentiated—perhaps a tad higher than animals or may be blessed with higher intelligence and deeply insightful. let's assume we utilize the entire 10% of brain's ability, or give the benefit of doubt, and allow 12% to 15% brain faculty, reflecting our reasoning competency which should manifest the way our contemporary world functions.

If so, then why become shocked when we decimate millions of our own kind in genocide or behave malevolently toward the innocent migrants with antiquated immigration laws as the war criminals displace millions of helpless people through malicious conduct since we bomb them and are conducive in making so many run for their lives, and as they come to us, we act upset and surprised, as if we do not see the elephant in the room, and the actual reason behind our problems, or even act surprised when the system so unjustly encourages extreme income inequality, which results in grotesque social and economic outcomes, and so forth. After all, we still have 90% of uncharted brain territories for accessing our brains' optimum level. It seems enlightenment is the only hope for saving humanity, as there are those with plenty of character flaws and beastly attitude in control of hydrogen bombs, atomic bombs, bacterial and chemical bombs, cluster bombs, and so on, in which they can with no doubt end life as we know it.

We live in a dangerous time, as beastly notions have outgrown good thoughts, which must collectively alert us to raise our antenna and notice the vile position that humanity is entangled with, since the culprits have the most dreadful technology to normalize repugnant ideas and are able to substantiate any evil feat at will, which can drive millions insane and form them into irresponsible and careless characters, as though robots have taken over.

The next crucial question should be whether there is hope for reaching light at the end of the tunnel—of course yes, but we must employ a system that is adamant to bring about radical changes that are user-friendly. When governments facilitate private mega arms corporations to make trillions by selling armaments to savages and barbarian regimes inhibited with one percentage brain activity, as their hooligans behave as pathogens and unfairly silent, and unjustly deaden dissidents via torture, and by murdering unarmed people, often through summary executions, then there is big problem.

When a governing regime allows colossal private enterprises to pollute the air we breathe and contaminate the water we drink and allows exterminating biodiversity, then the pharmaceutical corporation charges skyrocketing prices when the victims seek medical help and corporations charge money to sell water to famine and drought-stricken indigenous people, then, we should know we have a problem. When trash fields are controlled by so-called entrepreneurs and smaller companies, which charge a fee to let the poor secure clean food and clothing from the garbage to feed and cover themselves, we must know there is a problem. When we witness millions of refugees who have been militarily invaded and forced to camp out barricaded in the desert with no shelter, with no food or any amenities, we should know we have a big problem.

When we have the largest numbers of prisoners incarcerated in dire condition and inhumane correctional facilities that feed private institutions to maximize profit, because crime is going rampant, we need to know we have problem. Encouraging drug addiction with prostitution and human trafficking, since the pervasive porn industries are incessant to sexually exploit women even children for lucrative profiteering, we know we have a problem. When many sell their bodily organs via the black market to feed their loved ones, we should realize we have a problem, and so forth. The bottom line is that no capitalist system can honestly identify with humanism, since the system profits when there is war, the system profits when people are sick, the system profits when there is violence, fear, and distrust among different races. The system profits from toxic environments, making it necessary to reboot cultural, ideological, spiritual, social, political, and economic factors to put an end to constantly living in an alarming state and with high anxiety, which creates chronic stress and a host of other malignant and incurable diseases.

The commercially driven mass media worsens the outcomes because conglomerate news corporations do not operate in the public interest; they premeditate to lie, distort news, create fallacies, and distract consumers to damage control, to safeguard the entire system, and to disseminate what interests the mega-corporations. They decide what news is worthy and what is not; they control people's imaginations and ideas, they monopolize news media, distort the truth, and stampede to prevent what might degrade or discredit their bosses.

It is a vicious circle, since mega corporations contribute huge funds to campaign for their marionette (puppet) politicians, where dubious state representatives promise them much in return at the expense of ordinary people. The news media falsely creates "iconic images" that are deemed to elect those "sell-out politicians" for successive terms, while they broadcast lies to stir up people's emotions and dominate citizens' thoughts to control social apparatus, for reaching the menacing corporate objectives.

When we have an economic system that is destroying planet Earth and causes mass extinctions of species, exterminates biodiversity and the ecosystem, and then calls it "economic externalities," and causes economic terror and panic, we have a problem. They fleece ordinary people since they do not factor the so-called economic externalities as corporate costs, as they create "nature deficit disorder" endangering people's lives and declaring war on the entire planet.

The corporate media refuses to talk about the grotesque actions by the big money corporations that epitomize corrupt behavior and clandestine conduct. It has become a neurosis culture in denial, since it boycotts humanity from its natural inhabitants and separates so many from all of what nature has to offer that sustains us and the future generations. When they link human happiness to unconditional, un-relentless consumption, and unending growth, as they foster people's mindsets, as if this is quite natural. Where the matrix of human identity is measured by accumulation of wealth, material hording, and power that alienates people and encourages extreme individualism, then we should know we have a problem.

When we comprise 5% of the world's population, but have 30% of the world's prisoners, then we need to know we have a problem. It should be expected from correctional facilities that operate by taxpayers' money to deal and connect to inmates through professional entities, where the prisoners have a chance to be dealt with therapeutically and through correct psychoanalysis approach, since they should be taught to be emotionally honest and willing to look inward, to be "mindful" of their emotional reactions. And to question whether those reactions are coming from within ourselves, rather than wrongfully judging others with a biased eye, which perhaps has nothing to do with the way one feels.

Where pride, and not acting macho or ostentatious (pretentious) and not behaving in certain ways, should not mean emasculating, because many are emotionally unable to deal with their aggression and sometimes exhibit outrageous conduct without professional help, as they are faced against the odds, and a culture of violence that is shamelessly promulgated (declare, proclaim) and encouraged inside those hideous prisons, which victimize many who are sincerely seeking a way out of crime infested environments and their miserable situation with no avail. They manifest emotional honesty looking for a way out of jail, but feel guilt, as they are labeled weak, making them vulnerable preys of rape and other inhumane atrocities. Only the culture of force and manhandling rules inside those despicable cells and the so-called "correctional" facilities, which fear rules and force is predominantly the norm.

It is noteworthy that even in times of prosperity and the so-called economic discovery, the bottom 90% are not affected by the financial boom and fiscal expansion since they still experience extreme poverty. Where the cream of the crop consistently shifts to the upper 1% and goes to those at the top of the social echelon. Any ignorant economist should know the wages must be coherent and adjusted to unavoidable inflationary growth, since the system is structurally lop-sided and unequivocally bears precarious side effects such as recession, inflation, and because the system can only supply partial employment and is unable to produce full employment, as it also creates stagnation, depression, extreme income inequality, and misallocation of resources, as the market aims at making products that maximize profit, and not to manufacture need-based related goods and services. It helps to know what the cause to human suffering is and why some people act so indifferently toward others' pain, and not only that, but actually premeditate and plan to exploit the weak and the disadvantaged.

If dull-mindedness contributes to our lives' malaise, then it makes it imperative to further investigate the activities of the brain and how it functions. I am also curious if our destructive actions are proportionally related to the immature anatomical structure of human brain, not firing enough neurons to substantiate higher intelligence, and perhaps not viable to more brain cells opening. If so, is there any way out of life's hellholes that we have brought upon ourselves, as a human species. Adding to that mystery is the contention that humans "only" employ 10% of their brain. If regular folks could tap the other 90%, they as well could become savants who remember π to the twenty-thousandth decimal place, or perhaps even have telekinetic powers. Though an alluring idea, the 10% myth is so wrong it is almost laughable, says neurologist Barry Gordon at Johns Hopkins School of Medicine in Baltimore. Although there's no definitive culprit to pin the blame on for starting this legend, the notion has been linked to the American psychologist and author William James, who argued in *The Energies of Men* that "We are making use of only a small part of our possible mental and physical resources." It's also been associated with Albert Einstein, who supposedly used it to explain his cosmic towering intellect.

The myth's durability, Gordon says, stems from people's conceptions about their own brains. They see their own shortcomings as evidence of the existence of untapped gray matter. This is a false assumption. What is correct, however, is that at certain moments in anyone's life, such as when we are simply at rest and thinking, we may be using only 10% of our brains. "It turns out though, that we use virtually every part of the brain, and that [most of] the brain is active almost all the time," Gordon adds. "Let's put it this way: the brain represents 3% of the body's weight and uses 20% of the body's energy."

In the nervous system, there is a peculiar kind of cell recognized as a neuron/nerve cell. The marrow (main) element of the nervous system in general, and the brain specifically, is the neuron or nerve cell, the "brain cells" of popular term. A neuron is an electrically stimulated cell that advances and transmits information by electro-chemical signaling. They are different from other cells; neurons do not divide, and neither do they die off to be replaced by new ones. They normally cannot be changed after being lost with few exceptions. The specific structures of neurons permit them to forward signals to other cells swiftly and accurately. The cues (signals) are sent in the form of electrochemical waves (that travel along slender fibers/axons), which make chemicals (neurotransmitters) to be released at junctures known as "synapses." After this, we can ratify that synapses are constructions that permit signals/information from one neuron to be sent to another neuron. A normal neuron fires about five to fifty times in every second, as neurons form thousands of connections with other neurons to bestow a typical brain well over 1,000 trillion synapses. Neurons are cells that make nerve signals travel to and from the brain at speeds of 200 miles per hour, and more. Each neuron has a body (soma) and dendrites (signal receiver) and an extension or protrusion that is called an axon, which conducts the nerve signal to express messages. Neurons send electrical signals along axons; this causality is known as "conduction," through which the cell body of a neuron communicates with its own terminals by the axon. There are cells within the nerve system that communicate information to other nerve cells, muscles, or gland cells.

The average human brain conveys approximately 100 billion neurons (or nerve cells) and many more neuroglia (or glial cells) that support and protect the neurons. Every neuron is linked to up to 10,000 other neurons, transmitting signals to each other through as many as 1,000 trillion synaptic connections, equated by some estimates to a computer with a 1 trillion bit per second processor. The human brain's memory competency vastly differs from 1 to 1,000 terabytes, bear in mind that for comparison the 19 million volumes in the U.S. Library of Congress delineate about 10 terabytes of data. Distinct from other body cells, most neurons in the human brain are only able to divide to manufacture new cells via a process called "neurogenesis" during fetus development and for a short time after birth.

These brain cells may increase in size until the age of 18 years, but they are primarily designed to last a lifetime. Knowing that the only area of the brain where neurogenesis has been exhibited to endure throughout life is the hippocampus, an area inherent to memory encoding and storage. Each neuron asserts a voltage gradient across its membrane, due to metabolically driven differences in ions of sodium, potassium, chloride, and calcium within the cell, each of which has a different charge. If the voltage changes significantly, an electrochemical pulse called an action potential (or nerve impulse) is generated. This electrical pursuit can be measured and shown as a wave form called brain wave or brain rhythm.

Routinely related neurons couple to each other to constitute neural networks (known as neural nets or assemblies). The connections between neurons are not motionless, since they change over time. The more signals sent between two neurons, the stronger the connection grows, and the amplitude of the post-synaptic neurons response increases. With up to date information, new experience and with every remembered episode or fact, the brain slightly rewires its bodily structure. The interactions of neurons are not merely electrical, though, but electrochemical. Each axon terminal consists of thousands of membrane-bound sacs called vesicles, which each hold thousands of neurotransmitter molecules. Neurotransmitters are chemical messengers that relay, amplify, and modulate signals between neurons and other cells. The two most familiar neurotransmitters in the brain are the amino acids glutamate and GABA; other vitally important neurotransmitters include acetylcholine, dopamine, adrenaline, histamine, serotonin, and melatonin.

Our brain has the most intricate structure known in the universe; our brain is the product of many millions of years of evolution. Some of the structures exclusive to the human species have manifested relatively recently. For instance, only "about one hundred thousand years ago" the progenitors (forbearer) of modern man had a brain weighing approximately one pound; roughly one-third of the weight of the current version. Most of the grown weight is linked to the most striking feature of the human brain, the cortex—the two basically symmetrical (balance) and wrinkly hemispheres that sit astride (mounted) the central core. Almost all the jobs that seem tough for human beings, which are presently performed by computer generation are affiliated with processing in parts of the relatively new cortex. We should notice the chores that human beings often find easy, but are hard for a computer to execute, generally have a very long evolutionary history, since the most modern computers even after meticulous programing are typically weak at sensing their environment or coordinating movements. What humans find rather easy and straightforward, like recognizing someone's face, can be dreadfully difficult for a computer to manage because our human brain utilizes multiple levels of processing that have developed over millions of years.

Close to 5 million years ago, another type of cortex showed up in a new species, early man. In this brain, the exterior of the cortex was separately organized into columns, regions less than one millimeter wide but each conveying many millions of neurons. The new build permits much more elaborate protrusion (extension, bulge) to take place. Finally, about 100,000 years ago, this new cortex experienced speedy development with the advent of modern man. The present-day cortex holds something like two-thirds of all neurons, and weighs about three pounds, almost three times its weight only about 100,000 years ago. The human brain is comprised of three separate parts.

The first portion in the lower section, occasionally named the brain stem, consists of construction such as the medulla (controlling breathing, heart rate, and digestion) and the cerebellum (coordinating senses and muscle movement). Much of these components are innate "as is" from the reptilian brain.

The second portion shown as slightly inflated in lower vertebrates and magnifies in the higher primates and ourselves into the midbrain. The structures included here connect the lower brain stem to the thalamus (for information relay) and to the hypothalamus (that is meant for regulating drives and actions). The present is part of the limbic system.

The limbic system, inherently is identical in all mammals; it lies higher than the brain stem and beneath the cortex, which includes a number of interconnected structures. Researchers have connected these constructions to hormones, temperature, drives, emotion, control, and the hippocampus to memory formation. Neurons affecting heart rate and respiration appear focused in the hypothalamus and direct most of the physiological changes that accompany powerful emotion.

Forceful behavior is linked to the function of the amygdala that is next to the hippocampus. The latter enacts an important role in processing various forms of information as part of our long-term memory. Damage to the hippocampus will produce global retrograde (worsen) amnesia or the inability to obtain new stores of information. Most parts of the lower and midbrain are relatively simple systems able to register experiences and regulate conduct mainly outside of our conscious cognizance (i.e., we don't have to think to blink or remember to breathe).

Lastly is the third portion: the forebrain appears as a plain and simple bump in the brain of the lower life form, but swells into the cerebrum of higher life forms and covers the brain stem like the head of a mushroom. It has moreover evolved in humans into the walnut-like shape of right and left hemispheres (semicircle). The highly twisted and coiled surface of the hemispheres—the cortex—is approximately two millimeters thick and has a total exterior area of about 1.5 square meters. The edifice of the cortex is drastically complex. Its most "high-level" activities are associated to the mind. Some of its locality are highly particularized; for instance, the occipital lobes located near the rear of the brain are linked with the visual system. The motor cortex assists, coordinates the entire voluntary muscle movements. More neurons may be devoted to certain parts of the body than others; for instance, the fingers have many more nerve endings than the toes do. There is an approximate symmetry between left and right hemispheres; for example, there are two occipital lobes, two parietal lobes, and there are two frontal lobes. Although this symmetry is not precise; for example, the area connected with language appears on the left hemisphere.

The frontal lobes lodge the front part of the brain behind the forehead and put together portions of the brain most closely associated with "control" of responses to input from the rest of the system and closely related with making decisions and judgments.

In many people, the left hemisphere is preeminent (dominant, supreme, controlling) over the right in determining which response to make. The frontal lobes occupy 29% of the cortex in humans (as opposed to 3.5% in rats and 17% in chimpanzees).

In individuals with normal hemispheric dominance, the left hemisphere controls the right side of the body, deals with language and general cognitive functions. The right hemisphere, managing the left half of the body, deals with nonverbal processes, such as pattern recognition, attention, orientation, and the detection of complicated auditory tones. Even though the two hemispheres are in steady communication with each other, they function as independently parallel processors with corresponding occupation; the overriding left hemisphere appears most closely associated with a conscious self.

The average human brain weighs about three pounds and comprises the hefty cerebrum, which is the largest portion, and performs all higher cognitive functions; the cerebellum, responsible for motor functions, such as the coordination of movement and balance; and the brain stem, dedicated to involuntary functions like breathing. The majority of the energy consumed by the brain powers the rapid firing of millions of neurons communicating with each other. Scientists think it is such neuronal firing and connecting that gives rise to all of the brain's higher functions. The rest of its energy is used for controlling other activities— both unconscious activities, such as heart rate, and conscious ones, such as driving a car.

Although it's true that at any given moment all of the brain's regions are not concurrently firing, brain researchers using imaging technology have shown that, like muscles, most parts are continually active over a 24-hour period. "Evidence would show over a day you use 100% of the brain," says John Henley, a neurologist at the Mayo Clinic in Rochester, Minnesota. Even in sleep, areas such as the frontal cortex, which controls things like higher level thinking and self-awareness, or the somatosensory areas, which help people sense their surroundings, are active, Henley explains. Take the simple act of pouring coffee in the morning: In walking toward the coffeepot, reaching for it, pouring the brew into the mug, leaving extra room for cream, the occipital and parietal lobes, motor sensory, and sensory motor cortices, basal ganglia, cerebellum, and frontal lobes all activate.

A lightning storm of neuronal activity occurs almost across the entire brain in the time span of a few seconds. "This isn't to say that if the brain were damaged that you wouldn't be able to perform daily duties," Henley continues. "There are people who have injured their brains or had parts of it removed who still live fairly normal lives, but that is because the brain has a way of compensating and making sure that what's left takes over the activity." Being able to map the brain's various regions and functions is part and parcel of understanding the possible side effects should a given region begin to fail. Experts know that neurons that perform similar functions tend to cluster together.

For example, neurons that control the thumb's movement are arranged next to those that control the forefinger. Thus, when undertaking brain surgery, neurosurgeons carefully avoid neural clusters related to vision, hearing, and movement, enabling the brain to retain as many of its functions as possible.

What's not understood is how clusters of neurons from the diverse regions of the brain collaborate to form consciousness. So far, there's no evidence that there is one site for consciousness, which leads experts to believe that it is truly a collective neural effort. Another mystery hidden within our crinkled cortices is that out of all the brains cells, only 10% are neurons; the other 90% are glial cells, which encapsulate and support neurons, but whose function remains largely unknown. Ultimately, it's not that we merely use 10% of our brains; we only understand about 10% of how it functions. Some of us are already progressing into a criterion prone to control and manipulate memory at will, and to make certain past memories alive through extraordinary ability in detail retrospective to the extent of one's entire life; it seems we are going to enter a world that we cannot forget and wait for other unheard of mind power in the near future. Since the more neurons are created to fire and the more synapses connect and spark, dynamic revolutionary concepts are produced to unlock the mysteries of our universe. The new revelations in human natural aptitude will help to further advance civilization and give more hope for humanity to exit the life of turbulence and hopelessness.

This should indicate that unawareness has so sadly materialized social and political gridlocks, as so many keep quiet as they are oblivious to stark financial disparities forced on people, or they are well off and not wanting to notice deceitful and wicked financial cover-ups, which are not clear and conspicuous to the common man, since the rich keep getting richer and the poor become poorer. Hence, multitudes of precarious effects and misconduct escalate further, hurting billions globally for the worst and often beyond repair. It will help if we pay attention to the corporate capitalists and gigantic multinational firms that unethically delve into human subliminal terrain and unscrupulously devise their hideous plans, which creep into the realm of our subconscious mind and subtly manage to overwhelm our thinking brain and conscious thoughts without us having a clue. They adamantly bombard our subconscious mind through a very intricate conditioning mechanism, driving people into a bewildering state of thoughts and actions, but for the wrong reasons.

This transgression of behavior has molded our brain and burdened our mind into a web of uncertainties and mental defects, turning so many into addict consumerists, who are vulnerable to evermore spending and consumption, who act stoic and nonchalant to others' squalid living conditions and pain and suffering. It seems our mind is hypnotized and possessed by extraterrestrial agents into helplessness, cluttered with negative and trivial issues beyond our will, which has turned our conduct impervious to virtue, and has globally manifested a very sick environment, comprising it to become culturally chaotic, financially desperate, socially and environmentally tragic, and in need of desperate repairs.

This ongoing pejorative (insulting, derogatory) cascade of actions is not going to halt unless enlightened and courageous people collectively are inspired to seek justice and push for a better world. Einstein said, "The world is a dangerous place to live, not because of the people who are evil, but because of the people who don't do anything about it." We ought to know that our brain is interactively wired into a single monumental and conscious able entity. We forget we are a unified biological and mental organism qualified for existence, engulfed with cosmic and spiritual realm, and part of a destined universe premeditated with purpose, clearly mandated and objectified to reach its destiny.

Hence, humanity needs to accordingly defy these vicious circle of manufactured and sickly causes and effects that have strayed and derailed us from what is right. We need to constructively manage our life's objectives through enriched and practical curriculums, rather than becoming an easy target and vulnerable to everyday designed malice, which they produce constant anxiety, insecurity, fear, infested with traumatic political, social and economic events.

The system needs to stop controlling us like we are wild animals, saying there is no living outside of the corporate capitalists, as the survival of the fittest mentality should be the norm, where the meanest and the most horrible souls are to exploit and commoditize everything, including human lives to the point of exhaustion and collapse. And since anything outside of their pillaging ways and ruthless behaviors is not cool, since any conduct should identify with aristocratic kinds of civilization and relate to imperialistic culture, philosophy, science, selfish gene theory, and individualism, social and biological Darwinism. Where those with correct jaw lines and manufactured lies indicating advanced revolutionized head and scalp are anatomically ranked as progressive, and hence they are regarded as the embodiment of nobility and intelligence because they are from a superior race, since they pertain to high and preferable genotype, while others have yet to mature from the caveman mentality, and to further become developed in their physical and biological shortcomings.

Other ethnicities and indigenous natives were considered between human and animals that deserved to die. They did not have the intelligence to become duly compliant and civilized, as the Europeans exterminated millions of indigenous people ranking them as savages, which ethnic cleansing so tragically happened to Native Americans in North America, where premeditated genocide was to annex and steal all indigenous lands and their natural resources, meant to enslave the inhabitants by putting them to work just like beasts to produce valuable raw material and vital natural resources for the rich to plunder. That was also accompanied by religious mercenaries to discipline the natives into accepting the ideology that there is no salvation outside the church, as no life is worth living, if the unbelievers are not saved, as they should be indoctrinated into a trinity manifesto, which expresses the unity of Father, Son, and the Holy Spirit as three persons in one Godhead according to Christian dogma.

They perpetuate the individualism concept and perpetrate people to believe in the hierarchical culture and the systematic powers of God, spirit, angels, profits, religious, kings, queens, the country, men, women, minorities, indigenous people, animals, trees and plants, and non-animated beings. Infusing toxic thoughts and notions into our thought process to divide and conquer us, as they have, where no peace and justice and a life worth living is ever possible. They know when one is incarcerated and is put in solitary confinement long enough, one starts to hallucinate and basically go crazy, losing their mind, as simple as that, because we are group animals and cannot survive alone. This should awaken every caring soul to realize the vitality and the urgency of working together, and as co-ops to deal with corporate power and the cancerous individualistic based society they have imposed upon humankind. They have turned us into robots, in which we often haywire for the very reason of loneliness, and frequently not belonging because of many wrongs and unjustified reasons, so that the system can rule us with cruelty and with ease. It is time to prove capitalists' conniving ways and deceptive practices are wrong and stop their predatory behaviors, awakening them to do right in the name of God, humanity, and self-worth.

They can avoid subtle mass propaganda and not push for fanatical class-based societies, through subliminal and cleverly done messages and deactivate encouraging ideas that uphold "every man to his own mindset," which has permeated into many societies leaving horrifying effects, molding consumers into curse-like mentality of the "survival of fittest" ideology. They need to stop this monstrous notion that everything is for the grab in the name of profit, including desolating human lives and people's dignity.

Nick Harkaway, in *the Blind Giant* states that:

"Like casinos, large corporate entities have studied the numbers and the ways in which people respond to them. These are not con tricks—they're not even necessarily against our direct interests, although sometimes they can be—but they are hacks for the human mind, ways of manipulating us into particular decisions we otherwise might not make. They are in a way deliberate, undermining the core principle of the free market, which derives its legitimacy from the idea that informed self-interest on aggregate sets appropriate prices for items. The keyword is 'informed'; the point of behavioral economics—or rather, of its somewhat buccaneering (pirate, freebooter) corporate applications—is to skew our perception of the purchase to the advantage of the company. The overall consequence of that is to tilt the construction of our society away from what it should be if we were making the rational decisions classical economics imagines we would, and toward something else."

It seems no matter how we strive for a bit of happiness, it is with no avail, as we are still fettered with draconian circumstances and not free from the pipelines of uncertainties and anxieties facing ill maneuvers directed at the very core of our nervous system. And, hence, vanquishing the sovereignty of our mind, infusing it with ceaseless irrational thoughts and deceitful mental exercises where they manage to play us like a professional guitar player literally in control of frequencies of its instrument and how it should vibrate. So that the 1% that holds onto 99% of the resources can further amplify income inequality, turning people into sociopaths, agents in which consumers of toxic thoughts can exercise inhumane rivalries against each other through antisocial values engineered by the rich elites and the ruling class, which should remind us of "divide and conquer strategy."

Institutionalized sociopathic conduct is emanated into demented environment practices as the norm in which betokens self-interest as inherently instinctual that is laid at the very core of human morality and because from the system's point of view only the individual exists, which pushes so many to viciously compete with competitors and act psychopathically violent toward each other and behave abusive toward nature, as they exhaust natural resources and sabotage raw materials. They exploit workers through immoral use of child labor and take advantage of elderly working men and women for starvation wages.

Corporate oligopoly behaves in bad faith and deceptively exercises toward consumers and the less powerful nations. Because to corporate capitalists, nothing matters except profit, where unfettered growth drives their insatiable appetite to the point of exhaustion leveraged by insane propaganda and through false advertising compounded with hegemonic militarism and fear-mongering apparatus.

They are nimble in improvising policies that divide people and polarize wealth, where few elites can control the rest of the citizens. They cosmetically uphold democratic features and fake elections, since even the state resonates with the aristocrat's plans and unconstitutionally gives into their demands, where bribery and money make paradigms shift to illegally favor the influential elites. This abusive trend of thought and behavior has pushed the society from class system to a caste system, where the super-rich and the powerful elites are suppressing workers that are the backbone of the capitalist system that generates surplus values that are the foundation to the corporate capitalists' very existence.

Adam Smith said, "Civil government, so far as it is instituted for security of property, is in reality instituted for defense of the rich against the poor, or those who have property against those who have none at all."

The capitalist system should put an end to domesticating people and halt forcing them into the bottle to playing genie at the command of plutocratic government where billions are made miserable, since the poor are manipulated and degraded to function against their well-being and because of corporate selfish actions, the world is at grave risk of eradication and conduit to destruction. The super-rich must wake up in the name of virtue and what is right to actively take part in what is necessary to change the course of history in saving planet Earth and avoiding revolution through bloodshed and violence. And people also need to intelligently realize it is not appropriate to throw the baby out with the bathwater because it makes sense to save what works and understand that any new system is born from the womb of the old one and creatively makes a paradigm shift possible by introducing an innovative culture and new way of thinking. To grasp that rich are not evil by nature, Hitler, Mussolini, and Stalin were demonic by nature, and to ask if any one of us was put in their position, what would we honestly do, since most of us also are weak to harness human greed.

The actual problem stems out of greed and self-centeredness, since by nature, the capitalist economy differentiates classes via polarization of wealth, in which corporate oligopoly has worsened income inequalities, ignoring they have-nots leaving people with no choice, but to fight back for their survival. Where realistic social welfare and collective altruism is taken for a farce, barred and blocked by self-interest manuals, and dialogues, and misleading by individualistic culture and propaganda prevalent in families, active at schools, in communities and at work, even in churches and many other societal networks.

This basically implements policies against collectivism, which evokes the attitude of either to mesh in with customs and the norms or die in vain, even tainting those who are not accustomed to cynical behaviors and devious attributes, not wanting to act arrogant and egocentric, but often do, since one must blend in to make it. The ideology, the philosophy, the politics, and the cultural education of the system's objectives are to uphold and work accordingly to honor the powerful elites' viewpoints on how it should be done, and for people to robotically execute what they are programed with, and if they dare not to, they will be seen as not cool and perhaps an outcast or rebellious to social and civil order. Here is what many politicians and economists so naively say about inequality. Jason Welker said, "Politicians and some economists like to argue that income inequality is not as evil as many people make it out to be, and that greater income inequality can actually increase the incentive for poorer households to work harder to get rich, contributing to the economic growth of the nation as a whole. Allowing the rich to keep more of their income, in this way, leads more people to want to work hard to get rich, as they will be able to enjoy the rewards of their hard work." Welker correctly continues that, "The prevalence of income inequality in free market economies indicates that inequality may be the result of a market failure."

Those who are born rich are more likely to become rich, while individuals who are born poor are more likely to live a life of relative poverty. In a "free" market, it is believed, all individuals possess an equal opportunity to succeed, but due to a misallocation of resources in a purely market economy, this may not always be the case. The resources I refer to here are those required for an individual to escape poverty and earn a higher income. These include public and merit goods that those with high incomes can afford to consume, while those in poverty depend on the provision from the state, including: good education, dependable health care, access to professional networks, and employment opportunities they provide whenever a market failure exists. It can be argued there is a role for government in regulating the market to achieve a more optimal distribution of resources.

When it comes to income inequality, government intervention typically comes in the form of a tax system that places a larger burden on the rich and a system of government programs that transfer income from the rich to poor, including welfare benefits, unemployment benefits, health care for low income households, public schools, and support for economic development in poor communities. Going back in time, the Great Depression in the United States started after a fall in stock prices that began around September 4, 1929, and made worldwide news with the stock market crash of October 29, 1929 (Black Tuesday). The Great Depression went on between 1929 and 1932.

At this time, the whole system was struggling to recuperate from catastrophic economic and social dilemmas facing it. Then at some point, when the entire system was at the brink of war and potential for a bloodied and nasty revolution, President Franklin D. Roosevelt stepped in and mediated so that the rich could constructively spend some of their money to save the "profit system" or face a bloodied revolution as the capitalists would lose all their money.

In the meanwhile, the rest of the world provided the core capitalist system of western Europe, North America, and Japan, with very inexpensive natural resources, raw materials, and cheap labor. After so long of brutal exploitation, the workers all over the world, including western Europe, North America, and Japan, woke up and demanded a piece of the pie, which barely mitigated their miserable living conditions. This also gave birth to the liberal and middle class, and also made upper mobility relatively possible. Then, gradually globally transnational corporations eliminated the fair competition since neo-colonist rule of law was established through the entire world, giving them access to other developing nations with rich natural resources, oil, gas, minerals, silver and gold, uranium and so forth, and cheap labor.

Loyal dictatorial regimes and puppets were installed to implement the utter despotic rule of conducts by murdering, assassinating, torturing, raping, and imprisoning dissidents and anyone seeking justice or any call for human rights. Even in America the Native Americans, Mexicans, Irish workers and their families, the Jews, African-Americans, Italians, and Japanese suffered tremendously before they were recognized, even taking a gargantuan civil war between the south and the north, which claimed millions of lives, before establishing basic human dignity for all and the right to live where prejudice and discrimination were formally supposed to be abolished. We have reached an era in which unfortunately the death of liberalism has acted as a safety valve to save capitalism for so long, and the gradual wiping out of the middle class, which president Roosevelt worked so hard for and created, has basically desecrated the cushion that could have mitigated and perhaps avoid the clash and the possibility of bloodied violence between the extremely rich class and the poor in which the indigents face brutal poverty that are dissidents to economic tyranny and social, political injustice imposed on millions. And so many have become well-informed and cognizant enough to look for other viable economic systems to remedy their precarious position through elected social democratic government, or a viable co-op system as an alternative to the capitalist system, which unfortunately delegates for the success of the few, and not for the common good.

Both co-ops and a social democratic economic system prioritize the affair of the society based on having adequate employment, proper education, decent housing, and practical medical care, free public transportation, with an efficient financial safety net to back it up and kick in to protect citizens in times of need. A social democratic system is fueled with higher paid taxes, which then if the resources are allocated appropriately, the cultural architect and the socioeconomic infrastructures are fundamentally built from grassroots to efficiently benefit the people. As the entire resources are invested in the public sector to maximize return by producing competent and knowledgeable citizens who are not worried and frightened to death to lose their jobs, which some even kill themselves and enact a host of criminal activities when losing their vocation, and suddenly become devoid of their subsistence.

In his book, *The God We Never Knew: Beyond Dogmatic Religion to a More Authentic Contemporary Faith*, Marcus J. Borg writes, "The point is not that Jesus was a good guy who accepted everybody, and thus we should do the same (though that would be good). Rather, his teachings and behavior reflect an alternative social vision. Jesus was not talking about how to be good and how to behave within the framework of a domination system. He was a critic of the domination system itself."

In contemporary societies, quality education is not a right, but a prestige for the few. Education is scaled through politics and not influenced by skilled educators. Students are molded into what to think, rather than how to think, which this of course works to protect and preserve the very corporate capitalist system keeping many unaware of life-changing opportunities and a better future. Because they know that true education and literacy is the most potent force in existence and can relinquish viable knowledge and information to shake the core of deceptive practices of a decayed system of learning that exploiters are standing on.

Practical alternatives are a socialist democrat system, not in the form traditionally advocated through violence and bloodied revolution leveraged by a proletariat dictatorship, but via peaceful transition and evolutionary processes, where the activities of a social democrat government for the common good replaces the activities done by private corporate capitalists for the benefit of the few. Or via co-op institutions, which political and economic structures is peacefully shifted into workers' collective ownership. They are then elected as a board of directors, each entitled to one share, one vote into a democratically elected environment, where the transfer of wealth and productive forces into the hand of workers becomes possible, making the new realms of co-op business activities to gradually replace the status quo. Let's slightly elaborate on co-op institution and briefly explain how it manages to operate.

Co-ops are imbued with a humanitarian concept of doing business; its ideology is based on democracy at work, requiring collective participation of each worker with one share and one vote, solidifying the overall policy of the system's philosophy for the common good and not aimed at maximizing profit for the few. The workers are the actual owners of the means of production and are members of the board of directors that will decide what to produce, how to produce, where and when to produce, and what to do with the profit and the surplus values that the workers themselves created. Kofi Annan said, "Founded on the principles of private initiative, entrepreneurship and self-employment, underpinned by the values of democracy, equality and solidarity, the co-operative movement can help pave the way to a more just and inclusive economic order."

Annan further said, "In an age where community involvement and partnerships with civil society are increasingly being recognized as indispensable, there is clearly a growing potential for cooperative development and renewal worldwide."

The nucleus and the decency of the co-op system lays in the fact the no one is allowed to make 150 to 200 times more than other workers, making people's lives unbearable and almost impossible to keep up with the rapid pace of inflation and recessionary criteria, since their wages are stagnated and not raised accordingly, where top executives, the elites and CEOs and giant corporate owners make so much money, which creates horrifying inequality making a life of living hell for the majority of inhabitants. Martin Filler in Art, Force, Building said, "Despite the persistent image of the architect as a heroic loner erecting monumental edifices through sheer force of will, the building art has always been a highly cooperative enterprise."

The point is clear when the board of directors are the workers and the actual voters; they must live with the decision they make, then they sure will not vote to produce toxic products or pollute the water and the environment for worse, since their family and loved ones also will bear the consequences of their dire decisions. They will not commend and practice outsourcing and transferring the company to foreign lands to minimize their costs, practically destroying the locals and communities for the sake of making more money for a few greedy individuals. Because the corporate capitalists know no boundaries, understand no limit, are estranged to equity, do not believe in common good, but in maximizing profit, believe in collective and team work only to collect others fruits of labor, and throwing them bones for subsistence, and to keep them barely alive to produce more for the boss's lavish lifestyle.

They devour and exploit nature and humanity to the point of exhaustion, until collapsed with no remorse. Co-op workers are self-administered and will make sure to implement democracy at work where the hallmark of the entire system is there are no major shareholders who can override good decisions made on behalf of the community. People at the bottom would be in charge of their own destiny and institutionalize the power of production and enjoy the surplus values, which is a fresh way of organizing our life for the better and in reaching dynamic and progressive goals.

Kent Conrad said, "There are large cooperatives all across this country. Land O'Lakes is a $12 billion club functioning all across America. There are rural electric co-ops in 47 states. Ace Hardware is a cooperative." With many taxi cab companies and bakeries across the land giving hopes and future prosperities for all.

Arthur Potts Dawson said, "We are stronger as a group than an individual. Think in a cooperative, and communal way, set up local food hubs and create growing communities."

Boutros Boutros-Ghali said, "Co-operative enterprises provide the organizational means whereby a significant proportion of humanity is able to take into its own hands the tasks of creating productive employment, overcoming poverty and achieving social integration."

Workers owning their own companies at municipal institutions and co-ops, at credit unions, and so forth, with one share and one vote, true democracy at work should happen peacefully from local and state to national level. The evolutionary structure would gradually move from a system that is in decay, stagnated, and in state of deadlock to a genuine productive system of co-ops that could actually save people and direct them to control their destiny. And to make sure progressive movements do not get caught in a traditional socialist system or get deeper entangled in a traditional capitalist system or even a communist system, but where a democratic economy run by workers for improvement of the communities can take place addressing the well-being of the very people and community producing the goods and services, since the surplus value and all the profit is to be prioritized and allocated for the common good and not spent privately by mob-like characters in casinos like economy and wasted on no-good deeds.

This historical exchange should occur with no violence, through civil action, and by peaceful means, since innocent lives will be saved. The corporate cultural way of policing and repressive fascism can be instrumental with murdering, assassinations, torture, and imprisonment as any other totalitarian state would do. This collective overhaul effort and paradigm shift should occur from local to state and federal level, where social, and economic stagnation and deadlocks are able to change into dynamic production and a new way of life to preserve humanity and what is right.

History has taught us when people are forced into deplorable living conditions by stalemated regimes and systems in decay. They will learn their way out of their conundrum position and into a new social order. Unfortunately, contemporary corporate capitalists are facing stagnation and chaos and turning into a mundane system of corporate oligarchy.

But one should rest assure that ties will not positively turn unless aggressive legal and organized actions are taken, and everyone stands up for what is right and to reclaim the belief already ingrained into sociocultural ways of life, seeking justice.

And as the automation and robotic technology advances to replace jobs currently held by workers, so many will globally lose their jobs, adding grave problems to an already ill capitalist system that will further mature social rebellion, which will downshift against rich elites and tighten the noose around the system's neck. Unless creative and revolutionary economic plans are institutionalized to acutely abate the serious shortcomings of the private ownership of the means of production, humanity will have no choice but to act violently for mandating survival, which can face humanity with many bloodied uprisings and a huge debacle beyond perception.

The new system should shed light on education, economy, full employment, population control, decent housing, free public transportation, good public health system, clean environment, and stop global warming by activating renewable energy by going solar, looking into a zero carbon economy, and stopping fossil fuel usage, to lower greenhouse effect, provide clean water, institute quality immigration laws, and make due diligence to stop all the activities on atomic undertakings, and halt chemical and bacterial weaponries, halt cyber and drone attacks, and make all inhumane war machines obsolete. To stop wars of aggression and to act in concert with the rest of the world to unanimously stop terrorism and halt police brutality.

To further look into already obsolete marriage and family laws, and to prevent encouraging prostitution and inhibit commoditizing human beings for profit, and eliminate pornography industries, human trafficking, and harlotry (hustling, the selling of sex) as child sexual abuse and pedophilia is going as rampant. And in addition investigates religious fanaticism, stop prejudice against minorities and women, halt misogyny, discourage xenophobia, and thoughtfully look into gun control, and to stall other violent cultures and ugly traditions and to ameliorate the unbearable condition of the poor, who live way below the poverty line.

We should know how damaging a decentralized free market economy truly is, and be aware of corporate capitalists' philosophy that prioritizes profit even above human lives, since a free enterprise system knows no limit, but to monopolize and exhaust global natural resources and to exploit human resorts, as if their sadistic behavior should be celebrated and applauded as they are life-savers. Unless the role of multinational corporations and corporate conspiracy is truly exposed, which has since put an end to fair competitive market and made the death of the so-called laissez-faire possible, no renovated economic alternative will be possible.

The new system should insist on the culture of populism, instigate pluralism, and push for humanism, goad for social and cultural freedom to uphold and let public sectors manage decisive socioeconomic responsibilities, and to incite democratic party alliances and leverage the economic system of co-ops or give way to a social-democratic economic system, and to mean it when it bullhorns liberty and the pursuit of happiness for all, to ensure human rights and to live and let live.

To challenge dictatorial regimes and terrorism and aim at unfolding and educating people on perplex social and sometimes abstract moral and economic issues. To stoke concerns about divinity and God because people should connect with their maker and become liberated from the clutches of incredulity (cynicism, attitude of habitual disbelief) in grasping enlightenment, to enter into the realm of soul searching and spirituality. It should remind us of Kant's argument in idealism, critical (Kant) refers to Kant's theory of knowledge. The essence of critical idealism is Kant's sharp distinction between what is given to us in our experience (sense impressionist) and the structures (forms of intuition and the categories) which the mind uses to arrange, interpret, and evaluate that which is given.

Our senses can enslave and exploit us with worldly pleasures and make us addicted to money, power, and influence, where so many frequently burn with desires to unleash ruthless behaviors in serving lower selves, and sometimes at the cost of destroying millions of people's lives, with no remorse. We ought to be reminded that every time we serve power and prestige and overlook inhumane conduct or ignore the tyranny of the system imposed on the innocent because of self-interest, and in what material possession we hold dear that are financially at stake (in jeopardy), we disempower justice and cover up the truth against the fundamental rights of the republic, which sanctions so many from having to live the bare minimum, denying them a decent life, and leaving them with no choice but to vigorously fight back. And fairly so, since the right to life is questioned and liberty for all is choked, which has turned into just empty rhetoric and an opprobrious (derogatory, demeaning, insulting) slogan for billions, who are living gradual death. The fabric of diversity in living and peaceful coexisting in the name of compassion and humanity are insanely discouraged and falling apart; seeing each other as rivals is performed, as so many embark on a negative portrait of blacks, and the shortcomings of whites, and capitalize on the imperfect brown, the faulty red, and inconsiderate yellow, and so forth. Perhaps not knowing it is the system that feeds people with poisonous powwows (huddle, commune, discussion, consult) and plants virus in consumers' mind, as they irrigate mental tumors in people's memory and produce a toxic environment, mutating people into infectious diseases, turning inhabitants into monsters, and morphing millions into beasts against each other, making so many desolate from acting human.

Expert psychiatrists, clever psychologists, prominent social, political, and economic strategists, knowledgeable historians, expert anthropologists, and competent sociologists, financial advisers, and know-how culturists team up to muster vexed programs and make it into law through adept judges and skillful attorneys, as conniving law makers, and insincere media broadcasters, and dubious journalists publicize controversial issues, they encourage propaganda on troubling agendas, where the technology of spreading news and announcing information are communicated in subtle ways beyond the psyche of the common man to grasp many of complex subjects and troublesome programs; vicious outlets are causing menacing and ugly attributes among humanity.

The rich elite are well aware that no legal legislation or any law implemented can substantiate goodwill and bring peace to people unless a massive cultural change and intelligence undertaking are fulfilled to feasibly educate people and aim at bringing the good out of citizens for a radically positive change of heart, and if so, the humankind is definitely catered with good conscious to reach majestic heights where "no man has to live by the sword, and die by the sword" but will live in harmony with each other and the nature.

Until then, as Martin Luther King Jr. put it, "If a man has not discovered something that he will die for, he is not fit to live." We all live in alarming state of mind, which calls for worldwide humanitarian solutions, where uncorrupted ideas and pristine plans for better living should panoramically be witnessed and experienced by everyone. So forth, to change public opinion is the key before changing any politician, or any government for that matter, but I am afraid because the idea of kleptocracy (government by those who seek chiefly status and personal gain at the expense of the governed) is well alive and exercised, since the instrument that are utterly necessary to bring decisive lifesaving changes are controlled by public enemies.

The mega corporate media have become recidivists (falling back into bad behaviors), stifling the truth and manipulating the upper echelon of society into myopia, turning them into habitual fiction readers, rather than confronting and getting the populace to fight for so many tumultuous and covert matters created by the privileged class entrapping us all into horrendous situations where decisive social discourse are ignored by making so many people actually believe that politics is dirty and is best to stay away from politics, so just let's forget about it and go fishing and play golf. The plutocrats and their lackey corporate media place us exactly where they want us to be by keeping so many and specifically the influenced people silenced against their insidious and criminal activities.

We ought to know that we have reached an era where global consciousness is fertile enough to plant eye-opening seeds of enlightenment and since realized that we have the potential to constructively cultivate life and identify with each other from the perspective of humanity and progressive civil laws, and not due to a superiority complex or looking at the world with an inferiority complex and acting judgmental through narrow-mindedness.

It is time to condemn any damnable (wicked) socioeconomic factors designed to oppress people, either through an unfair monetary system, or any other cultural, political, and social prejudices. Since religious differences and many other manufactured ill agendas and troublesome issues, like violence, racial discrimination, prejudice, ethnicity, nationalism, sexism, extreme income inequalities, and class differences, has forced masses of people into isolation, as millions experience caste system societies. Because corporately induced democracy is too ambiguous (doubtful, equivocal, inexplicable) and amply ambivalent (uncertain, self-questioning), which has created an atmosphere where the state has become a sole servant to private institutions, since the public is devoid of basic public goods, such as free public education, health care, housing, decent employment, disability payments, public transportation, clean air and water, safe foods, paid vacation, secured retirement, and so forth as states are influenced by corporate elites for worse.

And the solution cannot be sought from the mainframe of a capitalist system, as no private enterprise is meant to created public goods, or any goods at all, without making maximum profit. But people are relentlessly persuaded by mega corporate media into believing that the only system efficiently feasible is the capitalist system, like it is ordained by God. It is a social economic system that can survive fake patriotism, class differences, militarism, ugly terrorism, and in avoiding concentration of wealth, halt catastrophic wars, and abort the threat of nuclear and biological war, stop sadistic mentality of divide and conquer, and put an end to the global warming catastrophe.

Corporate oligopoly insists on individualism through ideological domination and conditioning, where the entire global resources are deemed to be exploited for making money for the rich elites and denying the rest of the world basic needs. The solution to our problems is not more capitalism because a nonabusive relationships are not ever possible or should be expected form a capitalist system, other than victimizing the weak, and taking advantage of the billions of needy masses, exploiting people, exhausting human, and natural resources. Where they commoditize everyone and everything in the name of business to further nourish their sociopathic behaviors, which the capitalist regimes exercise to objectify making more money, no matter at what cost.

It is imperative to know we collectively evolve with nature to bring dynamic changes, rather than operating alone, as it is the aggregate efforts that materialize quality socioeconomic changes. The good news is that most people are receptive to quality times and resonate with what benefits them mentally, spiritually, emotionally, and financially rather than being enslaved and belittled, as the wealthy elites designed in turning billions of workers into producing machines as "division of labor" and assembly lines do, alienating them from their true beings and forcing so many into robots to specialize in producing specific products and ditch them at the employer's prerogative when they are no longer needed.

The alternative for having a communist system is just as too good to be true, which at this stage of our lives can only seem a utopia. Since our cultural intellect and ideological beliefs, our present socioeconomic expectations are yet to mature, to further appreciate the power of rationality, which requires colossal reasoning, might to convince the masses to accept revolutionary ideas and to digest the grand scheme (road map) on what Marx said about communism.

Marx stated that communism comes after socialism, which reveals full equality. That means there is no more state and no more money. Everything is run communally and owned by everyone, and there is no more scarcity since communist societies believe in "each according to his ability and contribution and to take according to his need." But if that should currently be the case and to actually take place at the present era. We will no doubt face "proletariat's dictatorship," which they staunchly believe in to implement and make transition from capitalist system to socialist and from socialist nations to communism possible, as Stalin did in Russia, Mao did in China, Pol Pot did in Cambodia, and Fidel Castro did in Cuba, and so forth, as they literally performed evil and inhumane actions to make the transition from socialist era possible to communism, with no avail because any kind of dictatorship and despotic behavior is certainly going to encounter an impasse and a very stiff resistance from freedom-loving people across the world.

To overcome what now seems a utopian state and in making these highly ambitious goals possible, a grandeur sociocultural revolution is definitely needed for humankind to take a giant leap toward self-denial and utterly believe in humanitarian agendas and productive communal work, rather than acting in self-interest alone. In which the state also needs to be eliminated, since no government is needed to enforce contracts and property rights, neither military nor police force is necessary, basically expecting the masses to act flawlessly making a piece of heaven possible.

I attest without transcending into a higher realm of consciousness and quality education affected with dynamic and progressive cultural revolution, which can carry the society into the premises of ideological enlightenment and welfare, no social reform of that magnitude can possibly take place. Because the average intelligence has not yet matured to rationalize and accept such a gigantic egalitarian task. Marx somehow exaggerates an ideological aspect of his material doctoring in "dialectical materialism," which Marx dictates is the real material of the world that shapes our ideas on which our life and our survival depends. It is as important as our ideas and mutually as important, since both materialism and idealism interact; he believed ideas come from the real world. This makes sense, but what Marx perhaps missed is that the real world is idea oriented, rather than materially based. We experience life and are in touch with matter in the realm of consciousness; it is not a senseless, motionless, unintelligent world with no purpose, when even matter does not lack energy, since every living and non-living being is subatomically energy-driven.

Dialectical materialism is a philosophy of science and nature based on the writings of Karl Marx and Friedrich Engels, inspired by dialectic and materialist philosophical traditions. It approves evolution of the natural world and the issuance of new qualities of being at new stages of evolution. Engels made continual use of the methodological intuition that the higher level of existence emerges from and has its foundation in the lower level; the higher level forms a new order of being with its irreducible laws and the process of evolutionary advance is ruled by laws of expansion, which contemplate basic properties of "matter in motion as a whole."

Hegelian dialectic accentuated on the idealist aspect that human experience depends on the mind's discernment. Marx developed Marxist dialectics, which highlighted the materialist observation that the world of concrete shapes, socioeconomic interactions, and those in turn determine sociopolitical reality. Some Hegelians hold responsible religious alienation for societal ills, but Marx and Engels concluded that alienation from economic and political autonomy, paired with exploitation and poverty, were the real problems. In keeping with dialectical ideas, Marx and Engels thus created an alternative theory, not only of why the world is the way it is, but also of which actions people should take to render it the way it needs. In Theses on Feuerbach (1845), Marx wrote, "The philosophers have only interpreted the world, in various ways. The point, however, is to change it."

Dialectical materialism is a version of the expansion subject of materialism, which believes the primacy of the material world. In short, matter precedes thought. Materialism is a realist philosophy of science, which holds that the world is substance, that all phenomena in the universe consist of "matter in motion," wherein all things are interdependent and interconnected and developed according to natural law. The world exists outside us and independently of our perception of it, that thought is a reflection of the material world in the brain and that the world is, in principle, knowable.

Marx criticized classical materialism as another idealist philosophy— idealist because of its transhistorical realization of material contexts. The young Hegelian Ludwig Feuerbach had disapproved of Hegel's idealistic philosophy and championed materialism. Despite being strongly influenced by Feuerbach, Marx rejected Feuerbach's aspect of materialism as incoherent. The writings of Engels, especially *Anti-Dühring* (1878) and *Dialectics of Nature* (1875-82), were the source of the main doctrines of dialectical materialism.

The idea of dialectical materialism comes from statements by Marx in the introduction to his magnum opus, *Capital*. There, Marx says he intends to use Hegelian dialectics but in renovated form. He retaliates and fights for Hegel against those who consider him a "dead dog" and then says, "I openly avowed myself as the pupil of that mighty thinker [Hegel]." Marx credits Hegel with "being the first to present [dialectic's] form of working in a comprehensive and conscious manner." But he then depreciates Hegel for turning dialectics upside down: "With him, it is standing on its head. It must be turned right side up again, if you would discover the rational kernel within the mystical shell."

Marx's criticism of Hegel stresses that Hegel's dialectics go awry (off track) in dealing with ideas with the human mind. Hegel's dialectic, Marx says, unsuitably concerns "the process of the human brain"; it focuses on ideas. Hegel's thought is in reality sometimes called dialectical idealism. Marx believed that dialectics should deal not with the mental world of ideas but with "the material world," the world of production and other economic activity. Marx's theory of dialectical materialism maintained the material basis of a reality constantly changing in a dialectical process and the priority of matter over mind, in which Marxist theory of history and society holds ideas, and social institutions develop only as the "superstructure" of a material economy.

For Marx, human history cannot be fitted into any domestic bovines (cattle, cows), a cathedral strategy. He explicitly rejects the idea of Hegel's followers that history can be understood as "a person apart, a metaphysical subject of which real human individuals are but the bearers" To interpret history as though previous social formations have somehow been aiming themselves toward the present state of affairs is "to misunderstand the historical movement by which the successive generations transformed the results acquired by the generations that predated them." Marx's rejection of this sort of teleology (the study of evidence in design, a doctrine that says the ends are imminent in nature) was one reason for his ebullience (though not entirely uncritical) reception of Darwin's theory of natural selection.

For Marx, dialectics is not a formula for generating predetermined outcomes, but is a mean for the phenomenal (experimental) study of social processes in terms of interrelations, development, and transformation. In his introduction to the Penguin edition of Marx's *Capital*, Ernest Mandel writes, "When the dialectical method is applied to the study of economic problems, economic phenomena are not viewed separately from each other, by bits and pieces, but in their inner connection as an integrated totality, structured around, and by, a basic predominant mode of production."

Marx's writings are almost restrictively concerned with comprehending human history in terms of systemic processes, based on modes of production (vastly speaking, the ways in which societies are structured to employ their technological powers to interact with their material surroundings). This is called historical materialism. It is within the structure of this general theory of history that most of Marx's writing is allotted to an analysis of the specific frame of reference and expansion of the capitalist economy.

Marx hyperbolizing (exaggeration) is clearly noticed when he so tightly consociates matter and economy as the fundamental parts of who we are, as our financial status affects our thought process, the culture of thinking, and he believes people's economic position significantly designates which caste they belong to, as economy denotes and simply characterizes the way people live. Classes struggle and violent revolution will give birth to a new classless society, which significantly equipoises (equilibrium) our lives and brings justice and fairness across the entire nation, and eventually the globe. As Marx ideologically resonated with matter, he assessed that dialectical materialism manifests the utter truth and the answer to our scientific and philosophical problems; since matter precedes ideas and correlates with human awakening and the cause to what we know as consciously oriented entity in human beings.

And how an economy directly relates to sociocultural, sociopolitical, science, philosophy, and economy influences the very core of our existence, as the world outside of us is a real world bound to scientific and historical materialism. Matter and ideas interact, and we are the products of our environment and how biological and social Darwinism do make sense, where technological mode of productions are the reason behind a historical change of events from slavery to the present capitalist economic system, and so on. Let's delve into energy and matter a bit to perhaps clarify some of the misunderstandings facing inquisitive minds.

We need to expand our horizons while knowing that of course the economic foundation is extremely vital, as Marx stated, but compare it to the infinite number of decisive forces involved. It is not savvy to draw ingenious conclusions on superannuating God (out of date) where ideological perspectives are compared with nickel and dimes of the economy to deny God or to denounce some unscrupulous religious traditions. "The fanatical atheists are like slaves who are still feeling the weight of their chains which they have thrown off after hard struggle. They are creatures who—in their grudge against traditional religion as the 'opium of the masses'—cannot hear the music of the spheres." — Albert Einstein

Anything one can hold, smell, or taste is made of matter; matter is comprised of everything you can see, for instance clothes, water, food, plants, and animals, which includes some of the things we cannot see, such as air or the smell of a rose. Matter is built of particles so tiny only the most powerful microscope can show them. Matter is divided into two groups: living matter like plants and animals and non-living matter like rocks. Not everything is made of matter; for example, the light from the bulb or the heat from the stove or from a fire, or the sound of an ambulance siren. One cannot hold, smell, or taste these things; they are forms of energy. Everything that exists can be classified as either a type of matter or a form of energy. Density is the amount of matter compressed into a space, for instance, a small cubicle of lead conveys a lot of matter congealed into a small space, which is why it feels heavy; comparably, flour weight is not as dense as lead weight.

All matter is made of extremely tiny particles called atoms. Atoms are way too small to see with our eyes, but scientists have figured out how small they are. There are many kinds of atoms. Sand grains are made of two kinds of atoms: oxygen and silicon. People are made of about 28 different kinds of atoms. Material properties depend on the sort of atom the material is made of. Grains of sand look like pieces of gravel when viewed through a microscope; they have different shapes and sizes. Each grain contains millions of atoms too small to see with a microscope. A sand grain the size of the full stop at the end of this sentence would contain about 10 million atoms. Democritus, Greek, 460-c. 370 BC, was one of the first philosophers (thinkers) to say that everything was made up of particles too small to be seen. He believed these particles could not be destroyed or split. Democritus said that all changes in the world could be explained as changes in the way particles are packed together. The bottom line is no matter how different in shape and size the atoms are, all matter and non-matter are energy driven, but naturally with different density. The reason we cannot just walk through a wall is because the wall is much denser in matter density than our body is, which comparably our bodily matter density is not as dense, making the wall impermeable, also making it harder and heavier. Human matter density is more compressed than air and water matter density, which is why we are able to walk and breathe through it, as clean air as well as clean water refreshes our soul.

Some of Marx's doctrine analogy holds relative truth, but it is naïveté in action to conclude senseless matter, exhausted of any intelligent preceding idea, since idea is energy driven, which is the sole reason for creation of the entire universe. We should make reference to quantum physics, which clearly concludes that in subatomic particles, there is no matter but there is energy, which cannot further split. And yes, the world is a reality outside of us, but we are an inseparable part of the nature, which without our collective mind, no existence can ever be perceived or observed.

Let's put it this way, referencing modern science "no matter" exists, where substance is in constant motion, as matter is energy driven, in which the real truth would be revealed if the human nervous system and senses were not limited to experiencing only the outside world, but also were able to decipher the world of the unseen, which is the sole reason for what we fathom and in what we apparently see. Marx and his predecessors cleverly mix philosophy and science, and interlace what is relatively the truth, and some ideas that are not fact and have pasted a mishmash of formula, prioritizing matter over mind, which to this day has puzzled scientists, not knowing where consciousness is situated in the physical brain. Saying "the brain secretes thought in the same way the liver secretes bile" if they believe not that our brain must be energy driven, and the brain itself must be a thought provocative entity before it can produce any energy oriented concepts; otherwise, the so-called materialist scholars must believe that our brain is substance based and lifeless, but miraculously generates energy driven, alive thoughts. Comparing brain and thoughts to the liver, which produces bile, is childish and irresponsible, which in this case, they should also accept liver as an intelligent part that works in concert with every cell in our body, taking instructions and intelligently responding to them, to play unified health music within the entire human body. I believe our brain acts as an intermediary, just like a cellphone or any other gadget. It is a receiver through which cosmic energy is permeated and received. And the more synapsis connections and neurons firing, the better we can receive the messages and how smartly we respond to the world around us. Just like one that owns current Apple or Samsung smartphone, with an excellent provider without interruptions or experiencing any other malfunctions.

Moreover, late century discoveries in physics (x-rays, electrons) and the beginning of quantum mechanics, philosophically challenged previous conceptions of matter and materialism; thus, matter seemed to be disappearing. But witness how Lenin the master mind of communist ideology and the ideologue of the materialist school of thought is so dogmatic in mending a huge flaw, which science explicitly rejects.

Lenin disagreed: "Matter disappears" should mean that the limit within which we have hitherto known matter disappears and that our knowledge is penetrating deeper; properties of matter are disappearing that formerly seemed absolute, immutable, and primary, and which are now revealed to be relative and characteristic only of certain states of matter. For the sole property of matter, with whose recognition philosophical materialism is bound up, is the property of being an objective reality, of existing outside of the mind.

Lenin was developing the work of Engels, who said that "with each epoch-making discovery, even in the sphere of natural science, materialism has to change its form." One of Lenin's challenges was distancing materialism, as a viable philosophical outlook, from the "vulgar materialism" expressed in the statement "the brain secretes thought in the same way the liver secretes bile" (attributed to 18th-century physician Pierre Jean Georges Cabanis, 1757-1808); "metaphysical materialism" (matter composed of immutable particles); and 19th-century "mechanical materialism" (matter as random molecules interacting per the laws of mechanics). The philosophic solution that Lenin (and Engels) proposed was "dialectical materialism," wherein matter is defined as objective reality, theoretically consistent with (new) developments occurred in the sciences. Lenin reassessed Feuerbach's philosophy and concluded that it is in line with dialectical materialism.

What I am saying is, it is all about energy driven ideas; it is all about our mind and how we are able to correctly conceptualize and deal with the problematic material world. We need to first reach a state of mindfulness, where gradually, and perhaps in near future we could be lucky enough to utilize 15 to 20% of our brain capacity from 100% potential brain neurons. Acquiring wisdom, information, and knowledge is the essence of progress and the key in unlocking troubles facing humanity. If dolphins use 20% of their brain, making them so intelligent, and as they utilize the most sophisticated sonar system and echolocation, then cannot human beings progress into a state where they could also run their affairs intelligently, using more brain power for rational behaviors. But then again "the time is always right to do what is right" — Martin Luther King.

To make change possible, we need intelligence and awakening minds that are able to present flawless leaders to replace those with wrong ambitions, and to make sure not to leave leadership a vacuum, when nations are in transition. In the meanwhile, let's be aware that leadership is one of those vague terms that has diverse definitions. The traits that make up a good governing leader or a leadership counsel depends on the nominee's ethical and economic background. It makes a difference if the leader, leaders, the president, or the party members never experience a day or two of utter poverty and have not identified with the poor, the working class, and millions of financially deprived people, but all they know is the life of luxury and life of plenty.

And, yes, individuals vary since everyone has a different personality and their own peculiarities that are innate. And since great leaders believe in humanity, they are aware of their strength and weaknesses, where they make sure to harness character defects and capitalize on their positive and constructive behaviors; they can inspire masses of people and motivate them to challenge and overcome difficult situations, as good leaders are excellent persuaders. They are honest, knowledgeable, respectful, well-focused, and they are passionate. They are goal-oriented, and no hard work can stop them from reaching their objectives. Good leaders believe in integrity. They are confident, disciplined, and serious at their work and they care. They also possess a sense of humor. They are efficient and collaborative; they are engaging and share vision and actions. They take responsibility and are able to delegate.

True leaders are compassionate and empowering, and they clearly communicate without hiding what is imperative to their constituents and other masses of people. They are courageous and fearless; they are not afraid to take risks. They believe in human rights, liberty, and the pursuit of happiness, as they are genuine and supportive. They mean well and believe in equity. They are not hubris and believe in modesty, and no power, no prestige, no wealth, or sexual rewards can ever influence them to compromise their principles. They are intuitive, but not opinionated or self-centered because they believe in teamwork and are committed to world peace. They value other nations' sovereignty, as they truly value human lives.

And above all, they are balanced and virtuous. They carry a strong sense of morality. They believe in God's wrath and mercy and know that no wrongdoings can ever go unnoticed by the omnipotent, omnipresent, and the omniscient God. They sincerely believe that "what comes around goes around" and no one can escape "karma"—even the strongest of them all, the presidents, the kings and the queens, or any dictatorial political party. And as Mahatma Gandhi put it: "We need to be the change we wish to see in the world." This should not preclude the powerful elites, as they should have indomitable will to bring good to the world. The system in question is faced with systematic crises and unable to advance because it is stagnated and entangled into a web of uncertainties and begins to deteriorate from within. Naturally other thoughts like "utopian communism" or "anarchism" also manifest progressive agendas, which again are not practical unless revolutionary ideas can make a paradigm shift into raising the citizens' overall knowledge and boost people's mentality through intelligent and adamant enough for detecting exploitation of any kind and rejecting impractical rhetoric.

Alexander Berkman, in *The ABC of Anarchism* (1929) originally asked, what is communist anarchism?

The more enlightened man will become, the less he will employ compulsion and coercion. The really civilized man will divest himself of all fear and authority. He will rise from the dust and stand erect. He will bow to no tsar either in heaven or on earth. He will become fully human when he will scorn to rule and refuse to be ruled. He will be truly free only when there shall be no more masters.

Anarchism is the ideal of such a condition, of a society without force and compulsion, where all men shall be equals and live in freedom, peace, and harmony.

The word anarchy comes from the Greek, meaning without force, without violence or government, because government is the very fountainhead of violence, constraint, and coercion.

Anarchy therefore does not mean disorder and chaos, as you thought before. On the contrary, it is the very reverse of it; it means no government, which is freedom and liberty. Disorder is the child of authority and compulsion. Liberty is the mother of order.

Alexander Berkman, in "Is Anarchism Violence?" from *The ABC of Anarchism* (1929).

Anarchism … rests upon the doctrine that no man has a right to control by force That is to say, that there should be no war, no violence used by one set of men against another, no … So anarchists generally believe that, whether as groups or individuals, no man who believes in force and violence is an anarchist.

It is not to say reaching such ambitious goals to truly free humankind from the yoke of oppressive powers is not possible; in contrary, they are very much practical. But not before reaching enlightenment and collectively realizing the true devilish nature of systems that are despotic and inhumane in their very structure and fundamental beliefs. We ought to understand it is our mind and our mental state of accepting something as true or not which is diagnosed in enslaving us or known to free us. Because there is no power ever created than the power of collective uprising and tsunami of masses resurrection; when fueled with adequate knowledge and information against what which is perceive as destroying humanity.

Historically speaking, the reason "slavery" and "feudalism" existed was because the overall mentality accepted such an abusive system and slaves and serfs were not conscious and enlightened enough to realize the collective power they held to overpower the tyranny of either one of the oppressive systems that were imposed on slaves by their masters and on serfs by land owners, known as feudalism. According to dictionary, feudalism was a system of political organization prevailing in Europe from the 9th to 15th centuries, having at its basis the relationship of lord to vassal (a person under the protection of a feudal lord to whom he has vowed homage, obligation, and fealty, a feudal tenant, one in a subservient or subordinate position) with all land held in fee as chief characteristics homage, the service of tenants under arms and in court, warship, and forfeiture, and with any of various political or social systems similar to medieval feudalism. Once a system is overhauled, all the institutions supporting, promoting, and encouraging it are bound for destruction, since the new system will bear and materialize its own progressive culture of thinking and its value system, which will be aggressively pursued until they sink in and are accepted as norms.

For instance, to promote capitalism, people like Walter Lippmann and Edward Bernays used the "Freudian theory" to deal with the public's conception of communism, as they believed we should not be easing the public's fear of communism, but rather promote that fear and play with the public's emotions of it. This theory was so powerful that it became a weapon of its own during the Cold War. They utterly believed people are not moved by rationality and the power of inference, but they should be manipulated by the power of emotion seducing them to call for their own exploitation, which they manifested through mass propaganda to foster fear and anxiety. By keeping people in a limbo state of mind and under psychosis of permanent war, they are leashed with agendas and cultural thinking which best serves their corporate bosses, and to keep the corporate oligopoly system intact by selling defective products to the masses of people to feed corporate profit. We ought to reckon that advanced socioeconomic techniques and socio-psychoanalysis are literally factored in to make us susceptible and influential with operating outside of our conscious ability and awareness. When hefty investors went to Edward Bernays and asked him to promote eggs and bacon for breakfast, Bernays reached 5,000 doctors and nutritionists to have them say that they highly recommend eggs and bacon for breakfast, which should signify the power of propaganda, since eggs and bacon are overwhelmingly preferred in the western hemisphere for breakfast.

Noam Chomsky said, "Bernays wrote a book called Propaganda around 1925, and it starts off by saying he is applying the lessons of the First World War. The propaganda system of the first World War and this commission that he was part of showed, he says, it is possible to 'regiment the public mind every bit as much as an army regiments their bodies.' These new techniques of regimentation of minds, he said, had to be used by the intelligent minorities in order to make sure that the slobs stay on the right course. We can do it now because we have these new techniques.

This is the main manual of the public relations industry. Edward Bernays is kind of the guru. He was an authentic Roosevelt/Kennedy liberal. He also engineered the public relations effort behind the U.S.-backed coup that overthrew the democratic government of Guatemala.

His major coup, the one that really propelled him into fame in the late-1920s, was getting women to smoke. Women didn't smoke in those days and he ran huge campaigns for Chesterfield. You know all the techniques—models and movie stars with cigarettes coming out of their mouths and that kind of thing. He got enormous praise for that. So he became a leading figure of the industry, and his book was the real manual."

In the era of capitalism and so-called modernity, millionaire and billionaire clubs are infested with hierarchical corruption going rampant. Mob-like organized crime groups act against the powerless by killing, maiming, torturing, and imprisoning the innocents and whomever is not complying with brutal and inhumane ways of treating the poor. Where the only crime of the helpless is their outcry for justice and wanting to live in peace. Because as profit is accrued at the top, miseries and squalid living conditions are built up at the bottom and the money made is meant to serve the ruling class and the powerful where laws are purposely made to keep people apart and hostile toward each other to preserve the status quo.

In the meanwhile, hopes are lost and the entire allocation of resources is unjustly distributed, and wealth is hugely polarized between the haves and the have-nots, where thousands are forced to lose their lives for one reason or another. They are not facilitated with the very basic standard of living, and billions live in subhuman conditions so that a handful few can live an unimaginable life of fortune and extravagance, where the super-rich hallucinate, that is God abundantly and so generously giving them money at the cost of horrific livings of the poor. The super-rich waste millions and billions of dollars on their lavish lifestyle.

But the moguls of fortune are not intelligent enough to realize that the entire life on planet Earth is seriously threatened and in need of immediate response and positive remedy. The system of plutocracy and corporate oligopoly refuses to see they are living at the people's devastating expense where thousands perish every day as the super-rich are literally enjoying a life of plenty and magnificent luxury, utterly acting indifferent to sordid condition of humankind and a destructive world facing its inhabitants.

How would you make prefund changes applicable to a system that used to do well, in comparison to a feudal system or slavery where dark ages were upon us and people were basically treated like animals? But then when old system had their runs and faced predicament and intricacies that generated irresolvable contradictions with antagonistic behaviors toward the very productive forces that gave birth to them, then, it was time to go. And yes, it took aggressive force and violence to get rid of them, and I am afraid sometimes of the loss of millions of innocent lives because of bloodied encounters.

Many are pumped up and refer to history where revolutionary changes take place through violence, and insist on no other viable peaceful solutions to make dynamic transitions possible; to them, moral imperative dictates that masses of people should overthrow the system, acting like barbarians. As if we everything is supposed to progress through evolutionary process, except the power of our wit and reasoning, despite enormous findings and accomplishments in every important scientific field and even putting human robots on the moon.

We just need not act so backwardly to resolve our social and economic differences, and the system of our governing by killing and through bloodshed and by lawlessness and savagery, like when slavery transitioned into feudalism via bloodshed and violence, as did feudalism into capitalism. We should realize we live in an age of consciousness equipped with enough intelligence to know better. If not, then we should all wonder if our mindfulness and the power of our reasoning has ever grown at all because our acting civil should steward us amidst turmoil and instability.

We should not be delinquent and deliberate in ignoring the unlocking of our cognitive ability, which literally takes place by gradually freeing more brain cells, in which it ascends and delivers humanity to realms beyond our imagination, when it does. And since it already has propelled us forward from the caveman mentality to what we experience as modern life, where the goal is to conquer other planets and perhaps harness them for the benefit of humankind. And in getting closer to fulfilling the eternal purpose in objectifying our human destiny, where reaching God and the higher power becomes so well-known and clearly manifested and since even the dumbest of us all can witness and resurrect against the stupidity and our clumsiness of truly claiming our creator.

Stop acting like beasts by mandating a global Holocaust where hell is to wait for us and start to pay attention to our evolutionary miracle-like brains and conscious to which has relentlessly endeavored and meandered (irregular trajectory, winding path) in accelerating its celestial task to save us from the clutches of ignorance and in moving toward its goal to arrive us into promised land, despite treacherous behaviors of the few, and their deviously ironclad-like conduct to obstruct what is just. This often impedes but is never powerful enough to halt the virtue of higher powers of the heavens. The contemporary challenges that are holding back societies are the fusion of state and corporate power, which since has reached the pinnacle of plundering, looting, and pillaging, where it seems the more powerful and privileged the ruling class becomes, the more deluded they are with business industrial complex backed up with military industrial complex against the forces that are keeping the system intact.

This myopia of acting and secret tribunals to restlessly conspire against people is not aligned with God's work and the time that is promised to capture the essence and the very reason we are here. This calls for the helpless to unanimously speak the undeniable truth to the powerful and make them understand these despicable conditions which so many are stuck with, and it should call for an amicable solution to humanity's problem. And there are potential dangers facing the entire system if no quality and plausible solution is to be expected soon.

The superrich should be warned and come to terms in grasping that human beings are a wholesome entity that must not be broken to pieces, and if so, the wrath of God will be upon us boomeranging everyone.

We already possess very destructible weapons to instantly annihilate what we know as human life. And hence, we must remind ourselves that no violence is an answer, as good breeds good and evil breeds evil; the gambling bet is on innocent human lives. And to realize any system change must occur peacefully to resolutely remedy our differences and the mess we have created, above all we must prove our non-hypocritical claim of believing in God we trust.

Why not live and honor in what we actually claim and built a humanitarian superpower rather than a military industrial complex where trillions of dollars are rampantly spent on unjustified military and logistics looking for an improvised enemy to justify the infinite numbers of armaments accumulated to force others into do-or-die situations, which counterintuitively threaten people and stifle the very foundation of virtues and what we stand for as a civilized nation. Our values and aspirations should relate to greed and other worldly seductions and can defy our values for sometimes unduly aspirations. We need to push for the truth and persist in balance; the solution is to actively participate in restoring goods, and not to act indifferent or delusional, as Ralph Nader says, "There are two kinds of people: one which believe everything, and the other which believe nothing, and both lack thinking." For one to act nonchalant, carefree, and often irresponsible is not the answer.

Just remember it is a republican state where our forefathers and so many good souls lost their lives, not a corporate state where greed, irresponsibility has shackled people with unbearable living condition. testing their limit and forcing them into acting desperate and suicidal. This should call upon consciously awakened people to feel accountable and get out of their comfort zone to make things right, where life would not be so damn hard for billions, and so ridiculously luxurious for just a handful of menacing souls.

We ought to know the era of awakening and responsibility, the era of consciousness and accountability, and the time parameter where so many are alerted and care to understand the structure of power, and the world that surrounds them is here. The truth is that at slavery's time or in the feudal era, the victims knew who was slashing, murdering, and raping them, and making them work harder than animals. But then the system of corporate capitalist became much more elaborate in its wrongdoing against its victims as they are hidden from the naked eyes, but are definitely relevant and the cause to human problems. Sheldon Wolin discusses this in an interview with "Truthdig" columnist Chris Hedges.

In his book *Democracy Incorporated*, inverted totalitarianism is different from classical forms of totalitarianism. It does not find its expression in a demagogue or charismatic leader but in the faceless anonymity of the corporate state. Our inverted totalitarianism pays outward fealty to the facade of electoral politics, the Constitution, civil liberties, freedom of the press, the independence of the judiciary, and the iconography, traditions, and language of American patriotism, but it has effectively seized all the mechanisms of power to render the citizens impotent.

Throughout his scholarship Wolin charted the devolution of American democracy, and in *Democracy Incorporated*, he details our peculiar form of corporate totalitarianism. "One cannot point to any national institution[s] that can accurately be described as democratic, surely not in the highly managed, money-saturated elections, the lobby-infested Congress, the imperial presidency, the class biased judicial and penal system, or, least of all, the media." Wolin continues: "Unlike the Nazis, who made life uncertain for the wealthy and privileged while providing social programs for the working class and poor, inverted totalitarianism exploits the poor, reducing or weakening health programs and social services, regimenting mass education for an insecure workforce threatened by the importation of low-wage workers."

Wolin writes: "Employment in a high-tech, volatile, and globalized economy is normally as precarious as during an old-fashioned depression. The result is that citizenship, or what remains of it, is practiced amidst a continuing state of worry. Hobbes had it right: when citizens are insecure and at the same time driven by competitive aspirations, they yearn for political stability rather than civic engagement, protection rather than political involvement. "If the main purpose of elections is to serve up pliant legislators for lobbyists to shape, such a system deserves to be called 'misrepresentative or client government.' It is, at one and the same time, a powerful contributing factor to the DE politicization of the citizenry, as well as reason for characterizing the system as one of anti-democracy."

The result, he writes, is that the public is "denied the use of state power." Wolin deplores the trivialization of political discourse, a tactic used to leave the public fragmented, antagonistic, and emotionally charged while leaving corporate power and empire unchallenged.

"Cultural wars might seem an indication of strong political involvements," Wolin writes. "Actually they are a substitute. The notoriety they receive from the media and from politicians eager to take firm stands on no substantive issues serves to distract attention and contribute to a politics of the inconsequential. In classical totalitarian regimes, such as those of Nazi fascism or Soviet communism, economics was subordinate to politics. But "under inverted totalitarianism the reverse is true. Economics dominates politics—and with that domination comes different forms of ruthlessness."

It is the time to hope for the change, but you must be the change and should stop taking the tranquilized medicine of non-activity, hoping others will do what everyone needs to do, without you lifting a finger. It is not an exaggeration to say we are sequestered into accepting illusions as reality and normal, and sometimes not humble enough to admit many issues that are killing us and wrongly so, which needs to be confronted with reason.

We should condemn our divisiveness, damn corporate greed, and halt bailing out the super-rich by taxpayers' money. We need to stop GMOs in food, global warming, and fight against contaminating the sources of our food and water supply, end polluting the air we breathe, and stop the trillions of dollars being spent on military industrial complex bleeding us dry, discourage outsourcing of jobs, and push rigorously to stop genocide and wars of aggression, make police brutality a thing of the past, and defy unlawful incarcerations, stop no due process of law against the apprehension of intellectuals and whistleblowers.

People of the civilized world should look into gun control and dishearten mega media and stop them from indoctrinating people with false reports and misleading information. They must stop defrauding billions, from people's hard-earned money, pushing them into foreclosures, and bankruptcies, where there are no regulations for unleashed bankers and corporation, forcing taxpayers to bail out bankers and huge financial institutions. The system should balance the budget and stop deteriorating the educational system, discontinue unemployment, create a savvy and efficient medical system, give housing subsidies, render educational subsidies, help with the horrendous infrastructure, and raise the minimum wage.

Challenge horrible immigration policies, terminate the exploitive tax system, and stop favoring the mega corporations and too big to fail entities at the expense of the ordinary people. Not to mention wrong ways of dealing with crimes, where violence is going rampant and ever present, do not support autocratic regimes, prosecute those who are guilty at the top, and do not put all the guilt on the little men with no executive power. Abort stifling all legislative activities by corporations and powerful lobbyists, stop fraudulent insider activity on Wall Street in which they defraud people out of billions, start up with using available and efficient alternative energy, implement and mandate more safe environmental policies, and regulative laws against big carbon monoxide producing companies.

Halt masquerading and distorting those with progressive thoughts and agendas. Stop beleaguering (attack from all sides, harass) democracy and insist on people's Constitutional rights, and for the love of God, do not rewrite the Constitution based on your taste and interest rather than upholding the interest of the republic for delivering the system futile. Stop marginalizing people and put an end to racial profiling, where intrusive activities are misconstrued by mapping, acting uncivilized, and without due process of the law and the misuse of power to illegally intimidate and apprehend minorities and ethnic groups.

Why not stop spewing hatred and venom toward so many, sowing fear and discord among millions of good souls who believe in our democracy system of government and sincerely try to become a productive member of the society? Stop giant corporate conglomerates from shoving toxic and inhumane conditions in our throats and forcing us to digest them, generating so many problems that no nation deserves. Discourage paying fealty to electoral politics to create allegiance against what needs to be done in which we can rescue people from this horrendous situation we call living.

If the government really cares to authenticate democracy and human rights and truly manifest the right to life and the pursuit of happiness for all and is perhaps adamant enough to save the system by peaceful means, then they should make dynamic changes that can resonate with the masses of people for financial security and for a life worth living. They should make a sincere effort to substantiate the emerging of a left-right alliance to dismantle the corporate state, stopping bureaucracies and getting rid of red tape. Stop bushwhacking (assaulting, ambushing) innocent citizens in the name of national security through spying, insidious surveillance, and eavesdropping. After all, this is a place nations under autocratic regimes look up to for guidance on freedom, democracy, justice, and human rights.

The politicians need to collectively support gradual changes into a co-op system of economic and modern social endeavors, and corporations and huge companies need to stop changing the nature of nature to maximize profit and stop burning food and burying cows, buffalos, pigs, lambs, poultry, and so forth to raise the price of meat and fowl in a desperately hungry world. In the meanwhile, make the corporations pay their fair share of taxes; most pay less than 2% of taxes or find loopholes to pay no taxes at all, while investing billions in places with no hardcore tax policies, since many authorities can be bribed and bought to turn a blind eye.

Why not decriminalize drugs for medical rehabilitation, since many users have health problems? Stop suppressing addiction, and start helping those through professional medical assistance and decisive therapy. Bring illegal drugs to the surface, and let's deal with it by educational means and taxing it higher, which will mitigate, and perhaps can get rid of, drug trafficking and its peripheral troubles and avoid the menace it causes for humanity. Put more women in higher posts and stop discriminating against women. And most of all, do not believe politicians who say the right things, but behave far from actuating them.

The culture to criminalize the fabric of society is ingrained in the monetary system, which has neurotically become the norm, as the ruling parties and the rich elites benefit from hoarding money, as they relentlessly pursue profit maximization even at the cost of human lives, where people's lives are compromised. The system must be fueled for reaching its economic objectives and because the business elites are adamant to fulfill their sadistic thirst for accumulation of wealth no matter at what cost.

And unless economic justice is prevailed, decriminalization and to avoid disparaging (degrading) the poverty-stricken people is not going to happen, in which economic equity can only uproot the very foundation of the society that is contemptuous toward the poor and belittling toward the deprived, forcing millions to do wrong to survive. The failed educational system has compounded the effects, since poverty and lack of education are tightly proportional to the rise of incarceration as so many people with no available opportunities and employment are mostly the victims, as society's crime rates has statistically skyrocketed, without any constructive and structural solution for the vast problems of crime-infested societies.

Apparently such squelching (triumph over, quelling, crushing, defeating) activities are intentionally planned to make repeated offenders, since many of the so-called felons have chronic mental sickness with no available medical therapy and professional help to rehabilitate and correct the situation that jailed them in the first place. This can help to make a safer neighborhood and a better atmosphere, where they are to reside in after they are released.

To make matters worse, the so-called felons are not clear and free from their insidious social and economic gridlocks, which haunt them even after they are released and have already paid their dues to society. They are labeled with the word "felon" and they are damned to carry it for the rest of their lives, which convicts them to unemployment, denying so many from earning the bare minimum wage, and without any other income, leaving a good reason to become a repeated offender and hostile toward a system that has declared war on them.

It seems there is no moral responsibility or conscious accountability left to face the problem of crimes head-on, where constructive resources should target social and economic shortcomings. But the legislative and the executive branch of government are heavily influenced by powerful lobbyists and private mega corporations, because the rich elites spend millions to hocus them into bribery, where no resolute or sensible public good is ever instituted, which has bewitched the entire society into self-destructive conduct and into accepting this weird crime-ridden criteria as normal, since so many have been brainwashed into complacency (self-content) as they utter, "It is what it is. Take it, or leave it." Forgetting that: Snowflakes eventually make avalanches.

In most cases, judges do not have the discretion to judge the accused since they have to follow certain guidelines that do not necessarily follow the expression: the punishment should fit the crime. And for humanity's sake, stop redefining and reconfiguring the Constitution to fit the oligarchical behaviors of the elites, which strips people of their fundamental rights and dignity. And halt changing the nature of Mother Nature; stop suppressing the poor and the very productive forces of society, the workers, who are the main reason for your deep pockets and surplus value.

Do not push further austerity on so many people who are already burdened and enslaved with a despicable and squalid lifestyle beyond human imagination, while producing robot-like people, as they are spellbound to behave indifferently toward others' suffering, but desire to consume more of what you unfittingly produce and relentlessly push to pursue.

Capitalists' moral mission is to see individuals and self-interest as the only propriety, as if we should accept altruism and grassroots social assistance as immoral, ignoring that it is why so many troubles have reflected humanity in undeniably ill ways. To protect corporate oligopoly, we have amassed the most mass surveillance, which has turned democracy into a sham, which has devalued our government of the people, by the people, and for the people, where the state is converted into autocracy by the corporate elites.

I strongly believe in so many intellectual and frontline fighters who struggle for justice, equity, liberty, and human rights. They are compassionate enough to risk their lives in many parts of the world for a better living condition and to save humanity. But I also believe that we have reached an age of consciousness and intelligence in which we must resolve our differences by peaceful means. I am sure no decent human being could ever ignore the loss of innocent lives through violence and criminal behavior. And the moral imperative should call for reasoning and humanely dialogues, since any one of us could act like the elites do, and perhaps even worse, if we were in the position of power.

It is the 21st century, we should act like it and not get stuck in caveman mentality where the dark ages are upon us. And, yes, history has proven that change has happened many times through violence and killing, but bear in mind, as many as those bloodied times, dynamic and authenticated changes have taken place by cooperation and peaceful means as well, rather than by killing; we should gracefully cherish nonviolent behaviors. That no violence should take over the power of wit and understanding when faced with complicated issues and to prove it just take a survey by the civilized world and ask if violence should be the answer.

Marx believed, "It is only possible to achieve real liberation in the real world. ... by employing real means ... slavery cannot be abolished without the steam-engine and the mule and spinning-jenny, serfdom cannot be abolished without improved agriculture, and ... in general, people cannot be liberated as long as they are unable to obtain food and drink, housing and clothing in adequate quality and quantity. 'Liberation' is a historical and not a mental act, and it is brought about by historical conditions, the development of industry, commerce, agriculture, and the conditions of intercourse, and so forth. Based on the theory of the productive forces and related perspectives, the economic systems of the former Eastern bloc and the present-day socialist states the state accumulated capital through forcible extraction of surpluses from the population for the purpose of rapidly modernizing and industrializing their countries, because these countries were not technologically advanced to a point where an actual socialist economy was technically possible,[1] or were a socialist state tried to reach the communist mode of production. The philosophical perspective behind the modernizing zeal of the Soviet Union and People's Republic of China was based on the desire to industrialize their countries."

Unless the global productive forces and the masses' consciousness is pinnacled, contrary to what Marx and Lenin and others, with the exception of Trotsky, believed: True communism is possible in one country where the industrial and economic forces have matured and will produce domino effects to the rest of industrial world with advanced and progressive cultures, when technology and human intelligence are mature enough and ripe. No economic and sociocultural meaningful changes are to take place. Either way an emotional or demagogic call for revolution by hostile means is not a viable option, when the proper forces to make a smooth transition possible are not available yet. If history should be an indicator, then we need to question why Russia, China, Vietnam, Cuba, Cambodia, and the like did not succeed their discourse. And still not rational enough to make sense of what they have started, since vacillating between capitalism, socialism, and acting revisionism, which are still very far away from adopting communism. They failed their bloodied revolution, losing millions of lives with no avail, because the fundamentals of productive force and the superstructures of feudal Russia and China at the time of revolt were not ready. And neither was the world for such exorbitant (drastic) social and economic changes to internationally assume and take place. So we need to harness the notion of emotional outrage, despite its justification and altruism, until the fundamentals of revolt have globally matured. Because no nation is an island anymore; we are all interactively connected.

Furthermore, should we think that slavery and feudal changes or the renaissance for that matter would ever be possible if the productive forces and the culture of thoughts, the ideology and awareness, would have not been ready to switch into the new system and to have reveled (celebrate) its outcome? But one thing is for sure: If the revolution were to take place in North America, then it would manifest itself with a much better result than in Russia, China, and others like them. The leverages for a dynamic and quality change are not cosmetic; we are not in a feudal state, but are living the era of a capitalistic society, which is the highest stages of capitalism known as imperialism rather than living in other primitive eras not suitable for reliable and progressive changes, which were doomed to failure.

Could our predecessors have expected the slaves to bring about the social changes that capitalists have or could they had expected the feudal to place a man on the moon and create the miracle inventions that capitalists have done in their time? Yes, our perceptions and incisive awareness and consciousness might be ready, which perhaps could overpower our momentary lapses of reason for a revolutionary idea to take place, but to be sure, we must have the fundamental forces of economic and social production available to induce such historical change. This should also awaken not only the masses of the poor, but the capitalists themselves to investigate the stalemated, stagnated, or matured system, which once was dynamically productive, to avoid bloodied upheavals, and if room is left for more progress and believing in social order and prosperity for all. Or is it really time for the capitalist system to go? Referencing history, the maturity of productive forces and the widening gap between the poor and the rich might have caused social uprising and turmoil. But also, more powerful governments, like the Persian empire, Egyptian empire, Arabian empire, Mongolian empire, Chinese empire, Greek and Roman empire, Ottoman empire, British empire, and so many others, felt like they needed to expand since they might have noticed their economic demise, or they just wanted to add territories to their empire. They attacked and destroyed other weak nations, especially if the less powerful nations owned valuable resources. This should remind us of today's modern warfare and militarism taking place in many parts of the world, where the corporate capitalists compete for the resources of developing countries by either unfair trade practices or through militarism.

Superpowers first stir trouble in many parts of the world, then talk about peace, democracy, and human rights, which is followed by sending trillions of dollars' worth of arms to dreadful and bloodied regimes of their choice to kill millions in the name of doing business and making money for the few. They are able to cause these inhumane atrocities because they are equipped with the technology that makes the world perceive the corporate mega media intended to comprehend as reality, but not the actual reality. This should remind us of fascist and autocratically orchestrated techniques that the few super-rich control and manifest, rather than democratic techniques and products people should control. To avoid making freedom-loving people of the globe lose and not to brainwash them to stay on the wrong side of justice and what is right. To change the status quo and to bring about a more just economic system, where true democracy and socialized goods can equitably be allocated among masses of people, where the workers enjoy the fruits of their labor. Where trillions of surplus value is not concentrated in the hands of the private enterprise, but will make sure the basic necessities of living are prioritized, including proper employment, retirement security, free education, free health care, subsidized housing, free transportation, and more.

Marx and others predicted that true social revolution is only possible in advanced industrial nations that have reached economic maturity; this does not historically fit the criteria and neither fits today's world social economic and cultural agendas. The truth is Marx did not predict that billions, even trillions, of dollars could electronically be transferred in seconds, where outsourcing has become the norm in many industrial and powerful nations since the multinational companies invest in countries with plenty of raw materials, with dirt cheap natural resources and labor. They also establish the puppet government of their choice, a neo-colonialist system of governing, which is the accomplice to exploiting native resources and cheap labor, murdering, torturing, and imprisoning their own citizens. They all work in concert as superior classes against the deprived and international working class, which has quelled most of the pressure in nations that have peaked industrially and are managing to avoid socialist revolution.

Marx did not predict the wars of aggression pursued by looting, plundering, and extortion; taking other helpless nations' natural resources and raw material has become the norm. He must have not expected the explosive power of computers, the advent of the internet with amazingly quick communication technology, and the super advanced jet engines, the power of outsourcing, the global economic expansion and counter-trade (a form of international trade in which purchases made by an importing nation are linked to offsetting purchases made by the exporting nation), and the potential for nuclear, chemical, bacterial, and cyber warfare and terrorism, which is shifting the national boundaries and making the entire world act like one village. Everything is immediately accessible by the international monetary system through trade and militarism.

Until the resources of the planet are depleted to the point of exhaustion and collapse, which we should already see the dire signs of, then, it is perhaps possible for the poor, the destitute, and the global working class to confront the murderous agents in decisive ways and make a worldly socioeconomic and cultural revolution compatible to the 21st century. This should be dynamic and progressive enough to carry humanity into the next couple of centuries, where the system can make meaningful life and happiness relatively possible and not be made to belittle God and trash humanity in the name of accumulating infinite wealth and power.

Our mental progressiveness and higher understanding of social and natural order can empower us to rationally conceptualize and induce dynamic intelligence, which is only possible in accordance to scientific breakthroughs, enabling society to perceive a culture of thinking that is interconnected with the advancement of technology and the industrial mode of production, which grants us a paradigm shift into new consciousness and assembly of thoughts that leverages humanity to enter into a new notion of civilization, enabling societies to digest and comprehend the dynamics of historical events. For example, "division of labor" and mass production were only possible because of the invention of assembly lines, which an industrial breakthrough made possible.

The problem is the relationship of the production that is an imprecation (curse), since it distorts and exploits nature, destroys humanity, and commoditizes everything and everyone in its path for profit—and not for the sake of creating public goods compatible with the sustainability of the social and natural order. This private opulence at the cost of public misery needs to end, as the poor are paying with their lives to feed a system that has become dull and indifferent to the suffering of so many bereft of basic necessities to sustain them. The system has turned fair competition and appropriate market functions into sociopathic individualistic nature.

The system has violated nature; it has disturbed class order to the extreme, where the middle class are becoming an endangered species, and the working class cannot make a living anymore. It has turned into sociopathic politics fed by corporations and mad institution to focus on wealth creation for the elites and the hell with everyone else. People are casted into dire positions where upper mobility is impossible, since the masses are stuck in terrible financial situations. This personality disorders and anti-social conduct must stop by the power of reasoning and in the name of human virtues, and not by murdering each other.

The philosophical perspective behind the modernizing zeal of the Soviet Union and the People's Republic of China was based on the desire to industrialize their countries. At this stage, the global dynamics and interconnectivities have grown too big to behave nativist, populist, or nationalist. We need to strive for international citizenry and strategize hallmarks for global governing and a worldwide transitory infrastructure to heighten our appreciation for one government, one nation, under God, in which our ethos should be directed at preserving humanity, rather than acting self-centered and narrow-minded in fortifying boundaries to separate humankind.

Let's break down the stereotype mentality and encourage the peaceful coexistence of man, which by the way, can exterminate so many excuses for having to go to war with the so-called enemy nations and boycott governments and their military industrial complex from wars of aggression, where no nation or any group can act genocidal toward the weaker countries or race. Let's move forward with virtual reality, which has surpassed and is beyond domesticated and inhibited forces of ignorance and authenticate the phrase "I know of no illegal human being."

I am sure if persevered enough, people can make the privileged elites open their eyes that are blinded with power and prestige. They should incessantly be reminded of acting delusional, which can be corrected, if pushed enough by the truth-teller to open the eyes of plutocracy and to avoid a bloodied class war. If keen enough, we can clearly see that Mother Nature, the very reason for our existence, works gradually and is an evolutionist in its pursuit of giving life and making dynamic and decisive apparatus possible for humanity to enjoy. We are part of nature and should act like it. For some, it might be easy to say the corporate tyranny must be overthrown no matter what cost, but this must not occur at the cost of millions of innocent lives, which violence will surely bring. Every time we are violent, we eviscerate (to remove, to deprive of vital contents) and insult the very intelligence and human mindfulness that has collectively enabled us to do the impossible. Resorting to force and barbarism will kill the civility of mind and manner and the power of compassion in all of us. It will breed more ills, demonic and horrific conduct, as it has in the past, if history is to remind us and is witnessed.

The mechanism of power that betrays those marginalized and the destitute, the powerless and the poor can be shifted. But then, what guaranty does anyone have if we are not educated and wise enough to keep others intact, which are supposed to govern and rule us from doing the same or even worse. If we are not mentally competent and do not possess the dynamics and the technology of thought to manage our literal problems with this corporate state now and resolutely manage to communicate savviness and wisdom to them, then what should make us confident that we can make it happen with the alternative system?

Discourage talks about sublime (exalted, elevated) madness and violent confrontations to deal with the system, where moments of extremity might call for revolt. The power of reasoning can unlock and speak the undeniable power of truth to the power and acclaim its sovereignty where no man should resist, unless wanting to act beastly and assume savage behavior.

We live in an era where our overall mentality bears enough intelligence to retaliate against the mechanism of powers that betrays those whom they are supposed to rule and care for, but it must happen in dignified and civilized ways because we are in profound need of humanity, and the daunting question should be, why not? Why not activate the potentiality of our human brain which collectively has the literal power to rescue humankind from the clutches of ignorance and where kinship and meaningful perspective could sooth our pain and anguish and replace breathing and living devastation?

Why procrastinate until is too late? And why not get out of this entrenched madness and act humane against the root causes of evil, which have caged and imprisoned our souls in the name of profit? Let our failure leverage and aim us at enlightenment where human spirit can kindle to do well and make peace and justice possible and to realize we are unbalanced and will extinguish faster if were to resort to nuclear, biological, chemical, and many other vicious weaponry, which can wipe us all out, making Holocaust-like tragedies many time over, where no day will be left to call it a day.

Let's necessitate, rehabilitate, and resuscitate our love for each other and become one against all atrocious and inhumane behavior. We must become warned of our abysmal mistakes we are making and condemn the real perpetrators of crimes and misconduct. Let's be human. Violence will end in revenge, and revenge is a very potent force that will travel the endless road of outrage and violence, which creates a vicious circle of beastly acts, until millions of lives are senselessly taken. It should be obvious that criminal behaviors are odious no matter which side is causing them.

We need to know that either through a conscious decision or a momentary lapse of reason, any violent action should be counted as human failure, which must not be challenged through the barrel of gun, because humanism should always be the answer. And hence all-out effort must be directed at bulls' eyeing and targeting the heart of raising the plural consciousness of the people and to equip them with correct information, higher education, and knowledge so they can truly digest and understand the complexity of the system which is rendering them helpless.

And to detect the anatomical structures of power and exploitation and replace it with a new manifesto to emancipate billions from the ironclad indecency and ruthless economic programs, as the financial despots and the Byzantines of today's world laugh at democracy and human rights, where they know their autocracy of corporate power rules. Truth diggers are incessant in their effort to stand against this behavioral hegemony, which is structured to put an end to inhumane living standards manufactured by the corporate power blinded with greed.

They cannot see the effect of giant corporate economy on the world, which has left a ruthless inefficiency on so many people who die every day because of food and water depravity and famine that has turned humanity into vast herds of prey and made the super-rich into a handful of predators hunting human beings, since they artificially raise prices and manipulate the world market to maximize their profit as they insanely fight the natural and social order, amassing 80-90% of the wealth into the hands of 1%, leaving 99% of the world's population to barely survive on 10-15% of the entire global resources.

This madness must be stopped if there is going to be a slight chance left for humankind to survive corporate atrocities, which have become a life and death situation for so many and an insurmountable challenge for the wise to overcome. It is time to realize that no nation or any society should be at the mercy of a power individual or influenced group because they will be victimized and will not fare well. No man can resist not abusing his power. We are social and self-interested beings. No one should prevail with one's self-interest agendas at the cost of common good and society, where social apparatus and the common goods should work well for the benefit of the entire society, with no one left behind.

The bottom line is that in individualistic societies individuals benefit at the cost of the group, war-like cultures—including racism, social injustice, prejudice against women and children, prejudice against the poor and the weak, against minorities, infinite wrong against the nature itself, religious resentment encouraged by the sectarian charlatans in making superficial difference. Where even God is not immune to their perils and toxic lectures to make money because no one is safe to the atrocities of human greed, which must be controlled. And authenticated altruism and much better humans are the products of a social and cooperative system; they are delivered in a less hostile and negatively competing environment, where common goods are truly recognized and prioritized.

Someone wise once said: "Don't ask God to guide your footsteps if you're not willing to pick up your feet." Take steps toward nullifying and dismantling the relentless efforts of corporate capitalists' system that have become numb to causing the destruction of the entire planet. Outlaw them for maximizing wealth in the name of taking lives; take their social license away and inactivate their murderous behaviors, and let's be delighted that we are not part of doing so much ill to humanity. Let's make sure to be congenial (to get along) and belong to the right side of history, as we must repeatedly remind ourselves that we are here for a short time, since we must return to where we came from sooner or later.

And when it is time to transcend to higher realms with a clear conscious, we can stand erect as if with a chip on our shoulder and keep our head up to answer with no hesitancy and say, "No. I did not murder. I did not rape or cause any irreparable harm to humankind." Socrates said, it is better to suffer wrong than to do wrong. We ought to know it is not the application of common sense that is lost, but greed and self-interest agenda which is gone haywire, and the premises encouraging its reckless behaviors, that is about to make humanity an endangered species if not wisely corrected or entirely stopped.

It is imperative for any progressive system to direct its goals and activities at a global scale where the greater good is to benefit everyone, to avoid acting small and narrow-mindedly and not become restrained in doing justice because of social, cultural, nationality, race, ethnicity, sectarianism, color, gender, religious, economic classification, or any discriminatory factors. Otherwise, it will lessen or sanction its overall objectives deemed at helping the entire humanity from reaching its full potential; the system should transcend beyond concocting nebulous (vague) and petty differences that are traditionally made to keep us apart. If prevailed, "no can manifesto" will be a thing of the past, where even seeing God the almighty should become explicitly clear and closer to one than one's jugular vein.

I believe we will overcome our malignant social and financial problems and will reach the mountaintop of human consciousness and become enlightened to shatter the old paradigms and unanimously vote for the common goods of the entire planet and its inhabitants. I also believe we have the means to substantiate quality changes that can empower us to expedite global social solidarity, where a better system can play a huge positive role and a catalyst in opening plural brain might and materialize a dynamic global educational culture to direct us in a right track at the end of the tunnel, where there is light, and away from predatory practices and beastly behaviors.

Disturbingly enough, so many keep silent to protect their interests and to dote (coddling, excessive attention) their positions to guaranty how high they stand in the ladder of life. Then we have to bear confluences of negative situations and dire ripple effects resulting in roguish (vicious) outcomes that would take years to correct and heal from.

It is not riddling (perplexing) to unravel the rationale behind what holds many back from grasping success and obviate (prevent) billions from ascending to decisive and gratifying positions since it is in our DNA to cultivate and search for a better life, but unless people's talent and might is unlocked by giving them a chance, an opportunity to exploit their full potential, billions would be denied to make the right choice, to play the music of living, and to orchestrate what is often a heavenly and beautiful sound. Because of greed and holding infinite resources in few individuals' hands with no clemency toward the financially deprived is not healthy, since it makes the atmosphere vulnerable to outburst and bound to violence from deprived masses of impoverished inhabitants and unhappy campers without any protection against the storms of life. This should be alarming since the biggest scam in the history of humankind is revealed, as so many are being plundered by so few, as it is obvious and not a conundrum anymore.

Let's not forget it makes a difference in how committed we are to accomplishing our goals, to gain prosperity and thrive for reaching happiness, but then, no matter how resilient we are and how willingly we should try, if there are no fertile grounds to spread potentiated seeds, it will prove futile. And yes, there are those manufactured cases where occasional talents are revered and decorated, as they are exhibited as paragons (symbols) and the hallmarks of true success, which since have surmounted their ultra-difficult position before reaching the pinnacle of victory.

This surely can motivate many and perhaps create hope for millions of eager souls, but the fallacies behind such tactics are plenty, since the actual winning numbers are one in millions, where real statistics sing much gloomier songs. Hence, it is imperative for a democratic system of governing to encourage and support viable grounds with golden opportunities for all its citizen and not only the chosen ones because reason dictates to help everyone and not be imbued with so much prejudice.

We should think insightfully and depend on what actually makes sense rather than becoming exposed to the malice of conditioning and not believe in what we see and hear, since we perceive what is visible and apparent, which in many cases victimizes and shackles millions in their engagement with the outside world. Regrettably, we often notice when it is already too late, damage is done. Not catching that, billions is spent to capitalize on propaganda and advertisements to lure people into the quicksand of accepting the wrong socioeconomic policies and dreadful political agendas, without noticing what is actually taking place; we are being hypnotized with phony programs and accepting lopsided ideas, which should accredit the phrase "seeing is believing." I am afraid this is also true in our private lives, in our family and marriage lives, in our finances, and in almost everything we participate in; sometimes we pay a heavy price to learn otherwise.

We should further discuss many issues in urgent need of our attention—for instance, "concentrated power." Have you not noticed when anyone, any network or group, government entity, organization, party, lobbyist, corporation, become too powerful? It always brings awful results that affect people in worse ways, even at a global level—especially now that the boundaries are collapsing. We are becoming a small village, and dynamic communications are as fast as lightening. And thanks God for some of the sincere media that is as vigil as eagles to report decisive news via marvelous technology leveraged by honest reporters and brilliant journalists.

It is true that with information and knowledge comes power, which needs to blend in with understanding and compassion to bear tolerance and give diversity in human concept a chance to grow and bind people's healthy relationships impermeable to any prejudice and not only exclusive to certain ethnicity or nationality but uniting the entire human race while leaving no one behind.

We should not have moral depravity and turpitude toward each other and ought to act in righteous ways as building blocks in every society. It is the tendency of human nature to become arrogant, psyched up, and pompous when we have too much power, like one should play God. But then can you imagine an unwise, rube, and unjust God because the problem can become colossally wicked so that sometimes it seems impossible to confront or manage to control.

The powerful tyrants are not frugal in ravaging human lives and do not hesitate to kill, maim, and destroy anyone standing in their mighty path since no opinion should be contrary to the despots' ruling or tolerated against their absolute command. They bulldoze unfavorable plans and destroy constructive programs if they are not meant to strengthen their position; the inhumane rulers wipe out any archetype (idea, model) believed to oppose their reign, which may endanger a dictator's ruthless status or activate ideas against the conglomerate allies and powerful network of fascist regimes. The problem worsens when many decipher to evoke a socialist system that glorifies "dictatorial of proletariat" as its focal point, believing a socialist system could set us free and render proper solution to our abstract sociocultural and socioeconomic dilemmas.

Forgetting that too much power in anyone's hand, any party or assembly, group, organization, will most definitely spell tragedy of a paramount size, and God forbid if the ruling party lacks knowledge and empathy to comprehend intricate human nature and perhaps is exhausted with wisdom, not able to understand the veracity and the complexity of our human soul that is undeniably part of cosmic energy where no socialist or communist ideology can fathom.

Any system worthy of ruling ought to identify with God and realize the prevalent cosmic energy, without which, no life is ever possible. The system needs to realize our individual, social, and cultural thinking, our emotions and spiritual longings, as part of divine intervention and not without meaning; no being lacks having a purpose because we undeniably are part of the entire picture called life, nature—or call it as you wish. It is extremely disciplined and magnificently orderly; it should awaken willpower, responsibility, accountability, determination, compassion, and cooperation in humankind to become aligned with nature and not stray from what can break us and make us if we constructively adhere to nature's heavenly offering.

Either through individual efforts or by collective urges and bargaining humanity we must find solutions for so many unanswered questions and unravel an enigma to millions of mysterious questions, to quench our thirst in finding the unknowns to serve human curiosity, to patent innovative and inspiring thoughts, to marvel and create groundbreaking ideas. Our search for happiness and the aesthetic is to look for truth and beauty. Our craving for divinity and piety, poetry, art and music, our hopes and dreams, human longing for freedom and democracy, and millions of other crucial human devotions, which cannot flourish in a despotic and dictatorial environment, where social calamities and unjustifiable rule of law will be rudimentary and can become a fundamental part of cultural and social norms.

Remember, no imperial hegemony has ever lasted for the very same reason of expanding their tyrannical power; no human beings want to be yoked and deprived of freedom. It is just part of man's nature. Not taking people's freedom away is wisdom, not to lapse in respecting human rights and democracy is righteous; balance and moderation is not only virtuous, but plays an essential role in holding power and the secret to survival. Having too much of anything means bad business, which should not exclude power and wealth.

We are conditioned to believe in what we see and hear. We perceive what is visible and apparent to our senses, which in many cases victimizes and shackles millions in their engagement with the outside world. Regrettably, we often notice when is too late; the damage is already done. Not catching that, billions is spent to capitalize on propaganda and advertising to lure people into the quicksand of accepting wrong socioeconomic policies and dreadful political agendas without even noticing what is actually taking place. We are being brainwashed and hypnotized, accrediting the phrase "seeing is believing." I am afraid this is also true in our private lives, in our family and marriage lives, in our finances and in almost everything we participate in; sometimes we pay a heavy price to learn otherwise.

It is not so that the empires of wealth and power do not have the means or cannot identify with the criteria of an adequate system of governing, which if the government of powerful elites chooses to saintly operate, it could give meaning to the word hope and make a better world possible. They just choose not to, since withering away of ecosystem, draconian lifestyle of the poor with continuously wasting human lives in crime-ridden societies and wars of aggression, has no impact on their soul, which leaves no ill repercussion to the wrongdoing of the mighty rich and the agents of horror.

In the meanwhile, the intrusive and bullying empires are flagrantly proud to cuddle and call the most despicable puppet regimes of terror allies, which operate mercilessly against what humanity stands for. As the whole world witnesses these incriminating fascist regimes and religious extremist states, they behave cowardly with continuous rancorous beheadings and publically display headless bodies, as they order demonic stoning, slashing, rape, despicable honor killings, encouraging misogyny, gay bashing, xenophobia, cruel and inhumane torturing of political inmates, and illegal imprisonment of the dissidents without any due process of law.

These totalitarian regime of terror stoop very low and act so condescending to breed fear and expect utter obedience to impose savage and prehistoric rules of conduct on their subjects. It seems the culprits are numb to the extremely robust and active international communication, where the newsworthy items spread so fast, since brave and talented journalists and whistleblowers are still available, which is neither engulfed with glamour, nor lost in the atmosphere of greed. They are adamantly decisive to let the vital information out and let the entire international community hear the good news and travesties of the world. The empires of misdeed and corruption have forgotten that.

In the contemporary world even the farthest dwellers of the planet Earth are unquestionably affected by political, cultural, and financial interactivities of the globe; the conglomerate (cartel, trust, consortium) media is leveraged to influence so many through modern telecommunication and technological innovations. Today's generation possesses advanced industries that can unfold superb thoughts and brilliant activities. We are able to disclose helpful breakthroughs and information via dynamic ways of communication. With so much science and great technological innovations, enormous military and puissant policing, also with massive accumulations of wealth and influence beyond anyone's imagination, the wealthy empires of the world can positively resolve many prolonged sinister sagas beholding humanity.

Imperial corporations can halt consolidated attacks from fiendish jihads and put an end into the prolonged purgatory state of mind, which has disturbed world peace and tranquility, where so many have yielded to subtle fear from small scale business meetings to large enterprise assemblies. People worry in every important gathering, communities, even in government entities, national and international airports, as millions of innocent visitors and travelers become nervous, not knowing where the terrorists have designated their next targets and when or how they are going to strike again and again.

They can stop religious extremists sporadic attacks and their fragmented inhumane terrorist behaviors at will. But they do not. The mighty powerful are an illusion that ordinary people, who unlike the super-rich have no protection against sinful terrorism and other wicked misconduct, can live in a bubble impervious from harm, since the powerful elites act so indifferent to people's suffering and very fragile situation. Many empires believe that wars give birth to advanced civilizations. Albert Einstein said, "the pioneers of a warless world are the [youth] who refuse military Service." Charles Sumner said, "Give me the money that has been spent in war and I will clothe every man, woman, and child in an attire of which kings and queens Will be proud. I will build a schoolhouse in every valley over the whole earth. I will Crown every hillside with a place of worship consecrated to peace."

And Eve Merria said, "I dream of giving birth to a child who will ask, Mother, what war was." President Thomas Jefferson said: "I recoil with horror at the ferociousness of man. Will nations never devise a more rational umpire of? Differences than force? Are there no means of coercing? Injustice more gratifying to our nature? Than a waste of the blood? Of thousands and of the labor of millions of our fellow creatures?"

The oligopolistic governments choose to kill people who kill people, to show that killing and maiming is barbaric, and since they do not concoct realistic plans for constructive peace and productive investments to improve people's lives, they rather steadfastly plan for wars and are antsy (fidgety, impatient, restless) to spend billions in bombing campaigns against common people and leave irreparable traces of hatred behind. It shouldn't take a genius to ask why thousands of young wannabe martyrs attach suicide vests, detonate explosives to end their own lives, and take innocent lives. The recruiters of hell swarm naïve and vulnerable individuals' poisoning their minds, seducing them into believing that life is much happier on the other side, and the act of suicide will put them in paradise where the angels of heaven can't wait to embrace them. I wonder should female martyrs expect handsome males as well to greet them in the heaven above?

They are quite successful in enchanting many into fools and deranging young cadets' minds to create time bombs since they literally facilitate and remind their prey of the primordial lifestyle and the bitter experiences that are structurally designed by the foreign corporate intruders backed by government hegemonies to colonies, and they exploit them into agonizingly poor condition, where there is no way out but to commit suicide and to kill innocent others in an act of revenge. Recruiters of hell radicalize potential suicidal cells by luring them into cul-de-sacs (blind alley, dead end) and making them understand the cause to their despicable poverty; the ruling despotic regimes are pumping oil and gas out of their backyards and extracting minerals and valuable stones from poor people's mines and territories without giving a damn about them, while forcing natives, who are the real proprietors of wealth, to live in a subhuman condition which is staunchly supported by the west. Entrenching them and their loved ones in pandemonium, since they are the ones rubbing them from what belongs to people and with impunity to those responsible for their misery. Human traffickers are successful since they capitalize on exploitation of the poor and desperately vulnerable individuals, which are the victims of social and economic disasters; they become prey into the hands of merciless profiteers, except for the so-called next martyr terrorist to be, remuneration (pay) is promised in the next life.

Natives' anger and hatred is coalesced (compounded) when seeing loss of loved ones, family members, friends, countrymen women, and other innocent human beings as well, asking why? As they are witnessing firsthand the harsh ramifications of an ugly war of aggression imposed on them, as they are being bombed with no mercy and for no apparent reason linked to ordinary people. Globalization has also marked its pervasively (ubiquitous, universal) irresponsible effects on millions of immature characters, where images of sex, glamor, and violence made by movie industries and news agencies exhibited through TV, satellites, the internet, and shown by thousands of internationally known social media channels have left a jagged view, skewed with narrow-mindedness, and misinterpreted outcomes, bewitching millions of youth into hallucination and leading them to perdition. Since they are apart from the real happenings, obscure from the reality, and unfamiliar with what actually takes place in the business world because they are also strange to the shark-like entertainment environment and the cutthroat venture societies, compounded with crude-mindedness, they are longing so naively for a piece of the action, as they thrive to become part of the powerful images. In making a name for themselves, so many of them are already looking for a cause to rebel. They wrongfully fall into the hands of demagogues and religious extremists with no way out of their decadent position, in which the predators evolve them into sublime madness to do the unthinkable.

Let's not forget that there is a dark and callow side to human nature that can become flammable and vulnerable to deception, since no one figuratively speaking is perfect. Charlatans and traders of evil know how to ignite others for reaching their sadistic objectives and beastly goals. The question is why should such a cruel apparatus and such demonic missions materialize in the 21st century. It really is an enigma—perhaps part of human genome. But then again, history has witnessed that literacy and education, wisdom, building knowledge, and gaining constructive information along with civility of mind and manner, professional therapeutic approaches, effective psychological trainings, and positive people around you, also the presence of decent role models and competent mentors can make a huge difference in dwindling violence and lessening vicious behaviors in human pathology and deviated conduct.

Sadly, the resources that are essentially needed to correct human maladies, to treat and improve byzantine (complex, convoluted) mental and psychological shortcomings, to further literate and enlighten the populace are held by corporate oligarchy and plutocratic governments for arriving at their inhumane objectives. This should leave no doubt that those running the global system have premeditated to eradicate us, as if they have found suitable ways to control population growth. The aggregate illusionism and deranged positivism have held so many hostage to metastatic (cancerous, wicked in nature) conditions, where dire reality is not an obstruction to our suckling dream-like desires and our insane ambitions, which since have infected our minds with autoimmune diseases and venom-like substances, forcing us toward self-cannibalism aimed at the very destruction of humankind.

It does not take an oracle to know the reason behind so many destructible forces that vortex billions collectively to the bottom of the abyss, where forces behind so many atrocities and rapacious behaviors unanimously operate behind closed doors, well-guarded by powerful, covert intelligence agencies, police forces, and the national guards and vast militarism.

So much of incompetency in self-control and limitless craving for greed should exist to turn us into some type of subhuman creature that must be protected to cause harm and institutionalize what actually hurts people and renders them helpless—privilege and power versus justice and truth. Why lack moral imperative to act indifferently toward people's pain, making citizens exposed to insensible socioeconomic maleficence and getting masses to retaliate, ready for a bloodied class war. It is urgently required for corporate autocracy and the powerful elites to unplug their myopic, cultic behavior to show funambulism (mental agility) and exist in this deteriorating and deadened state of mind to comply with human dignity, to ameliorate a harsh and unbearable situation that masses of ordinary people are so sadly experiencing.

The conglomerate capitalists ingratiated with global government empires, and their military industrial complex has grown too strong to let a Rwanda genocide, a Bosnian massacre happen, and to permit ISIS cleansing of innocent ethnics, and murdering other religious factions and denominations substantiate or let a Holocaust-like situation take place without a green light from the imperial powers. John Steinbeck puts it this way: "War is a symptom of man's failure as thinking animal." And George Washington said, "My first wish is to see this plague of humankind, war, banish from the Earth."

And Albert Einstein said, "I know not with what weapons World War III will be fought, but World War IV will be fought with stick and stone." But then, since there are powerful international forces in denial of ugly historical events, atrocities as such are to be expected redundantly without remorse and because the superpowers are very afraid of the word peace. They are skillfully able to brainwash people into systematic doubt and literally make citizens skeptical of their predatory and insane actions against humanity. The system of corporate capitalists should remind us of sociopathic behavior defined as: "having antisocial personality disorder. This disorder is characterized by a disregard for the feelings of others, a lack of remorse or shame, manipulative behavior, unchecked egocentricity, and the ability to lie in order to achieve one's goals."

Profiling a sociopath with narcissistic attitude:

Narcissistic personality disorder, also known as NPD, is a personality disorder in which the individual has a distorted self-image, unstable and intense emotions, is overly preoccupied with vanity, prestige, power, and personal adequacy, lacks empathy, and has an exaggerated sense of superiority, acting nonchalant with smooth charm, controlling, and conning. They do not acknowledge the rights of others and see their self-serving conduct as admissible. They appear to be entrancing (delightful), yet are furtively malicious and bossy, seeing their victims as merely agents to be taken advantage of. In a bold sense, they see what does not belong to them as their right. They are pathological fabricators, since they lie and act in falsehood. They have no difficulty lying easily and it is almost impossible for them to be factually coherent. No feeling of regret, abashment, or guilt—none. With rooted rage, which is cleaved off and restrained, they are roiled (disturbed) and do not see others around them as people, but only regard them as dupes (fools) and possibilities. Instead of friends or colleagues, they have targets and accomplices who end up as victims; at the end, they justify the means and allow no obstacle in their way. Superficial feelings and emotions. When they present what appears to be friendly, warmth, happiness, love, and empathy, it is more fake than experienced and serves an ulterior reason. Violent by insignificant stuff, yet linger to be unshakable and cool by what would fumble (upset) a normal person. Since they are neither genuine, nor are their commitments. They lack the ability for love and cannot truly belong. Desensitize with having no compassion, unable to sympathize with the suffering of others. They have only disdain for people's feelings of trouble and are ready to take advantage of them and lack concern with their ill impact on others and are morally insane, paranoid of the word revolution.

Other connected merits are:

Hateful to those who try to understand them. Do not believe anything is wrong with them. Covert, but try to keep conventional appearance. Has an emotional need to justify their crimes and therefore needs their victim's affirmation (respect, gratitude and love). Incapable of real human attachment to another. Not able to feel remorse or guilt;

they have a malignant personality and are radically narcissistic and ambitious. They may say readily that their objective is to conquer and rule the world, since only wealth, power, and influence can palliate their relentlessly zealous inhumane behaviors. Substantial (genuine, meaningful) religious agendas, virtuosity, morality or other human values play no part in their lives.

They have no feeling of mercy for others and are competent of violence. Under older psychological terms, they fall into the breed of sociopath, or psychopath, but unlike the typical psychopath, their behavior is masked by a shallow social façade, and they are habitual liars. The point is, such malfunctioning characters are holding extremely important posts that can put humanity at grave risk of total annihilation, if not dealt with sensibly and without violence. They have created hideous situations impregnated with fatal flaws and despair, but it can be improved and changed for better, if only the money spent on genocidal weaponry and in dropping bombs to kill unarmed men, innocent women, elderly and children that relegate contempt, plague, and despair could be allocated to assist the victims of wretched poverty. And to honestly try to implement peace and show the world we mean business, not in killing, but in saving lives, where billions of funds will be saved that are spent in a very large scale to keep the powerful elites and their global establishment's safe and to make their business entities immune and free from harm, to manage security for the super-rich universal investments. They should rather be put in good use to capitalize on educating young generations and showing them that we care, which in return they will be exhilarated to join the massive international workers making them productive human beings and not suicidal murderers.

The mighty elites need to generate constructive programs to bring deprived masses of people hope and prosperity, to stop alliances with oppressive regimes, and to make weapon embargos against dictatorial regimes. Fascist governments are in the business of mass murdering, mass incarceration, and horrific tortures and abuse, and ironically and quite chillingly are antipathetic toward freedom, liberty, democracy, human rights, economic opportunity, and they stringently campaign against sacred humanistic values.

We ought to be reminded that the west has come too far in preserving some precious and certain enlightening values, as many so-called allies and friends are not in favor of these progressive ideas; they are the very reason behind many cases of ill will and terrorism against the west, and in which the so-called allies play "wolves in sheep clothing."

Many wars of transgression are induced by transnational corporations to control weak nations, beating them into submission as they outsource jobs to designated parts of the world to gain access for cheap labor and free natural resources, to excavate inexpensive raw materials aimed at maximizing profit. And also have the luxury of not paying taxes, while bribing the authoritarian regime to suppress and keep the poor natives silent, which is the main reason for many illegitimate wars that the weapon industry is thrilled to have and who said "you cannot have your cake and eat it too."

The tyrannical regime has learned how to oppress citizens and keep them poor, where they incapacitate them by force not to fight back. Mark Twain once said, "Lack of money is the roots of all evil." And how true that is.

Corporations are financially so powerful and potently influential that they can manifest better living condition for billions of victims. They can economically leverage the natives with indigenous resources and national wealth to improve their infrastructures and lifestyle, so that no one would most likely care to be summoned for terrorism, keeping so many deprived and without any economic opportunity to improve their lives, as poverty is what puts them in trouble, as it has a lot to do with their insane conduct. Do not extort and take all the pie and confiscate what inherently belongs to the indigenous inhabitants; give them some of the pie. Let the impoverished majority share a bit of the liberty and the prosperity you abundantly afford to enjoy—after all, it is their money for God's sake and not yours. Try to earn your share of the pie by doing some good for humanity's sake and not in pirating people's wealth.

Allow people's standard of living to change for the better; let their ways of life positively alter and ascend. Give them a chance to rebel against the recruiters of hate and monstrosities, to deter them from entering the gates of hell and avoid becoming sitting ducks, victims so vulnerable to be hunted and perished. Help them to abstain from their inhumane terrorist mindsets and divert them from cruel behaviors and gruesome actions. If you, the mighty elites, illustrate the power of compassion and mercy that real human beings are blessed with, it will certainly bring them peace and happiness; show them that God exists.

The imperial elites should start constituting universal economic relief and manifest programs toward globalization, so that boundaries can gradually collapse and mobilize billions with education, skill, training, and realistic hope, and not just in rhetoric. Call for true culture of humanism, rather than the petty nationalism you crave—where no animosity toward any race, gender, or creed can be tolerated, and where the global natural resources, and the international wealth and productivity are fairly allocated, and for the right reasons too.

The global government and the powerful elites should cooperatively challenge nature for the best outcome, as climate injustice has undermined human rights all over the globe; no practical effort is ever taken by plutocracy of the corporate governments to mend the worst global warming ever experienced by humankind. And to rescue humanity from the clutches of hatred and warmongering actions, to discourage and halt sadistic conduct toward Mother Nature. It is time to ease off on international boundaries to cut down the legal barriers and let humanity mature to one government, one nation under God.

It is time to let diversities in racial, cultural, and religious differences become a blessing rather than a menace, which should help us have access to collective brotherhood. Let's lessen the national debt, balance the budget, control population growth, and have a global system competent enough to structurally create full employment, mollify income inequality, and control inflation, recession, depression, stagnation, and other socioeconomic maladies. Here is what Alan Greenspan, former chairman of the U.S. federal reserve, said about income inequality: "I consider income inequality the most dangerous part of what's going on in the United States."

Furthermore, let's socialize health coverage, subsidize housing, free public transportations, and above all, let's have a free educational system accessible to everyone, and let's have progressive retirement plans where social security and networks of financial and professional assistance can efficiently help retirees and protect the elderly, the seniors, and those unable to work. You might ask where the funds should come from to orient and constitute grave and humanly deeds, and I say rest assured with the wealth and the infinite resources that the rich 1% hold; the entire planet can be refurbished, and its population can epitomize good living 100 times over than what we are presently experiencing and for many generations to come, and still have plenty of funds left to deal with municipalities' concern for attending to imperative matters if professionally managed, prioritized, and suitably allocated.

And finally, let's give true meaning to civilized behaviors and not act hypocritical in bullying the weak into silence and submission while catapulting their natural and human resources for little compensation. And halt policing and destroying the world, since God has blessed and strengthened some nations with stupendous (awesome) technology and amazing instrumental power; it does not mean to wipe out the entire planet. Let's give meaning to "in God we trust" and earnestly practice true democracy, because you cannot choke off discourse and defend freedom.

It is true that either knowledge or wisdom should mature enough to substantiate an enlightening atmosphere to keep civility of mind and good conscious in check or refuge to force and dictatorial rule to keep peace where the average intelligence has not yet ripened. And of course, it is most appropriate if the ruling class and the powerful elites commit to people's education and invest in a constructive mental makeover for positive changes that can resonate with the entire nation.

But it seems awakening the masses to accede consciousness in acting with literal prudence, accessing the power of information and insightfulness discourages the financially imperial elites and makes them afraid of pushing for a global cultural revolution in higher education. This in turn can rise the collective understanding of how the system is unfairly managed since billions can then detect and realize the very cause to their miserable lifestyle is not the almighty God, but the way the system is so unjustly operated by the few that can endanger the ruling class's position, the aristocrat's fate, and put the entire plutocratic government at grave risk of falling.

They can only rely on brainwashing billions of people, intoxicating their minds for so long through dubious propaganda, luring them with insane positivism into collective delusional behaviors, which shroud the populace by uncertainty and in acting complacent, so that no meaningful changes could ever constitute, and to further linger to maintain the status quo.

To make sure the economic chokehold is not loosened on the rest of the world, where the powerful elites have to be reassured with exploiting the globe and its inhabitants with no remorse—despite so many infectious misdeeds and treacherously planned conduct against humanity, which has risen a high wall of prejudice, unfair and unjustified practices throughout the entire world by multinational corporations.

I believe globalization will progress to induce a world in which the boundaries collapse, and humanity should then inaugurate one system of government with one nation under God, where people could unanimously call themselves citizens of the world. Murray Gell-Mann in complexity, science, system, said, "Today the network of relationships linking the human race to itself and to the rest of the biosphere is so complex that all aspects affect all others to an extraordinary degree. Someone should be studying the whole system, however crudely that has to be done, because no gluing together of partial studies of a complex nonlinear system can give a good idea of the behavior of the whole."

We ought to persist on an effective system of ruling that digs into a host of vital issues indigenous to people's existence. It should plow into human activities and discourage immoral temperament and not malfunction with misdeeds and other ill characteristics, such as vile personality makeup infused and fortified with avarice for accumulating material wealth and power, which makes an environment of grotesque inequalities, forcing many to believe in the "survival of the fittest" attitude and a cutthroat society, where human lives and dignity are neglected, as atmosphere of crime, violence, corruption, and insatiable bodily joy becomes the norm and accepted as a natural way of life.

Individual quenchless thirst for money has alienated us from our values, from each other, and it has distracted so many from God and nature, as the culture of hoarding money has taken over, not as a medium of exchange, but rather a measure of wealth, influence, prestige, prosperity, and power. We are infatuated with money and are so tempted to produce huge wealth; it has undermined human veneration and because billions act herd-like, where they are distracted and cannot prioritize, making people lost in how they should objectify imperative issues in their lives and the world around them. We need to be inspired to constructively challenge life and to act collectively within balance, to accomplish quality living for all. Unfortunately, the entire monetary system—not to exclude financers, bankers, who are known as the high priests of finance, the corporate executives, and the so-called board of trustees—control our lives just like the Middle Ages, where religious tyranny was a curse upon humanity.

The invisible hand of the tyrannical financiers has replaced the invisible hand of the market and controls and influences our lives like in the medieval era, where Pope Innocent III declared, "Anyone who attempts to construe a personal view of God which conflicts with church must be burned without pity." So does poverty, which can burn us without pity as well; wretched poverty induces all sorts of crimes and vices, as did the word inquisition, where financially bankrupt people become so desperate that many could potentially do much wrong to survive, as the Roman Church was associated with murder, torture, robbery, treachery, lies, arson, deceit, rape, lust, hypocrisy, cupidity (avarice), holiness, which no other word in all languages is so abhorrent and owes its notoriety to its link with the inquisition's infamously hideous reputation, as the "financial terrorists" of our times, which should remind us of medieval religious atrocities.

The capitalist economy and its supporting political system is constantly faced with systematic failure, with no hope of actual recovery expected, we need to realistically find a viable option that can sustain humanity financially. The current economic system has become deadlocked, stuck, and dilapidating (decay, ruination), and policing is what keeps it from falling, where systematic brutality is contrary to what George Washington did remind us of: "The basis of our political system is the right of the people to make and alter the constitution of government."

Since a capitalist system of governing objectifies money as an ultimate end in dealing with everything we do, it is very crucial for such a monetary system to manage funds professionally, efficiently, justly, and in dynamic ways, so that streams of ill ripple effects do not paralyze the whole nation, and perhaps the entire globe. When an economic system becomes incompetent and full of irresolvable problems, it delivers the system stagnant and in ruination. And with discouraging better alternatives, it leaves no choice, but to make the loss of human lives inevitable. It enters into a game of Russian roulette that in every second looks for the next victim.

But then we smile like nothing is wrong and pretend that everything is all right, although inside it truly hurts. Rumi the Persian poet wrote, "these pain you feel are the messengers, listen to them."

And I say again and again: Isn't it amazing that we are all made in God's image, and yet there's so much adversities among us—those who do not deny God, but tell us God is a lie with their actions, and those who lose their very breath and die for a good cause to tell the rest of humanity, "There is a God." In the meanwhile, we need to keep pounding on the question of financial terrorism of our time, which has since kept a malignant tyrannical position facing humankind. We should incessantly ask, if not tyranny, then what is it that keeps societies from transforming to positive changes and better living conditions? We are not exhausted with no options, there are sensible alternatives, such as the economic system of co-ops, which if given a chance can flourish and significantly improve everyone's lives.

Having a democratically genuine system of co-ops, where the locals, communities, and the actual wealth creators, the workers can start bottom up companies, and own the means of production to assess the actual need of the market where necessary productions, sell and distribution can become authenticated. And as the profit is justly shared while the allocation of resources is fairly managed, and since innovation, ingenuity, true motivational force, and imagination, democracy and collective ownership of the means of production will replace a futile privatization enterprise system that needs constantly resuscitated (revive) at the expense of the taxpayers. If so, and it should be the tax payers' obligation to bail out these too big to fail institutional bankers and other humongous financial entities and keep rescuing them with no monetary return for the actual people who keep saving them. Why not let public ownership replace these monstrously big institutionalized corporations?

It is so sad that we are entering the era of the solar system, and yet some people behave so naïvely toward the inalienable rights of others. They support private opulence and negate public squalor, as they act so indifferently toward the suffering of billions of ordinary masses. This should call for a radical change in the landscape of the entire financial system, peacefully. In the meanwhile, we should make the idea of having a socialist and dictatorial party system remote, and detour from any perceived hostile revolutionary attitude.

The system of capitalists' coercion and monetary domination is not ordained by God, hence the modern life parameters clearly indicate the fallacies and wrongdoings of the system. By nature, the system has become stalemated and in decay, which is no longer fair play, and a dynamic force to reckon with. The capitalist system indoctrinates people to identify with its political and economic way of life that has institutionalized class differentiation, where extreme income disparity absolutely thwarts collective bargaining and social movements, which should be the essence of human interactivities. Human beings by nature gravitate toward collectivism and generally dislike to be isolated and reluctant in fairing alone; it is the essence of humankind to be cooperative. It is in our DNA; otherwise humanity would have not pulled through for billions of years from prehistoric times to the current civilization era.

We should not fall trap into believing that human species are some type of abstract beings, money-driven by nature that resonate with greed and self-centeredness. These types of analogies are nothing but shams, which since have created cosmetic pretext and intoxicating environments to direct and encourage the individualism school of thought that is the pillar of the capitalists' philosophy and its belief on how societies ought to run.

It has become necessary to rescue people from the power of greed and a dysfunctional system. Since there are other decent and efficient economic systems that can gradually work their way up democratically and make the actual evolutionary process a dream come true for billions of people without bloodshed and institutionalize the co-op system on a global scale from the very bottom up, locals and communities, and saving precious human lives can become mandatory and a priority, not optional and just more rhetoric. The system should aim to correct those who illegally hoard billions of dollars at the top with devious intent and disgraceful conduct, which has replaced God in their lives. They have accumulated so much wealth beyond comprehension and call it economic thriving for the blessed ones, as if deprived others are born from behind and have arrived from sub-terrains and are perhaps the citizens of inferior planets.

The system needs to mollify the concept of "everyone to his own philosophy" and avoid extreme individualist culture, where survival of the wisest can lead to collective moral intelligence and prosperities, rather than promoting self-centeredness through mischievous and cynical behaviors with irrational conduct. Financial predators, loan sharks, and economic hitmen devour their victims as they exhibit the most unrestrained and inhumane actions in the name of business and self-interest. They have implemented a toxic atmosphere of "not what you know, but who you know," which counts and makes upward mobility possible.

It is who you know that moves you up in treacherous zigzagging of life's walkways, making a mockery of fair play.

The powerful elites hunt their prey with impunity since no repercussion faces them, as if their barbarically unconstitutional practices, ferocious manhunt, and civil disobedient should be rewarded. The corporate plutocracy somehow believes no better living is ever possible without their incredulous and incriminating ways of dealing with society in the name of a free market economy, which unleashes its predatory behavior repressing the middle class, the working class, and the poor, and exploiting nature what has already caused so much damage to the entire globe beyond repair. What should be awakening are blatant atrocities and explicit violation of global human rights, nuclear race, global warming, war of aggression, religious extremists, terrorism, jihadism and radicalism, extreme income inequality, protecting dictatorial regimes, sexism, human trafficking, implicit racism, and other inhumane and ugly traits that urgently need to stop; and if not, it sure can become antecedent to a catastrophic nuclear, and in making it a war of weapons of mass destruction, ending life as we know it.

Let's dig into some of the mishaps as we need to figure out the root causes of the problems. We access our brain and try to act mindful for making sense of things from the simplest to most puzzling tasks, where the outcome should accordingly differ because some are blessed with a higher IQ and relatively potent intelligence than others. It is not facetious when scientists say we are basically utilizing about 10% of our brain capacity, which should mean 90% still constitutes gray matter bound to be explored. Yes, human brain is very complex because it performs millions of elegant and magnificent sublunary (worldly) acts, but then if we could tap into the remaining 90%, perhaps it would enable us to have telekinetic and novel (space age) power, which I am certain would positively rub on our civility and decent conduct too. The 10% notion has been linked to the American psychologist and author William James, who argued in *The Energies of Men* that "We are making use of only a small part of our possible mental and physical resources." It's also been associated with Albert Einstein for explaining his cosmic towering intellect. The myth's durability, Gordon says "stems from people's conceptions about their own brains: they see their own shortcomings as evidence of the existence of untapped gray matter, this is a false assumption, what is correct, however, is that at certain moments in anyone's life, such as when we are simply at rest and thinking, we may be using only 10% of our brains. Evidence would show over a day you use 100% of the brain."

Says John Henley, a neurologist at the Mayo Clinic in Rochester, Minnesota. Even in sleep areas, such as the frontal cortex, which controls things like higher level thinking and self-awareness, or the somatosensory area (being sensory activity having its origin elsewhere than in the special sense organs as eyes and ears), which helps people sense their surroundings, are active. He said, "What's not understood is how clusters of neurons from the diverse regions of the brain collaborate to form consciousness. So far, there's no evidence that there is one site for consciousness, which leads experts to believe that it is truly a collective neural effort. Another mystery hidden within our crinkled cortices is that out of all the brains cells, only 10% are neurons; the other 90% are glial cells, which encapsulate and support neurons, but whose function remains largely unknown. Ultimately, it's not that we use 10% of our brains merely that we only understand about 10% of how it functions."

I believe when Henley refers to using our 100% of brain usage, he should indicate 100% usage of the 10% available, which Einstein was able to manifest when he discovered his famous relativity equation; otherwise it is odd to relatively utilize 100% of our brain and only understand 10% of how it does actually function. And referencing historical evolution it makes sense to adequately perceive and acknowledge that no caveman from Stone Age times and prehistorical era could have had access to 10% of their brain, which is presently available to modern man, and if so, then billion years of evolutionary time span, which has molded a complex cerebral cortex (part of the nervous system, the thinking brain) should render futile; rather than accepting its tremendous progress in cognitive ability since the prehistoric era. Or perhaps we should accept that our modern and relatively civilized world is just an illusion, and we have not advanced and progressed a bit in our evolutionary concept of understanding the human brain. Besides, I also believe much of the gray area not in use is not just going to forever lay there idle; it is eventually going to be pushed to its limit.

If only regular folk could tap that other 90%, they too could become savants who remember π to the twenty-thousandth decimal place or perhaps even have telekinetic powers. Though an alluring idea, the 10% myth is so wrong it is almost laughable, says neurologist Barry Gordon at Johns Hopkins School of Medicine in Baltimore. Although there's no definitive culprit to pin the blame on for starting this legend, the notion has been linked to the American psychologist and author William James, who argued in *The Energies of Men* that "We are making use of only a small part of our possible mental and physical resources." It's also been associated with Albert Einstein, who supposedly used it to explain his cosmic towering intellect.

Further, I am only investigating statistics and numbers, no impropriety directed at anyone at all. But then, the provocative question should foment wonder and alert us to investigating human insightfulness as to why we behave the way we do.

Let's say animals are credited with only using 1% of their brain, and since not everyone is gifted to truly manifest the absolute 10% and within its full capacity, then relativity speaking, some should proportionally enact their intellect and savviness of their mind perhaps a tad higher than animals, since some could be trapped and framed in a lower percentage rate of mindfulness. And let's even assume it is the overall 10% mentality that reflects our societal reasoning, agendas, and the activities of our contemporary world. If so, then why should anyone be surprised or shocked and in a state of awe, when we decimate millions of our kind in a genocide manner or behave malevolently toward the helpless innocent with antiquated immigration laws, with hugely widened class derivative culture and so forth.

After all, we still have 90% of uncharted territories that must become urgently cultivated, which by the way, westerners somehow imply to be the forerunners of civilization and are supposed to be the cream of the crop. God help us with the rest. And urgently because we have some mentalities very close to behaving beast-like; they are in control of hydrogen bombs, atomic bombs, bacterial and chemical bombs, cluster bombs, and other weapons of mass destruction because with no doubt they can end life as we know it. The next crucial question should be whether there is hope, where we can reach light at the end of the tunnel, of course yes, but we must employ a system that is adamant to bring about changes that are user-friendly to human beings and their environment.

To be more precise, when a system of government permits and even encourages private mega-arm corporations to make trillions by selling armaments to savage and barbarian regimes limited with one percentage usage of their brain cells murdering innocents and the unarmed, there is a big problem. When a governing regime allows private enterprises to pollute the air we breathe and contaminate the water we drink and allows exterminating biodiversity, then charges a skyrocketing prices to seek medical help, and charges money to sell water to famine and the drought-stricken indigenous, then we should know we have an enormous problem. When so many globally are forced to sell one of their kidneys to find money desperately needed to pay for the emergency related operation of loved ones or sell blood to survive, we ought to know we have a problem.

When trash fields are controlled by so-called entrepreneurs and smaller companies that charge a fee to let the poor sequester clean food and clothing from the garbage to feed and cover themselves, we must know there is huge problem; when we witness millions of refugees who have been militarily invaded and are camping out in the desert barricaded with no shelter, with no food or any amenities, we should know we have a big problem. When there are the largest prisoners incarcerated in dire condition and inhumane correctional facilities that feed private institutions to maximize profit in the name of correctional institutions, compromising public safety, since crime is going rampant, we need to know we have a problem. Encouraging drug addiction with prostitution and human trafficking, where pervasive porn industries are incessant to sexually exploit people—even the children for lucrative profiteering—we know we have a problem.

The bottom line is that no capitalist system can honestly identify with humanism since the system profits when there is war, the system profits when people are sick, the system profits when there is violence, fear, and distrust among people, races, and societies. The whole system profits from a toxic environment, making it necessary to reboot cultural, social, political, and economic factors to put an end to constantly living in an alarming state and high anxiety condition, which creates chronic stress and a host of other incurable diseases unknown to humankind.

The concentration of the mass media in the hands of conglomerate news corporations is not in the public interest, as they premeditate to lie, distort news, create fallacies to damage control and to safeguard the entire system and what interests the mega corporations. It is a vicious circle, since mega corporations contribute huge and overwhelmingly campaign for their favorite news entities and dubious politicians who have promised them so much in return, at the expense of the people. They falsely create iconic images based on lies to elect them for successive elections, while wrongly stirring up people's emotions, dominating citizen's thoughts to strengthen social control in which they become an insurmountable (unable to overcome) difficulty.

We should wake up to this bitter fact that the conglomerate corporate media controls the airwaves; they have privatized news and information, the blood stream of what can arouse people or keep them as dull as possible, and at the mercy of corporate bosses, and their hound dogs.

When we have an economic system that is destroying the planet and causing mass extinctions of species, exterminates biodiversity and the ecosystem, and then calls it "economic externalities" and causes economic terror and panic, we have a problem. They fleece ordinary people and write these monstrous behaviors off at the people's expense and do not factor them as their corporate cost, which puts everyone's life in grave danger through acting as "nature deficit disorder." We should know they are declaring war on nature and humanity. The corporate media refuses to talk about the grotesque actions by the big money corporations, which epitomize corrupt and clandestine conduct and inhumane behavior. It has become a neurotic culture that is in denial since it boycotts humanity from its natural inhabitant and separates them from all of what nature has to offer, which sustains us and the future generation; then we should know we have a definite problem.

They link human happiness to unconditional, relentless consumption, and unending growth, and they foster people's mentality and mindset as if this is quite natural. Where the matrix of humanity and identity is measured by an accumulation of wealth and material hording, alienating people and encouraging extreme individualism, then we should know we have a serious problem. When we comprise 5% of the world's population, but have 30-35% of the world's prison population, then we need to know we have a problem.

It should be expected from correctional facilities that operate by taxpayers' money to deal and connect to inmates through professional entities, where the prisoners have a chance to be dealt with therapeutically and through a correct psychoanalysis approach, since they should be taught to be emotionally honest and willing to look inward, to be mindful of their emotional reactions. And to question whether those reactions are coming from within ourselves, rather than wrongfully judging others with a biased eye, which perhaps has nothing to do with the way one feels.

Where pride and not acting macho or ostentatious (pretentious) and not behaving in certain ways should not mean emasculating, because many are emotionally unable to deal with their aggression and sometimes exhibit outrageous conduct without professional help, as they are faced against the odds and a culture of violence that is shamelessly promulgated and encouraged inside those hideous prisons, which victimize many who are sincerely seeking a way out of crime-infested environments and their miserable situation with no avail. They manifest emotional honesty looking for a way out of jail, but feel guilt, as they are labeled weak, making them vulnerable preys of rape and other inhumane atrocities. Only the culture of force and manhandling rules inside those despicable cells and the so-called "correctional" facilities, which fear rules and force is predominantly the norm.

It is noteworthy that even in times of prosperity and the so-called economic discovery, the bottom 90% are not affected by the financial boom and fiscal expansion since they still experience extreme poverty. Where the cream of the crop consistently shifts to the upper 1% and goes to those at the top of the social echelon. Any ignorant economist should know the wages must be coherent and adjusted to unavoidable inflationary growth, since the system is structurally lop-sided and unequivocally bears precarious side effects such as recession, inflation, and because the system can only supply partial employment and is unable to produce full employment, as it also creates stagnation, depression, extreme income inequality, and misallocation of resources, as the market aims at making products that maximize profit, and not to manufacture need-based related goods.

I am afraid many keep quiet because they are oblivious to stark rancorous (antagonistic) financial disparities forced on people, or they are well off and not wanting to notice the unprofessional, deceitful, and wicked financial cover-ups that are not clear and conspicuous to the common man, as the rich keep getting richer and the poor become poorer. Hence, multitudes of precarious effects and misconduct escalate further, hurting billions globally for the worst and often beyond repair. It will help if we pay attention to the corporate capitalists and gigantic multinational firms that unethically delve into human subliminal terrain and unscrupulously devise their hideous plans that creep into the realm of our subconscious mind and subtly manage to overwhelm our thinking brain and conscious thoughts without us having a clue.

I adamantly believe our subconscious mind is deliberately bombarded with a sophisticated and very intricate conditioning mechanism driving people into a bewildered state of thought and action for the wrong reasons. This transgression of behavior has molded our brain and burdened our mind into a web of uncertainties and mental defects making so many vulnerable to ever more consumption, and addict consumerists who act stoic and nonchalant to others' squalid living condition and pain and suffering. It seems our mind is hypnotized and possessed by extraterrestrial agents into helplessness, cluttered with negative and trivial issues beyond our will, which has turned our conduct impervious to virtues. It has globally manifested a very sick environment, comprising it to become culturally chaotic, financially desperate, socially and environmentally tragic, and in need of desperate repair.

This ongoing pejorative (insulting, derogatory) cascade of actions is not going to halt unless enlightened and courageous people collectively are inspired to seek justice and push for a better world. Einstein said, "The world is a dangerous place to live, not because of the people who are evil, but because of the people who don't do anything about it." We ought to know that our brain is interactively wired into a single monumental and conscious able entity. We forget we are a unified biological and mental organism qualified for existence, engulfed with cosmic and spiritual realms, and part of a destined universe premeditated with purpose, clearly mandated and objectified to reach its destiny.

Humanity needs to accordingly defy these vicious circles of manufactured and sickly cause and effect that are strayed and derailed from what is right, making our life curriculum for survival infested with fear. The system needs to stop controlling us like we are wild animals, telling us there is no living outside of the corporate capitalists as the survival of the fittest mentality should be the norm, where the meanest and most horrible souls are to exploit and commoditize everything, including human lives to the point of exhaustion and collapse.

And since anything outside of their pillaging ways and ruthless behaviors is not cool, which should define their kind of civilization, science, selfish gene theory, social and biological Darwinism, since those with correct jawlines and manufactured lies about advanced revolutionized head and scalp, are anatomically structured progressive and hence they are regarded as the embodiment of nobility and intelligence. They are from a superior and preferred race, while others have yet to mature from the caveman mentality and to further become developed in their physical and biological shortcomings.

And other ethnic and indigenous natives were considered between human and animals, which deserved to die. They did not have the intelligence to become duly compliant and civilized, as the Europeans exterminated millions of indigenous people marking them as savages. So did happen this tragedy of action with Indians in North America in a genocide manner that, of course, was a made up hoax, where capitalists could annex and steal all the natural resources, which they meant to enslave the inhabitants by putting them to work just like beasts to produce valuable raw material and vital natural resources for the rich to plunder.

They also made sure to discipline people so that there is no salvation and any life worth living after they die outside the church; no matter what heinous crime one commits, one will be cleansed by the blood of our savior Jesus Christ in heaven above, if he or she belongs, because Jesus the almighty profit of God died for our sins. Misdirecting believers away from truth, not letting them realize that our good profit of God died because Jesus fought for what was right and against injustice, to show the light of compassion and understanding against the cruelty of the Roman Empire, but not for the Godly to act insane, as they can unleash sinful behaviors and be portrayed as being saved and assured of a pass to heaven.

This kind of interpretation can render green lights, especially to those callous minds to do as they wish, knowing they are already saved and not obligated to act as human beings, not knowing the laws of the universe will not allow abusing our free will, where people can distortedly utilize their conscious to kill, slaughter, maim, rape, and cause so many horrifying crimes and devilish misdeeds, and get away with it scot-free, reassured that they are already forgiven.

They perpetuate this notion of individualism and perpetrate people to believe in the hierarchical culture and the systematic powers of God, spirits, angels, profits, religions, kings, queens, the country, men, women, minorities, indigenous people, animals, trees and plants, and non-animated beings. Infusing toxic thoughts and notions into our thought process to divide and conquer us, as they have, where no peace and justice and a life worth living is ever possible.

They know when you incarcerate and put one in solitary confinement long enough, one starts to hallucinate and basically goes crazy, losing his mind, as simple as that, because we are group animals and cannot survive alone. This should awaken every caring soul to realize the vitality and urgency of working together as co-ops to deal with corporate power and the cancerous individualistic based society they have created. They can rule us with brutality, so it is time to prove capitalists' conniving ways and deceptive practices need to stop, and for them to start doing right in the name of God, humanity, and self-worth.

First by stopping mass propaganda for upholding and pushing for fanatical class based societies and to deactivate encouraging ideas of everyone on their own mindset, which has permeated many societies, actively leaving loathe (detesting) effects. Second, to stop this monstrous behavior that everything is up for grab in the name of profit, including desolating human lives and perishing dignity.

Nick Harkaway, the Blind Giant, states that: "Like casinos, large corporate entities have studied the numbers and the ways in which people respond to them. These are not con tricks—they're not even necessarily against our direct interests, although sometimes they can be—but they are hacks for the human mind, ways of manipulating us into particular decisions we otherwise might not make. They are in a way deliberate, undermining the core principle of the free market, which derives its legitimacy from the idea that informed self-interest on aggregate sets appropriate prices for items. The key word is 'informed'; the point of behavioral economics—or rather, of its somewhat buccaneering (pirate, freebooter) corporate applications—is to skew our perception of the purchase to the advantage of the company. The overall consequence of that is to tilt the construction of our society away from what it should be if we were making the rational decisions classical economics imagines we would, and toward something else."

It seems no matter how we thrive for a bit of happiness, it is with no avail, as we are still fettered with draconian circumstances and not free from the pipelines of uncertainties and anxieties facing ill maneuvers directed at the very core of our nervous system. And hence, vanquishing (to triumph over) the sovereignty of our mind, infusing it with ceaseless irrational thoughts and deceitful mental exercises where they manage to play us like a professional guitar player literally in control of the frequencies of its instrument and in how it should vibrate. So that the 1% that holds 90% of the resources can hold onto this inhumane income inequality, turning people into sociopaths, agents which exercise toxic ideas against each other, with antisocial values created by the elites and the ruling class, which should remind us of a "divide and conquer strategy."

Institutional ideology of sociopathic behaviors is emanated and reinforced into the larger environment as the norms, which propagates and pursues self-interest as the only good at the very core of morality of the system. From the system's point of view only the individual exists, which pushes so many to viciously compete with competitors and act psychopathically violent toward the environment, abusing natural resources, exploitation of workers and immoral use of child labor and elderly for starvation wages, consumers, and toward less powerful and less fortunate nations.

Because to the corporate capitalists nothing matters, except profit, where unfettered growth drives their insatiable appetite to the point of exhaustion leveraged by toxic propaganda and through false advertising which is backed up with corporate hegemonic militarism and inhumane apparatus. They have annihilated the societal and natural order by producing destructible products, which maximizes their profit and not directed at making public goods, which can positively change the fate of nations for better, if planned production was enforced, which can result in not wasting billions of dollars, which could be put in good use.

They are nimble in improvising policies to divide people and polarize wealth, where few elites can control the rest of the citizens; they cosmetically uphold democratic features and fake elections, since even the state resonates and gives in to their demands and illegal plans because of them bribing and because of money. This abusive trend of thought and behavior has pushed society from a class system to an entangled system, where the super-rich and the elites are suppressing workers who are the backbone of the capitalist system, which generates surplus values that is the foundation to the corporate capitalists' very existence. The system should put an end to domestication of people, forcing them into the bottle to play genie at the command of the oligopolistic behavior of the few at the cost of billions of inhabitants made miserable. The poor are financially and mentally manipulated to function against their well-being, also conduit to degradation and destruction of the world and the planet.

The super-rich must wake up in the name of virtue and what is right to actively take part in what is necessary to change the course of history in saving Earth and avoid change through bloodshed and violence. And people also need to intelligently realize it is not appropriate to throw the baby out with the bathwater because it makes sense to save what works and understand that any new system is born from the womb of the old one, making a new paradigm shift into expressing an innovated culture of thinking. To grasp that rich are not evil by nature, Hitler, Mussolini, and Stalin were demonic by nature, and to ask what honestly any one of us put in their position would do, if also weak to harness human greed.

The actual problem stems out of greed and self-centeredness, since by nature, capitalism is divisible via polarization of wealth, which corporate oligopoly has demonized it to the extreme, ignoring the have-nots, leaving them with no choice but to fight back for their survival. Realistic collective altruism is taken as a farce and subtly barred from flourishing, blocked by self-interest manuals and dialogue and misleading by the culture of hazardous individualistic propaganda prevalent in families, active at schools, in communities and at work, even in churches and many other societal networks, which basically implement policies against collectivism but are prone to possessing attitude of meshing in with the norms or dying in vain—even tainting those who are not accustomed to cynical behavior and devious attributes to act so arrogant and egocentric that no one else matters, since one must blend in to make it.

The ideology, the philosophy, the politics, and the cultural education of the system's objectives are to uphold and work accordingly to honor the powerful elites' view on how it should be done and for people to robotically execute what they are programmed with and, if dare not, they will be seen as not cool and perhaps an outcast or rebellious to social and civil order. Jason Welker, in Economic growth, incentive, income distribution curve, and market, poverty, and goods, standard, taxes, states: "Politicians and some economists like to argue that income inequality is not as evil as many people make it out to be, and that greater income inequality can actually increase the incentive for poorer households to work harder to get rich, contributing to the economic growth of the nation as a whole. Allowing the rich to keep more of their income, in this way, leads more people to want to work hard to get rich, as they will be able to enjoy the rewards of their hard work."

Jason Welker continues: "The prevalence of income inequality in free market economies indicates that inequality may be the result of a market failure. Those who are born rich are more likely to become rich, while individuals who are born poor are more likely to live a life of relative poverty. In a 'free' market, it is believed, all individuals possess an equal opportunity to succeed, but due to a misallocation of resources in a purely market economy, this may not always be the case. The resources I refer to here are those required for an individual to escape poverty and earn a higher income. These include public and merit goods that those with high incomes can afford to consume, while those in poverty depend on the provision from the state, including: good education, dependable health care, access to professional networks, and the employment opportunities they provide whenever a market failure exists. It can be argued that there is a role for government in regulating the market to achieve a more optimal distribution of resources.

When it comes to income inequality, government intervention typically comes in the form of a tax system that places a larger burden on the rich and a system of government programs that transfer income from the rich to poor, including welfare benefits, unemployment benefits, health care for low income households, public schools, and support for economic development in poor communities. Going back in time, the Great Depression in the United States started after a fall in stock prices that began around September 4, 1929, and made worldwide news with the stock market crash of October 29, 1929 (Black Tuesday). Between 1929 and 1932, the whole system was struggling to recuperate from catastrophic economic and social dilemmas facing it. At some point the entire system was at the brink of war and potential for a bloodied and nasty revolution. President Franklin D. Roosevelt stepped in and mediated so that the rich could constructively spend some of their money to save the "profit system" or face a bloodied revolution as the capitalists would have to lose all their money. In the meanwhile, the rest of the world provided the core capitalist system of western Europe, North America, and Japan with very inexpensive natural resources, raw materials, and dirt cheap labor. After so long of brutal exploitation, the workers all over the world, including western Europe, North America, and Japan woke up and demanded a piece of the pie, which barely mitigated their miserable living conditions. This also gave birth to the liberal and middle class and made upper mobility relatively possible. Then, gradually globally transnational corporations eliminated the fair competition since neo-colonist rule of law was established through the entire world, giving them access to other developing nations with rich natural resources: oil, gas, minerals, silver and gold, uranium and so forth, and inhabitants' cheap labor. Loyal dictatorial regimes and puppets were installed to implement the utter despotic rules of conduct by murdering, assassinating, torturing, raping, and long imprisonment of dissidents and against anyone seeking justice or any call for human rights. Even in America the Indians, Mexicans, Irish workers and their families, the Jews, blacks, Italians, and Japanese suffered tremendously before they were recognized, even taking a gargantuan Civil War between the south and the north, which claimed millions of lives, before establishing basic human dignity for all and the right to live where prejudice and discrimination were formally supposed to be abolished. We have reached an era which unfortunately the death of liberalism has acted as a safety valve to save capitalism for so long, and the gradual wiping out of the middle class, which President Roosevelt worked so hard for and created, has basically desecrated the cushion which could have mitigated, and perhaps avoided, the clash. The possibility of bloodied violence between the extremely rich class and the poor; the indigents face brutal poverty that are dissidents to economic tyranny and social political injustice imposed on millions. Since so many have become well-informed and cognizant enough to look for other viable economic systems to remedy their precarious position through elected social democratic government or a viable co-op system as an alternative to capitalist system, which unfortunately delegates for the success of the few and not for the common good.

Since both co-ops and social democratic economic system prioritize the affair of the society based on having adequate employment, proper education, decent housing, and practical medical care, free public transportation, with an efficient financial safety net to back it up and kick in to protect their citizens in times of need. Because a social democratic system is fueled with higher paid taxes, then the resources are allocated appropriately, since the cultural architect and the socioeconomic infrastructures are meant to efficiently benefit people. As the entire resources are invested in the public sector to maximize return by producing competent and knowledgeable citizens who are not worried and frightened to death to lose their jobs, which some even kill themselves and enact host of criminal activities when losing their vocation, and suddenly become devoid of their subsistence. In *The God We Never Knew Beyond Dogmatic Religion to a More Authentic Contemporary Faith*, Marcus J. Borg wrote: "The point is not that Jesus was a good guy who accepted everybody, and thus we should do the same (though that would be good). Rather, his teachings and behavior reflect an alternative social vision. Jesus was not talking about how to be good and how to behave within the framework of a domination system. He was a critic of the domination system itself." Jesus was not crucified because the Romans applauded Jesus; they tormented and nailed Jesus to the cross because they denied justice to people because Jesus in his Godly way rebelled against the tyranny of the Roman Empire to institute what can save people from the clutches of unawareness and to put an end to people's pain and suffering, to enlighten the masses with the words of God.

In contemporary societies, quality education is not a right but a prestige for the few, where education is scaled through politics and not influenced by skilled educators, where students are molded into what to think, rather than how to think. This of course boils down in how to protect and preserve the very corporate capitalist system, keeping many unaware of life changing opportunities and a better future. Because they know that true education and literacy is the most potent force in existence and can relinquish viable knowledge and information to shake the core of deceptive practices of a decayed system of learning that exploiters are standing on.

Practical alternatives are a socialist democrat system not in the form traditionally advocated through violence and bloodied revolution leveraged by proletariat dictatorship, but via peaceful transition and evolutionary processes, where the activities of a social democratic government for the common good replaces the activities done by private corporate capitalists for the benefit of the few. Or via co-op institutions, which political and economic structures are peacefully shifted into collective ownership of workers. They are then elected as a board of directors, each entitled to one share, one vote into a democratically elected environment, where transfer of wealth and productive forces into the hands of workers becomes possible, making the new realms of co-op business activities to gradually replace the status quo. Let's sidetrack into the co-op institution and briefly explain how it manages to operate.

Co-ops are imbued with a humanitarian concept of doing business; the ideology is based on democracy at work, requiring collective participation of each worker with one share and one vote, solidifying the overall policy of the system's philosophy for common good and not aimed at maximizing profit for the few. The workers are the actual owners of the means of production and are members of the board of directors which will decide what to produce, how to produce, where, and when to produce and what to do with the profit and the surplus values the workers themselves created. Kofi Annan said: "Founded on the principles of private initiative, entrepreneurship and self-employment, underpinned by the values of democracy, equality and solidarity, the co-operative movement can help pave the way to a more just and inclusive economic order." Annan further said, "In an age where community involvement and partnerships with civil society are increasingly being recognized as indispensable, there is clearly a growing potential for cooperative development and renewal worldwide."

The nucleus and the decency of the co-op system is in the fact the no one is allowed to make 150 to 200 times more than other workers, making people's lives unbearable and almost impossible to keep up with rapid pace of inflation and recessionary criteria, since their wages are stagnated and not raised accordingly, where top executives, the elites, and CEOs and giant corporate owners make so much money, which creates horrifying inequality making life a living hell for the majority of inhabitants. Martin Filler, in art, force, building, said, "Despite the persistent image of the architect as a heroic loner erecting monumental edifices through sheer force of will, the building art has always been a highly cooperative enterprise."

The point is clear when the board of directors, which are the workers, are the actual voters; they must live with the decision they make. They will not vote to produce toxic products or pollute the water and the environment for worse since their family and loved ones also will bear the consequences of their dire decisions. They will not commend and practice outsourcing and transferring the company to foreign lands to minimize their cost and hence practically destroying the locals and communities for the sake of making more money for the few greedy individuals. Because the corporate capitalists know no boundaries, understand no limit, it is estranged to equity and does not believe in common good, but in maximizing profit, believes in collective and teamwork only to collect others' fruits of labor and in throwing them bones for subsistence and to keep them barely alive to produce more for boss's lavish lifestyle.

They devour and exploit nature and humanity to the point of exhaustion until collapsed with no remorse. In co-ops, workers are self-administered and will make sure to implement democracy at work where the hallmark of the entire system is there are no major shareholders who can override good decisions made on behalf of the community. Since people at the bottom would be in charge of their own destiny and institutionalize the power of production and enjoy the surplus values, which is a fresh way of organizing our life for the better and in reaching dynamic and progressive goals.

Kent Conrad, States, Large, and Land, said, "There are large cooperatives all across this country. Land O'Lakes is a \$12 billion club functioning all across America. There are rural electric co-ops in 47 states. Ace Hardware is a cooperative." With many taxi cab companies and bakeries across the land giving hopes and future prosperities for all. Arthur Potts Dawson, Food, Create, Growing, said, "We are stronger as a group than an individual. Think in a cooperative and communal way, set up local food hubs and create growing communities."

Boutros Boutros-Ghali said, "Co-operative enterprises provide the organizational means whereby a significant proportion of humanity is able to take into its own hands the tasks of creating productive employment, overcoming poverty and achieving social integration."

Workers owning their own companies at municipal institutions and co-ops, at credit unions, and so forth, with one share and one vote a true democracy at work should happen peacefully from the local and state to the national level. Where evolutionary structure would gradually move from a system that is in decay, stagnated, and in a state of deadlock to a genuine productive system of co-ops that could actually save people and direct them to control their destiny. And to make sure progressive movements do not get caught in a traditional socialist system or get deeper entangled in a traditional capitalist system or even a communist system. But where a democratic economy run by workers for improvement of the communities can take place, addressing the well-being of the very people and community producing the goods and services, since the surplus value and all the profit is to be prioritized and allocated for the common good and not spent privately by mob-like characters in a casino-like economy and wasted on no good deeds.

This historical exchange should occur with no violence and through civil actions and by peaceful means. Innocent lives must not be wasted since a corporate culture of policing and repressive fascism can be instrumental with murdering, assassinations, torture and imprisonment, manifesting a totalitarian state of existence. This overhaul and constructive paradigm shift should occur from local to state to federal level, where social and economic stagnation and deadlocks are able to change into dynamic production and a new way of life to preserve humanity and what is right.

And because history has taught us when people are forced into deplorable living conditions by stalemated regimes and systems in decay. They will learn their way out of their conundrum and into a new social order, which unfortunately contemporary corporate capitalism is facing stagnation and chaos and turning into a mundane system of corporate oligarchy. But one should rest assured tides will not positively turn, unless aggressive legal and organized actions are taken, and for everyone to stand up for what is right and to reclaim the belief already ingrained into sociocultural ways of life, seeking justice. And as the automation and robotic technology advances to replace jobs currently held by workers, so many will globally lose their jobs, adding grave problems to an already ill capitalist system, which will further mature social rebellion, tightening the noose around the system's neck. Unless creative and revolutionary economic plans are institutionalized to acutely abate the serious shortcomings of the private ownership of the means of production, humanity will have no choice but to act violently for mandating survival, which can face humanity with many bloodied uprisings and huge debacles beyond perception.

A new system should shed light on education, economy, employment, population control, decent housing, free public transportation, good public health system, clean environment, stop global warming by activating renewable energy and going solar, look into a zero carbon economy and to stop fossil fuel usage, to lower greenhouse effect, clean water, quality immigration laws, stopping all activities on atomic, chemical, bacterial wars, and halt cyber and drone attacks, and to make other inhumane weaponry obsolete, stopping wars of aggression, unanimously acting in concert with the rest of the world to stop terrorism, halt police brutality, look into already obsolete marriage and family laws, and to stop instigating and commoditizing women for profit, eliminate sex industries, human trafficking, and prostitution, where child sexual abuse and pedophilia is rampant. And further investigate religious fanaticism, stop prejudice against minorities and women, halt misogyny, discourage xenophobia, and thoughtfully look into gun control.

We should to know how damaging a decentralized free market economy and corporate capitalist enterprise system can be. If the role of multinational corporations and corporate conspiracy is truly exposed, they would have since put an end to fair competitive market and made the death of the so-called laissez-faire possible. The new system should go into pluralism, social and cultural freedom, to uphold public sector responsibilities, and to push for social democratic alliance and to leverage the economic system of co-ops, to prioritize the right to live, and mean it when it bullhorns liberty, the pursuit of happiness for all, and to insure human rights.

To challenge dictatorial regimes and terrorism and aim at unfolding perplexing social, financial, environmental, and moral questions. To stoke concerns about divinity and God because people should connect with their maker and become liberated from the clutches of incredulity (cynicism, attitude of habitual disbelief) in grasping enlightenment, to enter into the realm of soul searching and spirituality. It should remind us of Kant's argument in idealism, critical (Kant), refers to Kant's theory of knowledge. The essence of critical idealism is Kant's sharp distinction between what is given to us in our experience (sense impressionist) and the structures (forms of intuition and the categories) the mind uses to arrange, interpret, and evaluate that which is given.

Hence, our senses can enslave and exploit us with worldly pleasures and make us addicted to money, power, and influence, where we burn with desires to unleash ruthless behaviors in serving lower selves and sometimes at the cost of destroying millions of people with no remorse. We ought to be reminded that every time we serve power and prestige, and overlook inhumane conduct or ignore the tyranny of the system imposed on the innocents because of self-interest and what we also hold at stake, we disempower justice and cover up the truth against the fundamental rights of the republic, which sanctions so many from having to live the bare minimum, denying them a decent life and leaving them with no choice but to vigorously fight back. And rightly so, since the right to life and liberty for all is a stranglehold and has turned into just empty rhetoric and an opprobrious (derogatory, demeaning, insulting) slogan for billions living a daily gradual death.

Since the fabric of diversity living and getting along in the name of compassion and humanity are insanely discouraged and fading away, we're seeing each other as rivals embarked on with demonic portrait of black, white, brown, red, yellow and so forth. This is exercised and accepted as the norm, perhaps not knowing it is the system that feeds and irrigates these cancerous diseases and toxic environment into good-natured people mutating them into monsters against each other, making many desolated from acting human. Expert psychologists and prominent social and political strategists design dubious programs and intricate media controversies, where the technology of spreading news and information is broadcast and communicated in very subtle ways beyond the psyche of the common man to grasp many complex and troublesome programs and vicious outlets causing menacing and ugly attributes among people.

The mega corporate media have recidivist (falling back into bad behaviors), stifling the truth, and manipulated the upper echelon of society into myopia and turning them into habitual fiction readers, rather that confronting and getting the populace to fight for so many tumultuous and covert matters created by the privileged class entrapping us all into horrendous situations, where decisive social discourse is ignored by making us actually believe politics is dirty, and it is best to stay away from politics, so just let's forget about it and go fishing and play golf. The plutocrat and their lackey corporate media place us exactly where they want us to be by keeping so many and especially the influenced people silent against their insidious and criminal activities.

We ought to know that we have reached an era where global consciousness is fertile enough to plant eye-opening seeds of enlightenment and realizing that we have the potential to constructively cultivate and identify with each other from the perspective of humanity, not through civil law violations and superiority complex and from looking at the world through narrow-mindedness and deliberately damnable (wicked) socioeconomic factors and cultural prejudices with entrenched racism. Since religious competition and many other manufactured ill agendas and troublesome issues, like ethnicity, sex, and class differences, have forced masses of people into isolation and a caste system. Corporately induced democracy is too ambiguous (doubtful, equivocal, inexplicable) and amply ambivalent (uncertain, self-questioning), which has created an atmosphere where the state has become a sole servant to private institutions, since even creating the public goods like free public education, health care, housing, decent employment, public transportation, clean air and water, safe foods, paid vacation, and so forth are influenced by corporate elites for the worse. And the solution cannot be sought from the mainframe of a capitalist system, as no private enterprise will create public goods or any goods at all without making maximum profit. But people are relentlessly persuaded by mega corporate media into believing that the only system efficiently feasible is the capitalist system, like it is ordained by God. It is a social economic system that can survive fake patriotism, class differences, militarism, and concentration of wealth, catastrophic wars, and the threat of nuclear biological war, divide and conquer, global warming catastrophe. Corporate oligopoly insists individualism through ideological domination and conditioning, where everything and everyone is treated as objects to be exploited for making money. The solution to our problems is not more capitalism because no abusive relationship is ever possible from a capitalist system, other than solely being taken advantage of and in becoming commoditized to nourish the sociopathic behaviors a capitalist regime enacts to objectify making more money—no matter at what cost. We must also realize we evolve collectively by nature in dynamic ways, rather than operating separately and alone to bring quality socioeconomic changes. The good news is that people become receptive and resonate with what benefits them, mentally, spiritually, emotionally, and financially, rather than belittling them and turning them into producing machines through "division of labor" and assembly lines alienating them from their very beings and turning so many into robots specialized in producing a specific product and discarding them at the employer's prerogatives.

The alternative to having a communist system is just too good to be true, which at this stage of our lives, can only seem a utopia. Since our ideological belief system to rationalize such grave expectations has not yet matured enough to accept what Marx said about communism, he stated that, "Communism comes after socialism, and in this society, there is full equality. That means there is no more state and no more money. Everything is run communally and owned by everyone, and there is no more scarcity." He also said, each according to his ability and contribution and to take according to his need. We are also going to face proletariat dictatorship, which must implement its role, as Stalin did in Russia, and Mao did in China, and Pol Pot did in Cambodia, and Fidel Castro did in Cuba, and so forth. They literally performed evil and inhumane actions to make the transition from socialist era possible to communism because any kind of dictatorship and despotic behavior is certainly going to encounter an impasse and very stiff resistance from freedom loving people across the world.

To overcome what now seems utopian states and in making these highly ambitious goals possible, humankind must take a giant leap toward self-denial and utterly believing in humanitarian agendas and productive communal work rather than acting in self-interest alone. Then the state also needs to be eliminated, since no government is needed to enforce contracts and property rights, neither military nor police force is necessary, basically expecting the masses to act flawlessly, making a piece of heaven possible. I attest without transcending into a higher realm of consciousness and quality education affected with a dynamic and progressive cultural revolution, which can carry society into the premises of ideological enlightenment and welfare. No social reform of that magnitude can possibly take place. Because the average intelligent and advanced rational mind has not yet matured to accept such a gigantic task.

What I am saying is we need to first reach a state of mindfulness, where we are lucky enough to utilize 15%-20% of our brain capacity to form 100% potential, which is likely to happen gradually with time; time and persisting to acquire knowledge and correct information is the essence and the key in unlocking troubles facing humanity. If it is possible for dolphins to use 20% of their brain making them so intelligent and playful since they utilize and maneuver by the most sophisticated sonar system and echolocation, then why not human progress into a state where they could also run their affairs with so much intelligence, using more percentage of their brain to accept communism without bloodshed. We're not able to do so now, since we can witness Russia and China, and Cuba, and so on failing socialism and communism. This should make us focus and emphatically insist on making more sense of things, and adapt to acquire more knowledge, information, and ascent into ever more rational minds, exploring meta intelligence and mindfulness to enjoy the fruits of utter enlightenment and understanding, which sure can bridge a safe way to human prosperity—then you can name it what you like.

To make change possible, we need intelligent and awakening minds compounded with proper timing, when the system in question is faced with systematic crisis and unable to advance because it is stagnated and entangled into a web of uncertainties and begins to deteriorate from within. Other utopian thoughts like anarchism also manifest progressive agendas, which again are not practical unless revolutionary ideas can make a paradigm shift into raising the overall mentality of the people and their intelligence and adamant enough for not accepting exploitation of any kind.

Alexander Berkman, in *The ABC* of Anarchism (1929) originally asked "What is Communist Anarchism?"

The more enlightened man will become, the less he will employ compulsion and coercion. The really civilized man will divest himself of all fear and authority. He will rise from the dust and stand erect: He will bow to no tsar either in heaven or on earth. He will become fully human when he will scorn to rule and refuse to be ruled. He will be truly free only when there shall be no more masters.

Anarchism is the ideal of such a condition, of a society without force and compulsion, where all men shall be equals, and live in freedom, peace, and harmony.

The word anarchy comes from the Greek, meaning without force, without violence or government, because government is the very fountainhead of violence, constraint, and coercion.

Anarchy therefore does not mean disorder and chaos, as you thought before. On the contrary, it is the very reverse of it; it means no government, which is freedom and liberty. Disorder is the child of authority and compulsion. Liberty is the mother of order.

Anarchism ... rests upon the doctrine that no man has a right to control by force That is to say, there should be no war, no violence used by one set of men against another; no anarchists generally believe that, whether as groups or individuals, no man who believes in force and violence is an anarchist.

It is not to say reaching such ambitious goals to truly free humankind from the yoke of oppressive powers is not possible; in contrary, they are very much practical. But not before reaching enlightenment and collectively realizing the true devilish nature of systems that are despotic and inhumane in their very structure and fundamental beliefs. We ought to understand it is our mind and our mental state of accepting something as true or not that is diagnosed in enslaving us or freeing us. Because there is no power ever created than the power of collective uprising and a tsunami of mass resurrection, when fueled with adequate knowledge and information against that which is perceived as destroying humanity.

Historically speaking, the reason "slavery" and "feudalism" existed was because the overall mentality accepted such an abusive system, and slaves and serfs were not conscious and enlightened enough to realize the collective power they held to overpower the tyranny of either one of their oppressive system that was imposed on slaves by their masters and on serfs by land owners known as feudal. According to the dictionary: feudalism was a system of political organization prevailing in Europe from the 9th to about the 15th century having as its base the relationship of lord to vassal (a person under the protection of a feudal lord to whom he has vowed homage, obligation and fealty, a feudal tenant, one in a subservient or subordinate position) with all land held in fee as chief characteristic homage, the service of tenants under arms and in court, warship, and forfeiture, and with any of various political or social systems similar to medieval feudalism. Once a system is overhauled, all the institutions supporting, promoting, and encouraging it are bound to destruction since the new system will bear and materialize its own progressive culture of thinking and its values system, which will be aggressively pursued until they sink in and are accepted as norms.

For instance, to promote capitalism, people like Walter Lippmann and Edward Bernays used the Freudian theory to deal with the public's conception of communism, as he believed that we should not be easing the public's fear of communism, but rather promote that fear and play with the public's emotions of it. This theory was so powerful that it became a weapon of its own during the Cold War. They utterly believed people are not moved by rationality and the power of inference, but they should be manipulated by the power of emotion seducing them to call for their own exploitation, which they manifested through mass propaganda to foster fear and anxiety. By keeping people in a limbo state of mind and under psychosis of permanent war where they are leashed with agendas and culture of thinking, which best serves their corporate bosses, and to keep the corporate oligopoly system intact by selling defective products to the masses of people to feed corporate profit. We ought to reckon that advanced socioeconomic techniques and socio-psychoanalysis are literally factored in to make us susceptible and influence with operating outside of our conscious ability and awareness.

Noam Chomsky said, "Bernays wrote a book called *Propaganda* around 1925, and it starts off by saying he is applying the lessons of the First World War. The propaganda system of the first World War and this commission that he was part of showed, he says, it is possible to 'regiment the public mind every bit as much as an army regiments their bodies.' These new techniques of regimentation of minds, he said, had to be used by the intelligent minorities in order to make sure that the slobs stay on the right course. We can do it now because we have these new techniques.

This is the main manual of the public relations industry. Bernays is kind of the guru. He was an authentic Roosevelt/Kennedy liberal. He also engineered the public relations effort behind the U.S.-backed coup that overthrew the democratic government of Guatemala.

His major coup, the one that really propelled him into fame in the late-1920s, was getting women to smoke. Women didn't smoke in those days and he ran huge campaigns for Chesterfield. You know all the techniques—models and movie stars with cigarettes coming out of their mouths and that kind of thing. He got enormous praise for that. So he became a leading figure of the industry, and his book was the real manual."

In the era of capitalism, and so-called modernity, millionaire and billionaire clubs are infested with hierarchical corruption going rampant. Mob-like organized crimes act against the powerless by killing, maiming, torturing, and imprisoning of the innocents, and against whomever isn't complying with brutal and inhumane ways of treating the poor. The only crime of the helpless is their outcry for justice and wanting to live in peace. Because as profit is accrued at the top, miseries and squalid living conditions are built up at the bottom and the money made is meant to serve the ruling class and the powerful where laws are purposely made to keep people apart and hostile toward each other to preserve the status quo.

In the meanwhile, hopes are lost and the entire allocation of resources is unjustly distributed, and wealth is hugely polarized between the haves and the have-nots, where thousands are forced to lose their lives for one reason or another. Because they are not facilitated with the very basic standard of living and for billions to live in sub-human conditions so that a handful few can live an unimaginable life of fortune and extravagance, where the super-rich hallucinate that it is God that abundantly and so generously gives them money at the cost of horrific livings of the poor. The super-rich waste millions and billions of dollars on their lavish lifestyle.

But the moguls of fortune are not intelligent enough to realize that life on Earth is seriously threatened and in need of immediate response and positive remedy. The plutocracy and corporate oligopoly refuse to see they are living at people's devastating expense where thousands perish every day as the super-rich are literally enjoying a life of plenty and magnificent luxury, utterly acting indifferent to the sordid condition of humankind and a destructive world facing its inhabitants.

How would you make changes applicable to a system that used to do well, in comparison to a feudal system or slavery where dark ages were upon us and people were basically treated like animals? But then when old systems had their runs and faced predicament and intricacies that generated irresolvable contradictions with antagonistic behaviors toward the very productive forces that gave birth to them, then it was time to go. And yes, it took aggressive force and violence to get rid of them, and I am afraid sometimes with the loss of millions of innocent lives because of bloodied encounters.

Many are pumped up and refer to history where revolutionary changes take place through violence and insist on no other viably peaceful solutions to make dynamic transitions possible; to them, moral imperative dictates that masses of people should overthrow the system, acting like barbarians. As if everything is supposed to progress through an evolutionary process, except the power of our wit and reasoning, despite enormous findings and accomplishments in every important scientific field and even putting human robots in the moon. We just need not act so backwardly to resolve our social and economic differences, and the system of our governing by killing and through bloodshed and by lawlessness and savagery like when slavery transitioned into feudalism via bloodshed and violence as did feudalism into capitalism. We should realize we live in an age of consciousness equipped with enough intelligence to know better. If not then, we should all wonder if our mindfulness and the power of our reasoning has ever grown at all because our acting civil should mean stewardship amidst turmoil and instability.

We should not be delinquent and deliberate in ignoring the unlocking of our cognitive ability, which literally takes place by gradually freeing more brain cells; in which it ascends and delivers humanity to realms beyond our imagination, when it does. And since it already has propelled us from the caveman mentality to what we experience as modern life, where the goal is to conquer other planets and perhaps harness them for the benefit of humankind. And in getting closer to fulfill the eternal purpose in objectifying our human destiny where reaching God and the higher power becomes so well-known and clearly manifested, and even the dumbest of us can witness and resurrect against the stupidity and clumsiness of truly claiming our creator.

Stop acting like beasts by mandating a global holocaust where hell is to wait us and start to pay attention to our evolutionary miracle-like brain and conscious which has relentlessly endeavored and meandered in accelerating its celestial task to save us from the clutches of ignorance and in moving toward its goal to arrive us into the promised land, despite treacherous behaviors of the few, and their deviously ironclad-like conduct to obstruct what is just. This often impedes but is never powerful enough to halt the virtue of higher powers of the heavens. The contemporary challenges that are holding back societies are the fusion of state and corporate power, which has reached the pinnacle of plundering, looting, and pillaging, where it seems the more powerful and privileged the ruling class becomes the more deluded they are with business industrial complex backed up with military industrial complex against the forces that are keeping the system intact.

This myopia of acting and secret tribunals to restlessly conspire against people is not aligned with God's work and the time that is promised to capture the essence and the very reason we are here. This calls for the helpless to unanimously speak the undeniable truth to the powerful and make them understand these despicable conditions that so many are stuck with, and it should call for an amicable solution to humanity's problem. And because there are potential dangers facing the entire system if no quality and plausible solution is to be expected soon. The super-rich should be warned and come to terms with grasping that human beings are a wholesome entity that must not be broken to pieces, and if so, the wrath of God will be upon us, boomeranging everyone. We already possess very destructible weaponry to instantly annihilate what we know as human life. And hence, we must remind ourselves that no violence is an answer, as good breeds good and evil breeds evil, and the gambling bet is on innocent human lives. And to realize any system change must occur peacefully to resolutely remedy our differences and the mess we have created, above all we must prove our non-hypocritical claim of believing in God we trust.

Why not live and honor in what we actually claim and build a humanitarian superpower rather than a military industrial complex where trillions of dollars is rampantly spent on unjustified military and logistics looking for improvised enemy to justify the infinite number of armaments accumulated to force others into do-or-die situation, which has counterintuitively threatened people and stifled the very foundation of virtues and what we stand for as a civilized nation.

That should be demanded by actively participating in restoring goods, as Ralph Nader said, "There are two kinds of people: ones which believe everything, and the other which believe nothing, and both lack thinking." Just remember it is a Republican state where our forefathers and so many good souls lost their lives to restore, and not a corporate state where greed irresponsibility has shackled people with unbearable living conditions testing their limits and into acting desperate and suicidal. This should call upon consciously awakened people to feel accountable and get out of their comfort zone to make things right, where life would not happen to be so damn hard for billions, and so ridiculously luxurious for just a handful of menacing souls.

We ought to know the era of awakening and responsibility, the era of consciousness and accountability, and the time parameter where so many are alerted and care to understand the structure of power and the world that surrounds them is here. The truth is that at slavery time, or at the feudal era, the victims knew who was slashing them and murdering and raping them, and who made the work harder than animals. But then the system of corporate capitalism became much more elaborate in its wrongdoing against its victims. As Sheldon Wolin discussed in his interview with Truthdig columnist Chris Hedges.

In his book *Democracy Incorporated*, inverted totalitarianism is different from classical forms of totalitarianism. It does not find its expression in a demagogue or charismatic leader but in the faceless anonymity of the corporate state. Our inverted totalitarianism pays outward fealty to the facade of electoral politics, the Constitution, civil liberties, freedom of the press, the independence of the judiciary, and the iconography, traditions, and language of American patriotism, but it has effectively seized all the mechanisms of power to render the citizens impotent.

Throughout his scholarship Wolin charted the devolution of American democracy, and in *Democracy Incorporated*, he details our peculiar form of corporate totalitarianism. "One cannot point to any national institution[s] that can accurately be described as democratic, surely not in the highly managed, money-saturated elections, the lobby-infested Congress, the imperial presidency, the class biased judicial and penal system, or, least of all, the media." Wolin continues: "Unlike the Nazis, who made life uncertain for the wealthy and privileged while providing social programs for the working class and poor, inverted totalitarianism exploits the poor, reducing or weakening health programs and social services, regimenting mass education for an insecure workforce threatened by the importation of low-wage workers."

Wolin writes: "Employment in a high-tech, volatile, and globalized economy is normally as precarious as during an old-fashioned depression. The result is that citizenship, or what remains of it, is practiced amidst a continuing state of worry. Hobbes had it right: when citizens are insecure and at the same time driven by competitive aspirations, they yearn for political stability rather than civic engagement, protection rather than political involvement. "If the main purpose of elections is to serve up pliant legislators for lobbyists to shape, such a system deserves to be called 'misrepresentative or client government.' It is, at one and the same time, a powerful contributing factor to the DE politicization of the citizenry, as well as reason for characterizing the system as one of anti-democracy."

The result, he writes, is that the public is "denied the use of state power." Wolin deplores the trivialization of political discourse, a tactic used to leave the public fragmented, antagonistic, and emotionally charged while leaving corporate power and empire unchallenged.

"Cultural wars might seem an indication of strong political involvements," Wolin writes. "Actually they are a substitute. The notoriety they receive from the media and from politicians eager to take firm stands on no substantive issues serves to distract attention and contribute to a politics of the inconsequential. In classical totalitarian regimes, such as those of Nazi fascism or Soviet communism, economics was subordinate to politics. But "under inverted totalitarianism the reverse is true. Economics dominates politics—and with that domination comes different forms of ruthlessness."

With all this said, it is the time to hope for the change, but you must be the change and should stop taking the tranquilized medicine of non-activity, hoping others do what everyone needs to do, without you lifting a finger. It is not an exaggeration to say we are sequestered into accepting illusions as reality and normal, and sometimes we are not humble enough to admit many issues that are killing us and wrong need to be confronted with reason.

We need to condemn our divisiveness, corporate greed and bailing out the super-rich with taxpayers' money, GMOs food, global warming and contaminating the sources of our food and water supply, polluting the air we breathe, trillions spent on military industrial complex bleeding us dry, outsourcing jobs, genocide and wars of aggression, police brutality, unlawful incarcerations, no due process of law against the apprehension of intellectuals and the whistleblowers.

Gun control, mega media indoctrinating people with false reports and misleading information, defrauding billions from people's hard-earned money, pushing them into foreclosures, no regulations for unleashed bankers and corporations, forcing taxpayers to bail out bankers and huge financial institutions, balance budget, deteriorating educational system, unemployment, no savvy and efficient medical system, no housing subsidies, no educational subsidies, horrendous infrastructures, not raising the minimum wage.

Horrible immigration policies, exploitive tax system, too big to fail entities, not to mention wrong ways of dealing with crimes, where violence is going rampant and ever present, supporting autocratic regimes, prosecute those at the top, and not putting all the guilt on the little men with no executive power. Stifling all legislative activities by corporation and powerful lobbyists, stopping fraudulent insiders on Wall Street from defrauding people out of billions, not using available and efficient alternative energy to implement and mandate more safe environmental policies, and regulative laws against big carbon monoxide producing companies.

Halt masquerading and distorting those with progressive thoughts and agendas. Stop beleaguering (attack from all sides, harass) democracy and insist on people's constitutional rights, and for the love of God, do not rewrite the Constitution to render the system futile. Stop marginalizing people and put an end to racial profiling where intrusive activities are misconstrued by mapping, acting uncivilized and without due process and the misuse of power to illegally intimidate and apprehend minorities and ethnic groups. Why not stop spewing hatred and venom toward so many, sowing fear and discord among so many good souls that believe in our democracy system of government and sincerely try to become productive members of society. Stop giant corporate conglomerates from shoving toxic and inhumane conditions in our throats and forcing us to digest them, generating so many problems that no nation deserves. Discourage paying fealty to electoral politics to create allegiance against what needs to be done to rescue people from this horrendous situation we call living.

If the government really cares to authenticate democracy and human rights and truly manifests the right to life and the pursuit of happiness for all, and perhaps is adamant enough to save the system by peaceful means, then, they should make dynamic changes that can resonate with the masses of people for financial security and for a life worth living. They should make a sincere effort to substantiate the emergence of a left-right alliance to dismantle the corporate state, stopping bureaucracies and getting rid of red tapes. Stop bushwhacking (assaulting, ambushing) innocent citizens in the name of national security, through spying, insidious surveillance, and eavesdropping. After all, this is a place nations under autocratic regimes look up to for guidance on freedom, democracy, justice, and human rights.

The politicians need to collectively support gradual change into a co-op system of economic and social endeavors, stop changing the nature of nature to maximize profit and stop burning food and burying cows, buffalos, pigs, lambs, poultry, and so forth to raise the price of meat and fowl in a desperately hungry world. In the meanwhile, make the corporations pay their fair share of taxes; most pay less than 2% of taxes or find loopholes to pay no taxes at all, while investing billions in places with no hard core tax policies, since many authorities can be bribed and bought to turn a blind eye.

Why not decriminalize drugs for medical rehabilitation since many users have health problems; stop suppressing addiction and start helping those through professional medical assistance and decisive therapy. Bring illegal drugs to the surface, and let's deal with it by educational means and taxing it higher, which will mitigate and perhaps can get rid of drug trafficking and its peripheral troubles and the menace it causes for humanity. Put more women in higher posts and stop discriminating against them. And most of all, do not believe politicians who say the right things but are far from actuating them.

Criminalization is the mode of the government and the culture we practically live in. And unless economic justice prevails, decriminalization is not going to materialize, which should uproot the very foundation of the society that is contemptuous and belittling toward those less fortunate and the deprived; so many are forced to do wrong to survive. And because of a failed education system that is proportional to the rise of incarceration of millions with no available opportunities as society's crime rates have statistically skyrocketed without any constructive and structural solution to the vast problem of crime. And if not intentionally planned to make repeat offenders, many so-called felons have chronic mental sickness with no available medical therapy and professionally help to rehabilitate and correct the situation that jailed them in the first place. Doing so can help to make a safer neighborhood and society to live in after being released. To make matters worse, the so-called felons are not clear and free from their insidious social and desperate economic status after they are released and have paid their dues to the society because they are labeled as a felon for the rest of their lives, which condemns them to unemployment and denying so many form earning the bare minimum wage, or any other income, leaving a good reason to become a repeat offender and hostile toward a system that has declared war on them. And there are no incentives for either legislative or executive branch of government that are heavily influenced by the powerful lobbyist and private mega corporations; no resolute public good is ever instituted. In most cases, judges do not have the discretion to judge the accused because they have to follow certain guidelines which do not necessarily follow the expression that "the punishment should fit the crime." And for humanity's sake, stop redefining and reconfiguring the Constitution to fit the oligarch behaviors of the elites, which strips people of their fundamental rights and dignity. And halt changing the nature of Mother Nature; stop suppressing the poor and the very productive forces of the society, the workers, which are the main reason for your deep pocket and surplus value.

Do not push further austerity on so many people who are already burdened and enslaved with despicable and squalid lifestyles beyond human imagination. Stop producing people by your mega media propaganda machine, as they are defective products bewitched to act as robots to consume more artificially desired stuff you homogenize and push to pursue.

Capitalists' moral mission is to see individuals and self-interests as the only propriety, and as the only accepted norm; then, we should accept altruism to be immoral, and that is why so many problems have repercussions and reflect to humanity in undeniably ill ways. To protect corporate oligopoly, we have amassed the most mass surveillance, which has turned democracy into a sham and the government of the people, by the people, for the people has converted into an autocracy controlled by the corporate elites.

I strongly believe in so many intellectual and frontline fighters who struggle for justice, equity, liberty, and human rights. They are compassionate enough to risk their lives in many parts of the world for a better living condition and to save humanity. But I also believe that we have reached an age of consciousness and intelligence in which we must resolve our differences by peaceful means. I am sure no decent human being could ever ignore the loss of innocent lives through violence and criminal behavior. And the moral imperative should call for reasoning and humane dialogue, since any one of us could act like the elites do, and perhaps even worse, if we were in the position of power.

It is the 21st century, we should act like it and not get stuck in a caveman mentality where the dark ages are upon us. And, yes, history has proven that change has happened many times through violence and killing, but bear in mind, as many as those bloodied times, dynamic and authenticated changes have taken place by cooperation and peaceful means as well, rather than by killing. We should gracefully cherish nonviolent behavior. No violence should take over the power of wit and understanding when faced with complicated issues, and to prove it, just take a survey by the civilized world and ask if violence should be the answer.

Marx believed, "It is only possible to achieve real liberation in the real world. ... by employing real means ... slavery cannot be abolished without the steam-engine and the mule and spinning-jenny, serfdom cannot be abolished without improved agriculture, and ... in general, people cannot be liberated as long as they are unable to obtain food and drink, housing and clothing in adequate quality and quantity. 'Liberation' is a historical and not a mental act, and it is brought about by historical conditions, the development of industry, commerce, agriculture, and the conditions of intercourse, and so forth. Based on the theory of the productive forces and related perspectives, the economic systems of the former Eastern bloc and the present-day socialist states the state accumulated capital through forcible extraction of surpluses from the population for the purpose of rapidly modernizing and industrializing their countries, because these countries were not technologically advanced to a point where an actual socialist economy was technically possible,[1] or were a socialist state tried to reach the communist mode of production. The philosophical perspective behind the modernizing zeal of the Soviet Union and People's Republic of China was based on the desire to industrialize their countries."

Unless the global productive forces and the masses' consciousness is pinnacled, contrary to what Marx and Lenin and others, with the exception of Trotsky, believed: True communism is possible in one country where the industrial and economic forces have matured and will produce domino effects to the rest of industrial world with advanced and progressive cultures, when technology and human intelligence are mature enough and ripe. No economic and sociocultural meaningful changes are to take place. Either way an emotional or demagogic call for revolution by hostile means is not a viable option, when the proper forces to make a smooth transition possible are not available yet. If history should be an indicator, then we need to question why Russia, China, Vietnam, Cuba, Cambodia, and the like did not succeed their discourse. And still not rational enough to make sense of what they have started, since vacillating between capitalism, socialism, and acting revisionism, which are still very far away from adopting communism. They failed their bloodied revolution, losing millions of lives with no avail, because the fundamentals of productive force and the superstructures of feudal Russia and China at the time of revolt were not ready. And neither was the world for such exorbitant (drastic) social and economic changes to internationally assume and take place. So we need to harness the notion of emotional outrage, despite its justification and altruism, until the fundamentals of revolt have globally matured. Because no nation is an island anymore; we are all interactively connected.

Furthermore, should we think that slavery and feudal changes or the renaissance for that matter would ever be possible if the productive forces and the culture of thoughts, the ideology and awareness, would have not been ready to switch into the new system and to have reveled (celebrate) its outcome? But one thing is for sure: If the revolution were to take place in North America, then it would manifest itself with a much better result than in Russia, China, and others like them. The leverages for a dynamic and quality change are not cosmetic; we are not in a feudal state, but are living the era of a capitalistic society, which is the highest stages of capitalism, known as imperialism, rather than living in other primitive eras not suitable for reliable and progressive changes, which were doomed to failure.

Could our predecessors have expected the slaves to bring about the social change that capitalists have or could they have expected feudalism to place a man on the moon and create the miracle inventions that capitalists have done in their time? Yes, our perceptions and incisive awareness and consciousness might be ready, which perhaps could overpower our momentary lapses of reason for a revolutionary idea to take place, but to be sure, we must have the fundamental forces of economic and social production available to induce such historical change. This should also awaken not only the masses of the poor, but the capitalists themselves to investigate the stalemated, stagnated, or matured system, which once was dynamically productive, to avoid bloodied upheavals, and if room is left for more progress and believing in social order and prosperity for all. Or is it really time for the capitalist system to go? Referencing history, the maturity of productive forces and the widening gap between the poor and the rich might have caused social uprising and turmoil. But also, more powerful governments, like the Persian empire, Egyptian empire, Arabian empire, Mongolian empire, Chinese empire, Greek and Roman empire, Ottoman empire, British empire, and so many others, felt like they needed to expand since they might have noticed their economic demise, or they just wanted to add territories to their empire. They attacked and destroyed other weak nations, especially if the less powerful nations owned valuable resources. This should remind us of today's modern warfare and militarism taking place in many parts of the world, where the corporate capitalists compete for the resources of developing countries by either unfair trade practices or through militarism.

Superpowers first stir trouble in many parts of the world, then talk about peace, democracy, and human rights, which is followed by sending trillions of dollars' worth of arms to dreadful and bloodied regimes of their choice to kill millions in the name of doing business and making money for the few. They are able to cause these inhumane atrocities because they are equipped with the technology that makes the world perceive the corporate mega media intended to comprehend as reality, but not the actual reality. This should remind us of fascist and autocratically orchestrated techniques that the few super-rich control and manifest, rather than democratic techniques and products people should control. To avoid making freedom-loving people of the globe lose and not to brainwash them to stay on the wrong side of justice and what is right. To change the status quo and to bring about a more just economic system, where true democracy and socialized goods can equitably be allocated among masses of people, where the workers enjoy the fruits of their labor. Trillions of surplus value is not concentrated in the hands of the private enterprise, but will make sure the basic necessities of living are prioritized, including proper employment, retirement security, free education, free health care, subsidized housing, free transportation, and more.

Marx and others predicted that true social revolution is only possible in advanced industrial nations that have reached economic maturity; this does not historically fit the criteria and neither fits today's world social, economic, and cultural agendas. The truth is, Marx did not predict that billions, even trillions, of dollars could electronically be transferred in seconds, where outsourcing has become the norm in many industrial and powerful nations since the multinational companies invest in countries with plenty of raw materials, with dirt cheap natural resources and labor. They also establish the puppet government of their choice, a neo-colonialist system of governing, which is the accomplice to exploiting native resources and cheap labor, murdering, torturing, and imprisoning their own citizens. They all work in concert as superior classes against the deprived and international working class, which has quelled most of the pressure in nations that have peaked industrially and are managing to avoid socialist revolution.

Marx did not predict the wars of aggression pursued by looting, plundering, and extortion; taking other helpless nations' natural resources and raw material has become the norm. He must have not expected the explosive power of computers, the advent of the internet with amazingly quick communication technology, and the super advanced jet engines, the power of outsourcing, the global economic expansion and counter-trade (a form of international trade in which purchases made by an importing nation are linked to offsetting purchases made by the exporting nation), and the potential for nuclear, chemical, bacterial, and cyber warfare and terrorism, which is shifting the national boundaries and making the entire world act like one village. Everything is immediately accessible by the international monetary system through trade and militarism.

Until the resources of the planet are depleted to the point of exhaustion and collapse, which we should already see the dire signs of, then, it is perhaps possible for the poor, the destitute, and the global working class to confront the murderous agents in decisive ways and make a worldly socioeconomic and cultural revolution compatible to the 21st century. This should be dynamic and progressive enough to carry humanity into the next couple of centuries, where the system can make meaningful life and happiness relatively possible and not be made to belittle God and trash humanity in the name of accumulating infinite wealth and power.

Our mental progressiveness and higher understanding of social and natural order can empower us to rationally conceptualize and induce dynamic intelligence, which is only possible in accordance to scientific breakthroughs, enabling society to perceive a culture of thinking that is interconnected with the advancement of technology and the industrial mode of production, which grants us a paradigm shift into new consciousness and assembly of thoughts that leverages humanity to enter into a new notion of civilization, enabling societies to digest and comprehend the dynamics of historical events. For example, "division of labor" and mass production were only possible because of the invention of assembly lines, which an industrial breakthrough made possible.

The problem is the relationship of the production that is an imprecation (curse), since it distorts and exploits nature, destroys humanity, and commoditizes everything and everyone in its path for profit—and not for the sake of creating public goods compatible with the sustainability of the social and natural order. This private opulence at the cost of public misery needs to end, as the poor are paying with their lives to feed a system that has become dull and indifferent to the suffering of so many bereft of basic necessities to sustain them. The system has turned fair competition and appropriate market functions into sociopathic individualistic nature.

The system has violated nature; it has disturbed class order to the extreme, where the middle class are becoming an endangered species, and the working class cannot make a living anymore. It has turned into sociopathic politics fed by corporations and mad institution to focus on wealth creation for the elites and the hell with everyone else. People are casted into dire positions where upper mobility is impossible, since the masses are stuck in terrible financial situations. This personality disorders and anti-social conduct must stop by the power of reasoning and in the name of human virtues, and not by murdering each other.

The philosophical perspective behind the modernizing zeal of the Soviet Union and the People's Republic of China was based on the desire to industrialize their countries. At this stage, the global dynamics and interconnectivities have grown too big to behave nativist, populist, or nationalist. We need to strive for international citizenry and strategize hallmarks for global governing and a worldwide transitory infrastructure to heighten our appreciation for one government, one nation, under God, in which our ethos should be directed at preserving humanity, rather than acting self-centered and narrow-minded in fortifying boundaries to separate humankind.

Let's break down the stereotype mentality and encourage the peaceful coexistence of man, which by the way, can exterminate so many excuses for having to go to war with the so-called enemy nations and boycott governments and their military industrial complex from wars of aggression, where no nation or any group can act genocidal toward the weaker countries or race. Let's move forward with virtual reality, which has surpassed and is beyond domesticated and inhibited forces of ignorance and authenticate the phrase "I know of no illegal human being."

I am sure if persevered enough, people can make the privileged elites open their eyes that are blinded with power and prestige. They should incessantly be reminded of acting delusional, which can be corrected, if pushed enough by the truth-teller to open the eyes of plutocracy and to avoid a bloodied class war. If keen enough, we can clearly see that Mother Nature, the very reason for our existence, works gradually and is an evolutionist in its pursuit of giving life and making dynamic and decisive apparatus possible for humanity to enjoy. We are part of nature and should act like it. For some, it might be easy to say the corporate tyranny must be overthrown no matter what cost, but this must not occur at the cost of millions of innocent lives, which violence will surely bring. Every time we are violent, we eviscerate (to remove, to deprive of vital contents) and insult the very intelligence and human mindfulness that has collectively enabled us to do the impossible. Resorting to force and barbarism will kill the civility of mind and manner and the power of compassion in all of us. It will breed more ills, demonic and horrific conduct, as it has in the past, if history is to remind us and is witnessed.

The mechanism of power that betrays those marginalized and the destitute, the powerless and the poor can be shifted. But then, what guaranty does anyone have if we are not educated and wise enough to keep others intact, which are supposed to govern and rule us from doing the same or even worse. If we are not mentally competent and do not possess the dynamics and the technology of thought to manage our literal problems with this corporate state now and resolutely manage to communicate savviness and wisdom to them, then what should make us confident that we can make it happen with the alternative system?

Discourage talks about sublime (exalted, elevated) madness and violent confrontations to deal with the system, where moments of extremity might call for revolt. The power of reasoning can unlock and speak the undeniable power of truth to the power and acclaim its sovereignty where no man should resist, unless wanting to act beastly and assume savage behavior.

We live in an era where our overall mentality bears enough intelligence to retaliate against the mechanism of powers that betrays those whom they are supposed to rule and care for, but it must happen in dignified and civilized ways because we are in profound need of humanity, and the daunting question should be, why not? Why not activate the potentiality of our human brain which collectively has the literal power to rescue humankind from the clutches of ignorance and where kinship and meaningful perspective could sooth our pain and anguish and replace breathing and living devastation?

Why procrastinate until is too late? And why not get out of this entrenched madness and act humane against the root causes of evil, which have caged and imprisoned our souls in the name of profit? Let our failure leverage and aim us at enlightenment where human spirit can kindle to do well and make peace and justice possible and to realize we are unbalanced and will extinguish faster if were to resort to nuclear, biological, chemical, and many other vicious weaponry, which can wipe us all out, making Holocaust-like tragedies many time over, where no day will be left to call it a day.

Let's necessitate, rehabilitate, and resuscitate our love for each other and become one against all atrocious and inhumane behavior. We must become warned of our abysmal mistakes we are making and condemn the real perpetrators of crimes and misconduct. Let's be human. Violence will end in revenge, and revenge is a very potent force that will travel the endless road of outrage and violence, which creates a vicious circle of beastly acts, until millions of lives are senselessly taken. It should be obvious that criminal behaviors are odious no matter which side is causing them.

We need to know that either through a conscious decision or a momentary lapse of reason, any violent action should be counted as human failure, which must not be challenged through the barrel of gun, because humanism should always be the answer. And hence all-out effort must be directed at bulls' eyeing and targeting the heart of raising the plural consciousness of the people and to equip them with correct information, higher education, and knowledge so they can truly digest and understand the complexity of the system which is rendering them helpless.

And to detect the anatomical structures of power and exploitation and replace it with a new manifesto to emancipate billions from the ironclad indecency and ruthless economic programs, as the financial despots and the Byzantines of today's world laugh at democracy and human rights, where they know their autocracy of corporate power rules. Truth diggers are incessant in their effort to stand against this behavioral hegemony, which is structured to put an end to inhumane living standards manufactured by the corporate power blinded with greed.

They cannot see the effect of giant corporate economy on the world, which has left a ruthless inefficiency on so many people who die every day because of food and water depravity and famine that has turned humanity into vast herds of prey and made the super-rich into a handful of predators hunting human beings, since they artificially raise prices and manipulate the world market to maximize their profit as they insanely fight the natural and social order, amassing 80-90% of the wealth into the hands of 1%, leaving 99% of the world's population to barely survive on 10-15% of the entire global resources.

This madness must be stopped if there is going to be a slight chance left for humankind to survive corporate atrocities, which have become a life and death situation for so many and an insurmountable challenge for the wise to overcome. It is time to realize that no nation or any society should be at the mercy of a power individual or influenced group because they will be victimized and will not fare well. No man can resist not abusing his power. We are social and self-interested beings. No one should prevail with one's self-interest agendas at the cost of common good and society, where social apparatus and the common goods should work well for the benefit of the entire society, with no one left behind.

The bottom line is that in individualistic societies individuals benefit at the cost of the group, war-like cultures—including racism, social injustice, prejudice against women and children, prejudice against the poor and the weak, against minorities, infinite wrong against the nature itself, religious resentment encouraged by the sectarian charlatans in making superficial difference. Where even God is not immune to their perils and toxic lectures to make money because no one is safe to the atrocities of human greed, which must be controlled. And authenticated altruism and much better humans are the products of a social and cooperative system; they are delivered in a less hostile and negatively competing environment, where common goods are truly recognized and prioritized.

Someone wise once said: "Don't ask God to guide your footsteps if you're not willing to pick up your feet." Take steps toward nullifying and dismantling the relentless efforts of corporate capitalists' system that have become numb to causing the destruction of the entire planet. Outlaw them for maximizing wealth in the name of taking lives; take their social license away and inactivate their murderous behaviors, and let's be delighted that we are not part of doing so much ill to humanity. Let's make sure to be congenial (to get along) and belong to the right side of history, as we must repeatedly remind ourselves that we are here for a short time, since we must return to where we came from sooner or later.

And when it is time to transcend to higher realms with a clear conscious, we can stand erect as if with a chip on our shoulder and keep our head up to answer with no hesitancy and say, "No. I did not murder. I did not rape or cause any irreparable harm to humankind." Socrates said, it is better to suffer wrong than to do wrong. We ought to know it is not the application of common sense that is lost, but greed and self-interest agenda which is gone haywire, and the premises encouraging its reckless behaviors, that is about to make humanity an endangered species if not wisely corrected or entirely stopped.

It is imperative for any progressive system to direct its goals and activities at a global scale where the greater good is to benefit everyone, to avoid acting small and narrow-mindedly and not become restrained in doing justice because of social, cultural, nationality, race, ethnicity, sectarianism, color, gender, religious, economic classification, or any discriminatory factors. Otherwise, it will lessen or sanction its overall objectives deemed at helping the entire humanity from reaching its full potential; the system should transcend beyond concocting nebulous (vague) and petty differences that are traditionally made to keep us apart. If prevailed, "no can manifesto" will be a thing of the past, where even seeing God the almighty should become explicitly clear and closer to one than one's jugular vein.

I believe we will overcome our malignant social and financial problems and will reach the mountaintop of human consciousness and become enlightened to shatter the old paradigms and unanimously vote for the common goods of the entire planet and its inhabitants. I also believe we have the means to substantiate quality changes that can empower us to expedite global social solidarity, where a better system can play a huge positive role and a catalyst in opening plural brain might and materialize a dynamic global educational culture to direct us in a right track at the end of the tunnel, where there is light, and away from predatory practices and beastly behaviors.

Why is it that one feels so alone even though surrounded by many? Is our loneliness, indifferences, and denial a self-defense mechanism against death so that we could live without fear of dying?

Or are we just ignorant pure and simple in making a culture of individualism so prevalent in which we choose not to notice the malevolence and vicious consequences of such arid human interconnection? We do the most atrocious, abominable, and horrifying crime against the helpless, did we think that would go unpunished? We act like nothing has happened, as we stage a theater-like lifestyle, where actions are artificially maneuvered and at the end everyone gets better off and goes their own merry way.

In the meanwhile, the only hope left for humanity is to depend on and believe in transformation of the human mind in becoming enlightened, as we could become mindful of an exquisitely created universe, breathtaking cosmos, and be fascinated with infinite miracle-like phenomena that are mind-boggling, which should mesmerize any bright mind and inquisitive soul since human beings are an inseparable part of this grandeur and amazing, purposefully built universe that should be honored and respected

James Joule put forth the first law of thermodynamics (on the conservation of energy). Joule also made important contributions to the kinetic theory of gases. The unit of heat known as the "Joule" is named after him. According to Joule, "There are many ways in which people are made aware of their power to believe in the supremacy of divine guidance and power: through music or visual art, some event or experience decisively influencing their life, looking through a microscope or telescope, or just by looking at the miraculous manifestations or purposefulness of nature."

We should not hibernate in our effort to profoundly acquire ulterior knowledge in knowing the glory of God, since deciphering the brilliance of God's majestic power is beyond the mind of man, which requires infinite knowledge to perhaps elucidate a tiny fraction of the awesomely spectacular and remarkably manifested God's creation. Because the more humanity ploughs, the more puzzled we become, which should acknowledge that we are not self-created, but belong to an omnipotent, omniscient God that is beyond the scope of our human senses. And remember the almighty God is beyond matter, space, and time and cannot be seen, as God's awesome power is palpable (perceptible) in attributes and its effects. Again and again we need to know that no matter what kind of a ruling system is to prevail, humanity must accord with the power of God and authenticate God's presence in our lives. "I believe that the more thoroughly science is studied, the further does it take us from anything comparable to atheism."

"If you study science deep enough and long enough, it will force you to believe in God," said Lord William Kelvin, who was noted for his theoretical work on thermodynamics, the concept of absolute zero, and the Kelvin temperature scale based upon it.

Believing in oneself is a superb idea, but one must not be frail and stray from heading toward our creator in one's mission.

We are alive because what we consume and drink is mixed with oxygen through the invisible processes burning food to create energy, making it possible for humanity to survive and nature to sustain itself, but it is not visible to the naked eye and cannot be seen, only felt. Marvelous human ideas, thinking process, and wisdom can only be seen after they're manufactured and formed; the power of memory and remembering and the amazing thinking ability cannot be seen. Information captured from our human senses or produced by thought is developed in many parts of the brain. Some are responsible for processing sensory data, like sound, sight, taste, touch, and smell, and others, such as the cortex and cerebellum, issue commands that invoke or coordinate voluntary moves, but are not seen. Human consciousness is part of elaborate cosmic energy and awakened conscious cosmos and is not seen, but definitely is alive. The invisible world of sub-atomically manifested particles, the world of quarks and quantum is what makes the exposed world possible, which carries the real essence behind the physical cosmos. All the fundamental forces of the universe, including gravity, electromagnetic force, the small and big atomic energy forces, and so on, cannot be seen, but are available and mandatory to sustain life as we know it. Perhaps millions of other earthly and intergalactic energy oriented forces cannot be detected by the human nervous system and are not yet recognized through our minds, but they exist. The power of human emotion, love, hate, and resentment, the power of human intuition and potent premonition cannot be seen, but they can be felt. Billions of messages rendered at the speed of light to our brain through our senses via spinal cord and trillions of cells and other vital organs in our body cannot be seen, heard, or detected in any way, but the effect of such unseen mechanism is the evidence of their existence.

The bottom line is not to be fooled by the glamorous physical world and carelessly do so much wrong to cause decadent malice; there certainly exists an unseen absolute power, which seems to be testing us, but for unknown reasons. We should not be derelict (negligence) in understanding life's purpose and why we are here; perhaps then it could help us not to become reductionists in our search for God, since we know so little about something infinitely larger than our human mind. This also might percolate to those avarice souls not to relentlessly pursue the wealth built upon a game at any cost, and should remind them of Machiavelli's definition that is indicative of their grotesque actions: "the end justifies the mean." And it is okay to use clever and fraudulent conduct, dishonesty, lies, and tricks in order to get or achieve something, which I believe any pathological behavior should be held in contempt of civil and criminal court.

We are at the crossroads where because of technology we can see the unraveling of human doom days, which urgently calls for reclaiming our human civilization and stop pushing people to the edge, to take our blinders off and realize the sacredness of a gifted life where solidarity and collective cooperation could perhaps indemnify us all and alert us to avoiding the extinction of millions of species, unambiguously threatening the very existence of Earth in its entirety. The politics of manipulating people through fear, manufacturing lies and fabrications needs to stop, and politicians need to put an end to relishing the disagreements among various factions and people to control society for more profit and halt boosting dreadful greed. Policies need to shift into reverencing the sanctity of all living beings and organisms. Make the powerful and the privileged stall abusing Mother Earth, and not to further endanger the position of billions of inhabitants, since their livelihood is overwhelmingly being compromised; life is integrally interdependent, but unless the good people's voice is reflected and truly heard, no convergence of any kind is going to lift these repressive and ugly situations burdening humankind.

We must redefine all deadened and destructible ideas that have disillusioned us into seeing them as constructively creative works; they have worsened and impaired our present condition beyond repair. And unless we are collectively awakened to the spreading of infectious diseases of the mind meticulously implemented by an ill-intended powerful few, we will not recuperate. Many mendaciously preconceived notions are skillfully incubated and stimulated by unpropitiously (menacing, ominous) adept characters hired by the influential elites, to further ensure optimal accumulation of wealth. We should indisputably oppose being indoctrinated by what seems unending ill will and viruses of the mind programmed in our brain to further haunt humanity, as we are hardwired into behaving self-destructively once our mission to benefit the rich is accomplished. We are just a number in billions of statistics. We need to unblock and modulate how a real human being is to think, as we are definitely an inseparable part of divine cosmic energy encapsulated and geared into experiencing the human body.

In primitive times where our ancestors lived in caves, survival was the only issue and shockingly challenging. I am certain even then, so many were driven by savagery, jealousy, intimidation, murder, robbery, rape, and other beastly behaviors to fulfill their needs and for satisfying their sexual impulses while victimizing and forcing the weak to act against their will.

The answer to why criminal conduct as such would materialize in those times most probably would be: They were ignorant, not intelligent enough to know better, and perhaps had no conscience and of course were not educated. They were not enlightened or awakened and they would act on instincts without thinking. But in today's world, if you ask a neurologist why someone would act not normal or behave criminally, he most probably would say that when a thought actually forms in one's mind, an intricate set of electrochemical charges takes place in different parts of the brain, which can also illustrate evidence of brain damage in designated areas and makes the patient unable to operate in a savvy and civilized manner. A psychologist might characterize the patient having certain unfulfilled drives or perhaps an ugly past with acute trauma; the individual might have experienced severe psychic mental and emotional disorders.

An anthropologist would probably diagnose the person with having bad hereditary genes and analyze his forefathers and predecessors through time and space, physical characteristics, environment, culture, and social relation. And a priest, a rabbi, or a mullah might throw the baby out with the bathwater and say he is just ungodly, morally corrupted, and deserves to die. And while some thoughts can be so detrimental and damaging to self and society, relatively speaking, the proper answer should be that we are the product of our environment, and unless we are educated, trained, and imbued (permeated, influenced) with good thoughts into our brain and nervous system, where an environment of peace and tranquility is creatively designed to manifest positive and productive attitudes in a large scale, which should allow us to experience compassionate, knowledgeable, and trusting role models and encourage society to observe matters beyond the physical world into the world of the unseen, which is the spiritual world and the driving force beyond what we see and experience.

In the contemporary world, the power of technology and overloading information relates to human intelligence, but does not necessarily comply with wisdom and the might of reasoning. It seems possession of technology and information are inversely related to wisdom, since wisdom should encourage humility and not arrogance. Also a search for meaning and insight does not resonate with violence and barbaric thoughts within a human family. Extraordinary technology with surpassing information and devoid of adequate judgment can embolden governments to put human civilization at grave danger where fear becomes a force to reckon with. The government can encounter times where right and wrong is deluded and literally lost, especially when they have to make a difficult choice, compromising and endangering millions of innocent lives.

A wise and caring system of governing can grow virtues, where strategic political, social, and economic contributions can make humanity responsible enough to avoid letting 85 to 90 powerful individuals own half of the world's wealth, while billions are deprived of the basic necessities to survive a very rudimentary lifestyle or declare wars of aggression and genocide on weak nations. The problem is that ill thoughts and infectious viruses of the mind travel like a wildfire, creating so much harm, while intuitive knowledge and rational knowledge, which can make a decisive and noticeable improvement in our lives, do not get a chance to flourish, and once they do, they are denied leverage and prove incompetent. We are at a choice between insightfulness and catastrophe, which calls for a big jolt to awaken nations into making the right choice before it is too late.

And just because we are a five senses being, we should not destroy the less intelligent entities so irrationally for profit, as these planetary crises need to resonate with everyone and for each of us to exercise higher consciousness, where human propensity to advance would be based on sensible ability, compassion, and peace. To irradiate (to enlighten intellectually, spiritually) humanity and find sanctuary in diversities and mutual cooperation because diversity is beautiful, rather than perpetuating violence toward each other. We must not aim at eradicating the essence of life, which gives bountifully, whence it is gratifyingly divine and invitingly enchanting. Humanity has to have patience to truly redeem ourselves and not become victims of this nanosecond fast pace and hurry up culture, where masses have to obsessively pursue making money to survive. The elites are callously fettered by the power of avarice and mentally duped by denial, not wanting to see the rat race society that corporate oligopoly system has financially constituted to exploit, and they politically have engineered humongous feat to protect it, manifesting a caste system in which the plutocrats behave so absent-mindedly toward people's excruciatingly painful and suffering lifestyle.

As the mighty rich act obnoxiously cold, not identifying with problems of billions of indigents and wretchedly poor, as if the elites appeared from other planets not noticing their meritocracy conduct that is detrimental to social order. In which the super-rich should learn not to foster unconscious stereotyping of the disadvantaged majority and stop preferential treatment of the handful few since it hyphenizes and plummets people into adversity, manifesting hostile performance in the social realm, which effects the core of our human well-being. The super-rich gauge and carefully watch to prevent any progressive change for the people as they diligently try to maintain the status quo, knowing that collective apparatus and cooperation will eventually prevail and benefit people, which can devolve and turn the suppressor class into an endangered species.

People are ceaselessly facing violence, unjustified wars, genocide, terrorism, massive displacement from their homeland (refugees), consumption of genetically modified food and chemically ridden ingredients, sexual abuse, massive economic fraud, redacting truth, market monopoly, structural income disparity, spying, extortion, rigged elections, scamming, illegal insider trading, twisted and implicit racial inequality, lack of empathy, police brutality, undermining democracy, mass incarceration of the oppressed since they have to keep 90% occupancy to reach the targeted profit, anti-social behavior, as they act so oblivious to the struggle of the disadvantaged and so much other atrocious and malicious conduct baked into the ideological premises and institutional practices, which have evidently become the tools of trades for the global economic mafia. Let the courage become contagious to state the undeniable truth to the powerful, where the power of logic and reasoning should be evermore present to fuel against financial bullies of our time and to overcome this gargantuan corporate maneuverability, which is hideously designed to undermine people and adamant to confiscate the wealth of the nation. And unfortunately, when people justify the concentration of so much wealth in the hands of the few, then the conglomerate media labels them with warmongering and class warfare, in which the institutional control so unreasonably kicks in to quell and suffocate any progressive movement in its infancy.

We ought to know life is about balance and moderation, the accumulator of wealth realizes that: Their deliberate action can bring destruction to an entire nation, but they still persist on carrying out with hording so much wealth, which abnormally differentiates and classifies people, causing a very wide gap in social classes and hierarchical system with huge income disparity between the haves and the have-nots, while ignoring treacherous social, financial, legal, and political consequences. And unless societies are educated to indiscriminately follow a moderate economic system, so that humanity willingly gives up this ugly trait of greed and carelessness about other fellow human beings, trouble will consistently behold us. And if you think one cannot make a difference, then think of Gandhi, Abraham Lincoln, the Dalai Lama, Nelson Mandela, Mother Teresa, Martin Luther King Jr., Roosevelt, Sir Isaac Newton, Thomas Edison, Albert Einstein, or Mao, and for the worst, Hitler, Stalin, and Mussolini, and so on. We should also remember that we can never be apart from God, nature, and humanity; when we choose to separate people and segregate human beings, people act indifferently toward each other and animosity starts to break loose in which we pay a heavy price. Review the history and let's meditate on that. So many are at peace and profess to have faith and hope for a better situation without making any attempt to correct undesirable issues while billons are hungry and struggle to barely stay alive.

Camus wrote: Life is a struggle for Camus, Sisyphus typified all human beings in Greek methodology of pushing the huge rock upward, only to roll back down before reaching the peak. Again pushing the rock each time, and the struggle itself toward the height is enough to fill a man's heart. One must imagine Sisyphus' happiness. We must find meaning in a world that is unresponsive or even cruel and hostile to us. What Camus believed affirms life choosing to go back down the hill and pushing the rock again and again, only to relapse each time, as life is a constant struggle and unending battle that should be the core of our satisfaction. And yes life can be harsh and human beings are intelligently equipped to collectively deal with some of the difficulties life and Mother Nature throw at them, but Camus' anecdote and millions other motivational prospects like it should not be interpreted as bearing manufactured scenarios as designed to exploit and enslave billions, making them sitting ducks for the sake of maintaining the insanely luxurious lifestyle of the few.

People need to know the everyday stressful lifestyle does project its morbid effects on billions, victimizing so many by cutting their very lives short or in making them very ill and bedridden with no viable solution for this way of life and culture of madness. It forces people to work stringently hard, making their lifestyle very difficult, so that the top 1%, their lackeys, and the fascist puppet governments can so unjustly rule the entire world. We ought to know mental anguish and agitated state of mind, especially financial distress can pressure our body, where adrenal glands produce cortisol; the levels in the blood may become elevated in response to physical or psychological agony induced by unbearable lifestyle. It is a hormone known as the "fight or flight hormone." It does help our body and mind to have an extra boost to deal with a rough and dangerous situation. When we are entangled physically, mentally, and psychologically and are in a worrisome position, cortisol is induced to remedy a seemingly unresolvable dilemma. Or when we are sad and in a state of sorrow or shocked for any reason, our body responds producing cortisol "so to speak also known as a relief remedy." That is secreted in our blood to mollify and to make it less harsh and bearable to an extent.

When we put our body under too much pressure and stress, either physically or mentally, the brain does not recognize the difference, and either way releases cortisol. But we should know too much of anything is damaging and would not be good or pleasant for you. This is why sometimes you hear that, so and so athlete died or was transferred to hospital because of too much physical exertion or exaggerated physical activities or getting too excited, which when cortisol is overproduced; not only does it not mitigate the dismal situation, but it simply compounds the hazardous risk, increasing the probabilities of heart stoppage. Cortisol hormone is also produced when the human digestive system has to put up with so much bad consumption, especially with chemically induced and genetically modified, processed food. And because masses of people cannot afford organic wholesome ingredients, then troubles amalgamate when eating too much bad food with no time to exercise or mobile enough for our body to burn the cortisol off; so many are involved in sedentary office work repeating the same chore for years, which increases their stress level for the worse. When the cortisol hormone stays in our body it makes us obese. It is scientifically known that the cortisol level in our body is correlated with stress, fat, and obesity. High level of this hormone makes us overweight if no activities are done to curb and burn it off.

It is always good to have faith, but it is much better to have faith and believe in the might of reasoning, to apply logic in assessing what we should do and how we need to sensibly execute things and what positive things should we expect when putting our glorious mind to work.

We must let the charlatans know we are not acting only on faith but also acting on powerful wisdom to prove them wrong. Because they are so cunning and surreptitious and would immediately know when we act only based on faith and hope that tides will turn our way, and they detect when we utilize our intelligence to literally turn the table to our advantage.

They immediately comprehend there are high probabilities that we decide based on emotion and function irrationally, which gives them the very upper hand they need that consequently places so many helpless people in a very awkward and entangled position where they do not belong. It is clear that multinational corporate monopolies need to break up and let market practice true competition, or for public ownership to take over the private power structure that has rendered the market static and obsolete, except for few oligopolies, which are diametrical to let the real producer of wealth to prosper.

It is true that having faith alone not only is not enough, but will make an illusion of confidence, as we should have faith, but avoid being misled, since the premises and the cultures in which we are interacting are about self-interest, where many act egotistical and follow the ruthless maxim of a cutthroat environment.

The only time I do not need to acquire or challenge the circumstances with rationality is when I am alone and meditating with our creator, our supreme being, the omnipotent and the almighty God. Knowing there is no expectancy from this very powerful and potent source but giving love, as it is so magically justified.

This is when I surrender myself to faith because I feel serenity of mind, body, and spirit, knowing I am being exuded with true love and happiness from the divinity. Knowing nothing, and I mean absolutely nothing, is biased and prejudiced in our relation with the divine and sanctified God.

Further evolution in mind expansion and human genius is the only captivating force exultant enough to substantiate enlightenment in distinguishing actual right from wrong and to dedicate one's life for practicing justifiable means in God's itinerary path, which can manifest light at the end of the tunnel. And to recognize manufactured and fake propaganda that is targeted to construe brainwashing the masses for lobbying the majority of votes to objectify what is not true. They are adamant in practicing treacherous behaviors under the name of God and the zeal for more profit. The globally dominated system knows no boundaries in acting precarious and demonic; it is strongly influenced by greed and violence exercising moral turpitude and misconduct, which has morphed into behaving schizophrenic, utterly numb to the environment, of suffering, of the destitute and wretched condition of the helplessly poor.

This should emphatically remind us to capitalize on what makes us human beings to educate and strengthen us with belief in God, to nourish our mind with the spirit of goodness, to act intelligently rational and competent enough to learn barbarism appears in a variety of forms, not to exclude financial tyranny imposed on the innocent, which sure catches billions off-guarded as so many get caught against the savage waves of monetary depression, nimbly architected to give them the kiss of death and discard them as collateral damage. Another word we must thrive to bring out is the best in us, which should leave no excuse for any system of governing to abuse and unaccountably enforce their power in the name of the people; otherwise it makes governments utterly necessary, since no man is an angel. As James Madison puts it: "If men were angels, no government would be necessary." But a government must follow a strict code of conduct that is morally and virtuously applicable to each and every one of its public servants. Their purpose should be to efficiently serve people who help to put them in power. The system is obligated to mandate plans and programs which follows a doctrine that: Believes in wisdom, education, decency, sincerity, gratitude, consideration, respect, dignity, attentiveness, supportive and helpful, encouraging, cooperating, prudency, active participation, good judgment, invigorating, having good fiscal, and social sound policies, to believe in diversity, ethics, virtue, positivity, integrity, reliability, creativity, trustworthiness, dependability, caring, listening, persistency, justice and fairness, equity, accountability, responsibility, honor, loyalty, peace and tranquility, freedom and democracy, human and civil right, compassion, transparency, truth, due process of the law, acts consistence. This is also competent to brilliantly negotiate and appropriately manifest viable strategies to make friends across the globe and not enemies and above all believe in God. To make the entire body of governing run smoothly and to meet its inhabitants' need to the best of their knowledge and ability, where no one is biased, discriminated against, or left behind. I know it perhaps reminds us of a piece of heaven, but it is sure possible if we put our mind to it. We possess the attributes and the means to make a just world possible.

The system should act responsible to encourage the prevalence of an enlightening culture of novelty and to permeate the socioeconomic atmosphere with wise planning and through a constructive educational system and to modulate programs conducive to human nature for the common good and better living. Because the system is well-aware that people are influenced by their surroundings and subject to what they are taught as they are the products of their habitat relatively. In today's world, even the furthest dwellers are unquestionably affected by cultural interactivities, financial and political decisions, making of the mighty influential elements of the international community in which a conglomerate media monopoly acts like a mercenary devoted to the spread of unjustified news, which is highly leveraged to sharply influence so many people through modern telecommunication and technological innovations.

We possess advance industries that can unfold thoughtful activities; we are able to disclose helpful breakthroughs and information via dynamic ways of communication. I believe this trend of action is soon going to be directed and progress toward a globally induced society, in which the boundaries are collapsing and will head on to constitute one system of government and one nation under God. Murray Gell-Mann in complexity, science, system, said, "Today the network of relationships linking the human race to itself and to the rest of the biosphere is so complex that all aspects affect all others to an extraordinary degree. Someone should be studying the whole system, however crudely that has to be done, because no gluing together of partial studies of a complex nonlinear system can give a good idea of the behavior of the whole."

An effective system of ruling should dig into a host of vital issues indigenous to people's existence. It should plow into human activities and discourage immoral temperament and malfunctions, avoid misdeeds, and other ill characteristics and vile personality makeups, ingratiated with greed for accumulating material wealth and power, which sometimes makes an environment of grotesque inequalities, forcing many to believe in the "survival of the fittest" attitude and a cutthroat society, where human lives and dignity are neglected, as an atmosphere of crime, violence, corrupt, and insatiable bodily joy becomes synchronized and accepted as the norm in our lives. Are violence and a culture of savagery meant to entertain us? As it is prevalent despite societal alluding to cosmetic civility and in resuming a theater-like lifestyle.

The system should aim to correct those who illegally hoard billions of dollars at the top with devious intent and disgraceful conduct, which since has replace God in their lives. And because wrongdoings have denied many from their self-worth and depleted them from behaving decent with righteous attributes. It should warn us that mega-capitalists are never a good judge of what is good for society, and when unleashed, they will not hesitate a minute to crush everything in their path to make an extra buck. In one of his speeches, President Reagan stated, "we are going to place the bear in permanent hibernation, and turn the bulls loose." And they did, turning the bulls loose and unquestionably backing the conglomerate corporations, which resulted in merging mega corporations that stampede the working class, the middle class, and the very poor, since none of them escaped being horned right in their guts. As so many victims still have not recuperated to this date from the sharp and deep wound they suffered, in which too many did not even survive to make it since this wrong and inadequate financial policy was enforced, giving the green light to a handful of corporations to gobble everything and leave the majority of the entire nation with zilch and to ingest their own saliva. The system needs to mollify the concept of the "you are on your own" philosophy and avoid extreme individualistic culture, where "the survival of the wisest" and not "the survival of the fittest" can lead to collective intelligent property and prosperity for all, rather than promoting self-centeredness through mischievous and cynical behaviors and irrational conduct with braggadocio attitude. Predators devour their victims as they exhibit the most unrestrained and inhumane actions in the name of ethical business and self-interest.

Corporate elites cultivate predatory conduct; they hunt their prey with impunity and because of no repercussion facing them, as if their barbaric practices and ferocious manhunt and civil disobedience should be rewarded and accepted as natural as gravity and nature itself.

The corporate plutocracy somehow believes no better living is ever possible without their incredulous and incriminating ways of dealing with society and in the name of a free market economy that has already caused so much damage beyond repair.

Fundamentally speaking, the market economy is hostile and not user-friendly since it creates irresolvable crises and often is impossible to troubleshoot. This oligopolistic capitalist system defined as "from Ancient Greek (olígos), meaning "few", and (polein), meaning to sell, is a market form in which a market or industry is dominated by a small number of sellers (oligopolies). Oligopolies can result from various forms of collusion, which reduces competition and leads to higher prices for consumers. Oligopoly has its own market structure.

It cannot align with human nature; it is alien to public welfare since it is tightly controlled by the financially elite and the powerful few, as it causes fear and anxiety, misallocation of resources, extreme income inequality, stress, depression, and a host of other psychological disorders, violence, which is the most prevalent and often originated because so many come to the brink of a life and death situation. So many simply cannot afford to live anymore and are pushed to risk everything to stay alive, again because of the privatization of the means of production and most natural and common resources, and profit is strictly manipulated by the few, which puts public and social welfare constantly at grave risk of survival. And instead of recognizing the malice of the economy and identifying with the problematic ruling system and to honorably renounce the shortcomings ingrained in the political and free market system facing them.

They so blatantly label social and public assistance as "handouts." Where millions of indigents are well suited for exclusive technical vocations if available and capable of becoming a productive member of society, but are utterly denied work and statically cast aside because of incompetency of the system to absorb them since it is unable to substantiate full employment. When a high magnitude earthquake registering above 7.0, strongly trembles and shakes out the floor you are standing on, where one's entire foundation is destroyed, it only makes sense to struggle to save loved ones and the self and struggle to survive; it is just in human nature. People must not be placed in desperate positions where they are forced to do wrong where they are compelled to barely hang onto life; it is just a plain bad policy. Do not give me the cock-and-bull story of "life is not fair." It has nothing to do with life being unfair and it has everything to do with a system that malfunctions and gets exponentially worse because of greed and ignorance, which looks and deals with human lives wasted as another statistic.

Let's dig into some of the mishaps as we need to figure out the root causes of the problems. We access our brain and try to act mindful for making sense of things, where the outcome accordingly differs because some are blessed with a higher IQ and relatively more potent intelligence than others, and since one's belief depends on one's level of understanding. It is not facetious when scientists say we are basically utilizing 7-10% of our brain capacity, which should mean roughly 90% is still gray matter bound to become explored. Yes, the human brain is very complex entity because it performs millions of elegant and magnificent sublunary (worldly) acts, but then if we could tap into the remaining 90%, perhaps would enable us to have telekinetic and novel (space age) power, which I am certain it would positively rub on our civility of mind and manner too. The 10% notion has been linked to the American psychologist and author William James, who argued in *The Energies of Men* that "We are making use of only a small part of our possible mental and physical resources." It's also been associated with Albert Einstein, who supposedly used it to explain his cosmic towering intellect.

The average human brain weighs about three pounds but uses 20% of its energy and comprises the hefty cerebrum, which is the largest portion and performs all higher cognitive functions; the cerebellum, responsible for motor functions, such as the coordination of movement and balance; and the brain stem, which keeps the brain awake and brisk (active). Human consciousness is applicable by an arousal system situated in the brain stem known as the "reticular activating system," which locates incoming sensory information through pathways of nerve fibers; this also sends activating signals via the midbrain to the cerebral cortex dedicated to involuntary functions, like breathing, posture, and hear rate. Information obtained from the senses or produced by thought is processed in many parts of the brain. Some parts are responsible for processing sensory data, like sight and sound, and other parts, like cortex and cerebellum, issue commands that create voluntary movement. The hypothalamus is an area that contains a number of small nuclei with a variety; it is the size of an almond in humans. In concert with the pituitary gland, these nuclei monitor and regulate our body temperature, our sleep-wake cycle, blood flow, water and salt in our body, hormonal activities, and determine our response to other crucial activities and emotions, such as fear and anger. Majority of the energy consumed by the brainpower, the rapid firing of millions of neurons communicating with each other. Scientists think it is such neuronal firing and connecting that gives rise to all the brain's higher functions. The rest of its energy is used for controlling other activities—both unconscious activities, such as heart rate and conscious ones, such as driving a car.

Some scientists say that although it's true that at any given moment all of the brain's regions are not concurrently firing, brain researchers using imaging technology have shown that, like muscles, most parts are continually active over a 24-hour period. "Evidence would show over a day you use 100% of the brain," says John Henley, a neurologist at the Mayo Clinic in Rochester, Minnesota. Even in sleep, areas such as the frontal cortex, which controls things like higher level thinking and self-awareness, or the somatosensory areas, which help people sense their surroundings, are active, Henley explains. Take the simple act of pouring coffee in the morning: In walking toward the coffeepot, reaching for it, pouring the brew into the mug, leaving extra room for cream, the occipital and parietal lobes, motor sensory, and sensory motor cortices, basal ganglia, cerebellum, and frontal lobes all activate.

A lightning storm of neuronal activity occurs almost across the entire brain in the time span of a few seconds. "This isn't to say that if the brain were damaged that you wouldn't be able to perform daily duties," Henley continues. "There are people who have injured their brains or had parts of it removed who still live fairly normal lives, but that is because the brain has a way of compensating and making sure that what's left takes over the activity." Being able to map the brain's various regions and functions is part and parcel of understanding the possible side effects should a given region begin to fail. Experts know that neurons that perform similar functions tend to cluster together. For example, neurons that control the thumb's movement are arranged next to those that control the forefinger. Thus, when undertaking brain surgery, neurosurgeons carefully avoid neural clusters related to vision, hearing, and movement, enabling the brain to retain as many of its functions as possible.

The myth's durability, Gordon says "stems from people's conceptions about their own brains: they see their own shortcomings as evidence of the existence of untapped gray matter, this is a false assumption, what is correct, however, is that at certain moments in anyone's life, such as when we are simply at rest and thinking, we may be using only 10% of our brains. Evidence would show over a day you use 100% of the brain."

Says John Henley, a neurologist at the Mayo Clinic in Rochester, Minnesota. Even in sleep areas, such as the frontal cortex, which controls things like higher level thinking and self-awareness, or the somatosensory area (being sensory activity having its origin elsewhere than in the special sense organs as eyes and ears), which helps people sense their surroundings, are active. He said, "What's not understood is how clusters of neurons from the diverse regions of the brain collaborate to form consciousness. So far, there's no evidence that there is one site for consciousness, which leads experts to believe that it is truly a collective neural effort. Another mystery hidden within our crinkled cortices is that out of all the brains cells, only 10% are neurons; the other 90% are glial cells, which encapsulate and support neurons, but whose function remains largely unknown. Ultimately, it's not that we use 10% of our brains merely that we only understand about 10% of how it functions."

I believe when Dr. John Henley neurologist Doctor John Henley refers in using our one-handed% of brain use, He is indicating the 100% usage of the 10% available, which Einstein was able to manifest when he discovered his famous relativity equation; because if history and evolution are to be adequately acknowledged, then I am sure no cave man or our processors from stone and dark ages could sure have access 10% of their brain, if so then, we should accept that our modern and relative civilized world is just an illusion, and we have not advanced and progressed a bit in our evolutionary brain. Besides, also it is noteworthy to fathom this fact that some people are smarter than others, which should denote higher IQ signifying their expansion in brain cells validating their openness in mind and intelligence. I also believe much of the grey area not in use, is not just going to forever lay there idle, it is eventually going to be pushed to its limit. And it would make more sense for prominent scientists and neurologist to realize that: consciousness is cosmic energy and not the byproduct of any particular part of our physical brain, no wonder it cannot be located anywhere in our brain, as neurologist John Henley states.

Further and with all due respect I am only investigating statistics and numbers, no rudeness or impropriety directed at anyone at all. But then, the provocative question should foment wonder and alert us into investigating human insightfulness to why we behave the way we do. Let's say animals are credited with only using 1% of their brain, and since not everyone is gifted to truly manifest the absolute 10% and within its full capacity, then relativity speaking some should proportionally enact their intellect and savviness of their mind perhaps a tad higher than animals, since some could be trapped and framed in lower percentage rate of mindfulness.

And let's even assume it is the overall 10% mentality which is reflecting our societal reasoning and contemporary to the activities of governing body.

If so, then why should anyone be surprise or shocked and in state of awe when we decimate millions of our kind in genocide manner, or behave malevolent toward the helpless innocent with antiquated immigration laws, with hugely widened inequality, and extreme class derivative culture, and so forth. After all we still have 90% of uncharted territories that must be urgently cultivated, which by the way westerners claim to be the cream of the crop, if so, God help us with the rest. And why urgent, because we have the mentality very close to beasts that are in control of hydrogen bombs, atomic bombs, bacterial and chemical bombs, cluster bombs, and so on, since they with no doubt can end the life as we know it. So what is the point, the point is that the conductors of this evil empire refer people's misfortune and miseries to God's doing and insinuate a colossal lie that it is the God's will to destine each and every one of us, as some people are blessed since God favors them, and some are not, what a hoax. What kind of God would he then be, which wouldn't have been called a dictator, if God was to put his nose into every bit of decision which man was to make. If God was to interfere 24/7 in everything and all of what we decide to do; then, I am certain no one would have agreed and consented to such oppression and blatant control.

Instead the almighty knowing of all the best, gifted and endowed human beings with a marvel of an entity called "the god of brain and the god of mind" and has left the scene which can accomplish miracles if rightly utilized and manifested. And this is how we should know that human beings are created free, since our creator does not meddle with the things we do, the choices we make and our being free since our creator does not mess with our freedom and the will to choose.

If God made us to be self- governed, why then any man in his right mind should dare to take our autonomy away, or infringe in our sovereignty. The sinister issue is that no amount of intelligence, brilliancy and creativity, or any other positively decisive factor can decisively operate in a magnificent and productive manner, when the entire global resources and economic system is tightly controlled and scrutinized by few financial tyrants of the world which will implement the language of force and bully anyone or any constructive network or group through policing and militarizing where they deem necessary; which dissidents with different views, or other trend of thought and action would face persecution and retribution if not compliance with their policies, and perhaps is not in accord with their way of implementing exclusive plans, which is meant to keep them in absolute power. There is a saying that: "People who lose from change hold all the power, and the people who will gain from change have no power."

Rumi the Persian poet said quote: "why do you stay in prison, while doors are wide open." Our God left doors open, we can choose to be stalemated, we can crawl, we can walk, or even choose to run, with enough light, accomplish miracles if rightly utilized and manifested. And this is how we should know that human beings are created free, since our creator does not meddle with our being free, and does not mess with our freedom and the will to choose.

There are powerfully notorious elements and influential networks which support this nefarious global system acting as mercenaries.

Mercenaries, they do come in many shape and form, they participate in murdering innocent people and assassinating oppositions. They serve merely for wages and have no principle, and since act with no conscious.

Other kind of mercenaries are the lackeys of corporations, they come in form of media play, as they first bellow the horn of propaganda, misleading the public, and softening the road for godfathers of crime and their mischievous conducts in the name of profit and for accumulating more wealth fueled with spilling blood, where ever deemed necessary.

Joseph Pulitzer said quote: "A cynical, mercenary, demagogic press will in time produce a people as base as itself."

They act profoundly undemocratic and without the consent of people, since they implement covert missions with significant wrong doing. The main stream media funded by multi-national corporations propagate scripted narratives to brainwash people into complicit partners to act nonchalant and indifference toward the most outrages deceptive practices of the system, as if people are experiencing twilight zone.

And Henry A. Wallace said quote: "A fascist is one whose lust for money or power is combined with such an intensity of intolerance toward those of other races, parties, classes, religions, cultures, regions or nations as to make him ruthless in his use of deceit or violence to attain his ends."

Then, we are faced with the worst kind of mercenaries, which are religious mercenaries, for them God is an excuse to reach their filthy objectives. They are fake at heart and malignant in nature, since they behave hypocritical and aim at raping and murdering in the name of Allah (God). Which should alert freedom loving people to stay away from being dragged into the war of religion, because that is what they are after, the war of ideology where doctrines of many denominations are to supposedly clash and to eventually slaughter millions of innocent lives under the allegiance and duty for one's faith.

These culprits and the messengers of hate, they are ignorant enough not to realize humanity has reached the age of awakening, and will not be mouse trapped into medieval cultural of thinking, and enslaved by their dirty scheme; since wise and Conscious able people of the world are enlightened enough to take side with democracy, liberty, and human rights as they will stand united to protect lives and the pursuit of happiness.

Dalai Lama said quote: "There is no need for temples, no need for complicated philosophies. My brain and my heart are my temples; my philosophy is kindness."

And Yehuda Berg wonderfully said it, quote: "I do believe that the original sources of all religions should be taught, because with that we will find our similarities, not just our differences. I believe that if Mohammed, Buddha, Jesus, and Moses all got together they would be best of friends because the spiritual basis of all religions is something that builds unity."

These mercenaries of evil disseminate fear and choke off the opposition, no matter how significant and justified are the opposition in their decent demand for a better life. They have premeditated to obliterate anyone and anything which stands against their horrifying ways of bringing up the so-called "orderly world."

They cannot get it that modern man is adamant to get rid of back warded ways of living, and to ward off Stone Age mentality, since he is decisive to eradicate the culture of superstition, and therefore, persevered in adapting to a new way of life, which accords with the dynamics of 21st century and its ruling.

Mahatma Gandhi said quote: The essence of all religions is one. Only their approaches are different.

Many saints rightly believe quote: "However many holy words you read, however many you speak, what goodwill they do you if you do not act on upon them?"

Even our educational system is being hijacked as cultural propagators, educators, teachers, and the entire literacy administrators are molded into misrepresenting the truth.

The next crucial question should be whether there is hope, where we can reach light at the end of the tunnel; of course yes, but we must first employ a system adamant to bring about changes that are user-friendly for human beings and their environment. To be more precise, not to support a system of government that permits and even encourages private mega-corporations to make trillions by selling armaments to savage and barbarian regimes limited with one percentage usage of their brain cell murdering innocents and the unarmed. There is a big problem. When a governing regime allows private enterprises to pollute the air we breathe and contaminate the water we drink, and it allows exterminating biodiversity, then charges a skyrocketing prices to seek medical help and charges money to sell water to famine and drought stricken indigenous people, then we should know that we have an enormous problem. When trash fields are controlled by so to speak entrepreneurs and smaller companies that charge a fee to let the poor sequester clean food and clothing from the garbage to feed and cover themselves, we must know there is huge problem. When we witness millions of refugees who have been militarily invaded and camp out in the desert barricaded with no shelter, with no food or any amenities, we should know we have a big problem. When there are the largest number of prisoners incarcerated in dire condition and inhumane correctional facilities that feed private institutions to maximize profit in the name of compromising public safety, since crime is going rampant, we need to know we have problem.

When we have an economic system destroying Earth, the environment, and makes mass extinctions of species, exterminates biodiversity and the ecosystem, which we are tightly attached to and inseparable from and calls it "economic externalities" at people's expense, putting everyone's lives in grave danger through acting nature deficit disorder; since it does not factor these life-threatening and horrifying destruction into their corporate cost, then, we should know they are declaring war on nature and humanity. It is a neurosis culture that is in denial since it boycotts humanity from its natural habitat and separates them from all of what nature has to offer, which sustains us and the future generation, then we should know we have a definite problem. When they link human happiness to the unconditional, relentless consumption, and unending growth, since they foster people's mentality and mindset as if this is quite natural, where the matrix of humanity and identity is measured only by the accumulation of wealth and material hording, then we know we have a serious problem. When we comprise 5% of the world's population, but have 30% of the world's prisoner population, then we need to know we have a problem. It should be expected from correctional facilities that operate by taxpayers' money to deal and connect to inmates through professional entities, where the prisoners have a chance to be dealt with therapeutically and through correct psychoanalysis approach, since they should be taught to be emotionally honest and willing to look inward, to be "mindful" of their emotional reactions. And to question whether those reactions are coming from within ourselves, rather than wrongfully judging others with a biased eye, which perhaps has nothing to do with the way one feels.

Where pride and not acting macho or ostentatious (pretentious) and not behaving in certain ways should not mean emasculating because many are emotionally unable to deal with their aggression and sometimes exhibit outrageous conduct without professional help, as they are faced against the odds and a culture of violence that is shamelessly promulgated and encouraged inside those hideous prisons, which victimizes many who are sincerely seeking a way out of crime-infested environments and their miserable situation with no avail. They manifest emotional honesty, looking for a way out of jail, but feel guilt, as they are labeled weak, making them vulnerable preys of rape and other inhumane atrocities. Only the culture of force and manhandling rules inside those despicable cells and the so-called "correctional" facilities, which fear rules and force is predominantly the norm and since we should honestly know we have a serious problem.

I am afraid many keep quiet because they are oblivious to stark rancorous (antagonistic) financial disparities forced on people, or they are well off and not wanting to notice the unprofessional, deceitful, and wicked financial cover-ups that are not clear and conspicuous to the common man, as the rich keep getting richer and the poor become poorer. Hence, multitudes of precarious effects and misconducts escalate further, hurting billions globally for the worst and often beyond repair. It will help if we pay attention to the corporate capitalists and gigantic multinational firms that unethically delve into human subliminal terrain and unscrupulously devise their hideous plans, which creeps into the realm of our subconscious mind and subtly manages to overwhelm our thinking brain and conscious thoughts without having a clue. I adamantly believe our subconscious mind is deliberately bombarded with a sophisticated and intricate conditioning mechanism, driving people into bewildered state of thought and action and for the wrong reasons.

This transgression of behavior has molded our brain and burden our mind into a web of uncertainties and mental defects, making so many vulnerable to ever more consumption and addicting consumerists who act stoic and nonchalant to others' squalid living conditions and pain and suffering. It seems our mind is hypnotized and possessed by extraterrestrial agents into helplessness, cluttered with negative and trivial issues beyond our will, which has turned our conduct impervious to virtue and has globally manifested a very sick environment, comprising it to become culturally chaotic, financially desperate, and socially and environmentally tragic, which is in need of desperate repair.

This ongoing pejorative (insulting, derogatory) cascade of actions is not going to halt unless enlightened and courageous people collectively are inspired to seek justice and push for a better world. Einstein said, "The world is a dangerous place to live, not because of the people who are evil, but because of the people who don't do anything about it." We ought to know that our brain is interactively wired into a single monumental and conscious able entity. We forget we are a unified biological and mental organism qualified for existence, engulfed with cosmic and spiritual realm, and part of a destined universe premeditated with purpose, clearly mandated and objectified to reach its destiny.

Humanity needs to accordingly defy these vicious circles of manufactured and sickly cause and effect that are strayed and derailed from what is right, making our curriculum for survival infested with fear. The system needs to stop controlling us like we are wild animals, telling us there is no life outside the corporate capitalists, as the "survival of the fittest" mentality should be the norm where the meanest and the most horrible souls are to kill and exploit and commoditize everything, including human life to the point of exhaustion and collapse. Anything outside of their pillaging ways and ruthlessness is not cool. Defining their kind of civilization, science, selfish gene theory, social and biological Darwinism, which should rule; those with correct jaw lines and manufactured lies about advanced revolutionized head and scalp are anatomically structured as advanced and should be regarded as the embodiment of nobility and intelligence, hence they are from a superior and preferred race, while others have yet to mature from the caveman mentality and their physical and biological shortcomings. And because other ethnic and indigenous natives were considered between human and animals, which deserved to die. Since they did not have the intelligence to become duly compliant and civilized, as the Europeans exterminated millions of indigenous people, marking them as savages. So did happen this tragedy of action with Indians in North America in a genocidal manner that of course was a made up hoax, where capitalists could annex and steal all the natural resources, which they meant to enslave the inhabitants by putting them to work just like animals to produce valuable raw material and vital natural resources for the rich to plunder. They also made sure to discipline people so that there is no salvation and any life worth living after they die outside the church. They perpetuate this notion of individualism and perpetrate people to believe in the hierarchical culture and the systematic powers of God, spirit, angels, profits, religious, kings, queens, the country, men, women, minorities, indigenous people, animals, trees and plants, and non-animated beings. Infusing toxic thoughts and notions into our thought process to divide and conquer us, as they have, where no peace and justice and a life worth living is ever possible. It shouldn't be an enigma to figure out a system that is run by the rich and the elites generates hundreds if not thousands of ways to addict people into money-making machines, turning them into habituation puppets with trouble oriented issues like drugs, gambling, alcoholism, shopping, hoarding, sex, pornography, gluttony, and so on. The system is very good at temporarily treating the symptoms, but so hideously feeding the root causes of actual troubles; it is not an exaggeration to say we live in an addicted society where everyone is addicted to something, and no one is immune. To make matters worse, they throw people off by lecturing them with gibberish, making people delusional into believing addictions are hereditary and perhaps a miracle should occur to make one an addiction-free member of society. They know when you incarcerate and put one in solitary confinement long enough; one starts to hallucinate, and basically go crazy, losing his mind, as simple as that, because we are group animals and cannot survive alone. This should awaken every caring soul to realize the vitality and the urgency of working together and as a co-op to deal with corporate power and cancerous based society, which they have created. So that they can rule us with cruelty; it is time to prove capitalists' conniving ways and deceptive practices need to stop, and they need to start to do good in the name of God, humanity, and self-worth. First by stopping the mass propaganda in class-based ideologies and pushing for an ever more dividing mindset, which might have been permeated by the systems into many societies, leaving horrifying effects. Second, to stop this monstrous behavior that everything is for the grab in the name of profit, including human life and decency, through deceptive trades and war of aggression.

According to Nick Harkaway, the Blind Giant:

"Like casinos, large corporate entities have studied the numbers and the ways in which people respond to them. These are not con tricks—they're not even necessarily against our direct interests, although sometimes they can be—but they are hacks for the human mind, ways of manipulating us into particular decisions we otherwise might not make. They are also, in a way, deliberate undermining of the core principle of the free market, which derives its legitimacy from the idea that informed self-interest on aggregate sets appropriate prices for items. The key word is 'informed'; the point of behavioral economics—or rather, of its somewhat buccaneering (pirate, freebooter) corporate applications—is to skew our perception of the purchase to the advantage of the company. The overall consequence of that is to tilt the construction of our society away from what it should be if we were making the rational decisions classical economics imagines we would, and toward something else."

It seems no matter how we thrive for a bit of happiness, it is with no avail, as we are still bonded and fettered within the range of draconian circumstances, and not free from the pipelines of uncertainties and anxieties facing ill-maneuvers directed at the very core of our nervous system. And hence, vanquishing the sovereignty of our mind, infusing it with ceaseless irrational thoughts and deceitful mental exercises where they manage to play us like a professional guitar player, literally in control of the frequencies of its instrument and in how it should vibrate, so that the 1% which hold onto 75-80% of the resources can hold onto this inhumane income inequality, turning people into sociopaths, agents which exercise toxic ideas against each other, with antisocial values created by the elites and the ruling class. We ought to be awakened and fight back intelligently and challenge these brood of evils not by hate mongering conduct but by becoming more educated, through inference and the power of reasoning since further evolution in mind expansion and human genius is the only captivating force exultant enough to substantiate enlightenment in distinguishing actual right from wrong and to dedicate one's life for practicing justifiable means in God's itinerary path, which can manifest the light at the end of the tunnel. And to recognize manufactured and fake propaganda that is targeted to construe brainwashing the masses for lobbying the majority of votes to objectify what is not true. They are unifying and adamant in practicing treacherous behaviors under the name of God and the zeal for more profit. A globally dominated system knows no boundaries in acting precarious and demonic, since it is strongly influenced by greed and violence exercising moral turpitude and misconduct, which has morphed them into behaving schizophrenic, utterly numb to the environment of suffering of the destitute and wretched condition of the helplessly poor.

Institutional ideologies of sociopathic behaviors are emanated and reinforced into larger environment as the norms, which propagates and pursues self-interest as the only good at the very core of the morality of the system. Since into the system's eye only the individual exists, which pushes so many to act psychopathically violent toward the natural resources, the environment, exploitation of workers and child laborers, their competitors, and the consumers, and toward less powerful and less fortunate nations. Because to the corporate capitalists, nothing matters except profit, where unfettered growth drives their insatiable appetite to the point of exhaustion leveraged by toxic propaganda and through false advertising, which is backed up with corporate hegemonic militarism and inhumane apparatus. They have annihilated the societal and natural order by producing destructible products, which maximize their profit, and not directed at making public goods, which can positively change

214

the fate of nations for the better. They are nimble in improvising policies to divide people and polarize wealth, where few elites can control the rest of the citizens; they cosmetically uphold democratic features and fake elections since even the state resonates and gives in to their demands and illegal plans because of them bribing and because of money. This abusive trend of thought and behavior has pushed the society from class system to an entangled system, where the super-rich and the elites are suppressing workers that are the backbone of the capitalist system, which generates surplus values, that are the foundation to the corporate capitalist very existence.

The system should put an end to domestication of people, forcing them into the bottle to play genie at the command of the oligopolistic behavior of the few at the cost of billions of inhabitants made miserable. The poor are financially and mentally manipulated to function against their well-being, also conduit to degradation and destruction of the world and planet Earth.

The super-rich must wake up in the name of virtue and what is right to actively take part in what is necessary to change the course of the history in saving the planet and avoid change through bloodshed and violence. And people also need to intelligently realize it is not appropriate to throw the baby out with the bathwater because it makes sense to save what works and understand that any new system is born from the womb of the old one, making a new paradigm shift into expressing an innovated culture of thinking. To grasp that rich are not evil by nature, Hitler, Mussolini, and Stalin were demonic by nature, and to ask what honestly any one of us put in their position would do, if also weak, to harness human greed.

The actual problem stems of greed and self-centeredness, since by nature capitalism is divisible via polarization of wealth, which corporate oligopoly has demonized it to the extreme, leaving the have-nots with no choice but to fight back for their survival. Where any collective altruism is taken as a farce and barred from flourishing blocked by selfishness and self-interest manuals and dialogues and ill propagandas, which are taught in families, at schools, in communities, at work, and even in churches, and many other social and connective societal networks. This basically implements policies prone to possessing an attitude of do to mesh in or die in vain, even if it is not in one's character and attributes to act individualistic, one must blend in to make it. Since the ideology, the philosophy, the politics, and the cultural education of the system's entities work accordingly to uphold and honor the elites' view on how it should be done and for people to execute what they are told, and if they dare not to, they will be seen as not cool and perhaps an outcast or a rebel. It is so sad where a few so-called business pundits with so little information are playing God as they should make decisions to answer so much problem for billions of people that are facing realistic and irresolvable troubles beyond anyone's imagination, and to cast them as unfit, or imply that the rich are favored by God and the rest are destined to be anguished and helpless. What the rich elites forget is the tenacity of the masses for positive changes, which can make them erupt to triumph over economic repression and cruel behavior of the accidentally inherited financial moguls. The relentless purpose to free the poor should prevail for the deprived to reach their destiny where everyone can have the opportunity to grow and enjoy the fruits of one's labor and put an end to exploitation and prevent the mean moguls from confiscating what does not belong to them and save the world from further demolition and detractions. The pandemonium experienced by the innocent people of the entire globe does take place by the anonymity of the corporate system, where they unanimously have coup d'etat against the ordinary people of the world destroying the very means of people's subsistence in the name of modernity and economic growth. Yes it is possible to dream the impossible through peaceful means and to change the course of history where the next and the next, and so on, generation would not have to experience a pirate economy and a horrendously divided world, where the poor and people of color are not "implicitly biased" just because of who they are and people are hugged by a mothering hand of sacred nature to celebrate who they are, where color blindness is not an issue anymore, but the fortunate and the mighty are enlightened enough to be class conscious, and let everyone live without fear and anxiety, and actually have a future to be proud of, where no financial disparity, racial or color blindness, religious bias, gender or national superiority, or any other form of prejudice can exist or play a decisive role. It should not be beyond human comprehension to make a more justified world—just ask why and believe in a viable and progressive answer where the norms can be broken and your vision is extraordinary. This is how life works; we take initiatives toward the impossible, because we cannot thrive without the well-being of others. We can collectively accomplish what seems not possible, because we are connected to the universe and the entire cosmos. The future of course is challenging for sustaining projects and a culture of thinking that would let a capital paradigm shift in equality to substantiate, but curriculums toward such grave objectives need to be directed at designing plans now to make such a goal possible, perhaps the near future or for the next generation to come.

Here is what many politicians and economists so naively said about inequality. Published by Jason Welker under economic growth, incentives, income, income distribution, curve, market, poverty, goods, standard, taxes : "politicians and some economists like to argue that income inequality is not as evil as many people make it out to be, and that greater income inequality can actually increase the incentive for poorer households to work harder to get rich, contributing to the economic growth of the nation as a whole. Allowing the rich to keep more of their income, in this way, leads more people to want to work hard to get rich, as they will be able to enjoy the rewards of their hard work."

Jason Welker continues that, "The prevalence of income inequality in free market economies indicates that inequality may be the result of a market failure. Those who are born rich are more likely to become rich, while individuals who are born poor are more likely to live a life of relative poverty. In a 'free' market, it is believed, all individuals possess an equal opportunity to succeed, but due to a misallocation of resources in a purely market economy, this may not always be the case."

The resources I refer to here are those required for an individual to escape poverty and earn a higher income. These include public and merit goods that those with high incomes can afford to consume, while those in poverty depend on the provision of from the state, including: good education, dependable health care, access to professional networks and the employment opportunities they provide whenever a market failure exists. It can be argued that there is a role for government in regulating the market to achieve a more optimal distribution of resources. When it comes to income inequality, government intervention typically comes in the form of a tax system that places a larger burden on the rich and a system of government programs that transfer income from the rich to poor, including welfare benefits, unemployment benefits, health care for low income households, public schools, and support for economic development in poor communities.

Going back in time, the Great Depression in the United States started after a fall in stock prices that began around September 4, 1929, and made worldwide news with the stock market crash of October 29, 1929 (Black Tuesday). Between 1929 and 1932, the whole system was struggling to recuperate from catastrophic economic and social dilemmas facing it, which then at some point, the entire system was at the brink of war and potential for a bloodied and nasty revolution. President Franklin D. Roosevelt stepped in and mediated so that the rich could constructively spend some of their money to save the "profit system" or face a bloodied revolution, which then the capitalists would lose all their money. In the meanwhile, the rest of the world provided the core capitalist system of western Europe, North America, and Japan with very inexpensive natural resources, raw materials, and dirt cheap labor. After so long of brutal exploitation, the workers all over the world woke up and demanded a piece of the pie, which barely mitigated their miserable living conditions. This also gave birth to the liberal and middle class, and also made upper mobility relatively possible. Then, gradually, global and multinational corporations eliminated the fair competition since neo-colonist rule of law was established through the entire world, giving them access to other developing nations with rich natural resources, primary oil, gas, minerals, silver and gold, uranium, and so forth and with inhabitants' cheap labor.

Loyal dictatorial regimes and puppets were installed to implement the utter despotic rules of conducts by murdering, assassinating, torturing, raping, and long imprisonment of dissidents and against anyone seeking justice or any call for human rights. Even in America, the native Indians, Mexicans, Irish workers and their families, the Jews, blacks, Italian, and Japanese had to suffer tremendously before they were recognized, even taking a civil war between the south and the north, which claimed millions of lives, before establishing basic human dignity for all and the right to live where prejudice and discrimination were formally supposed to be abolished. We have reached an era where, unfortunately, the death of liberalism, which has been acted as a safety valve to save capitalism for so long, and the gradual wiping out of the middle class, which President Roosevelt worked so hard for and created, has basically desecrated the cushion which could have mitigated. Perhaps this will avoid the clash and the possibility of bloodied violence between the extremely rich class and the poor, facing brutal poverty, dissident to economic tyranny, and social political injustice imposed on them. And since has made so many cognizant enough to look for other viable economic systems to remedy their ill position through a social-democratic system of governing or a viable co-op system, an alternative to the capitalist system, which unfortunately delegates for the success of the few and not for the common good.

Co-ops and a social democratic economic system prioritize the affair of the society based on having adequate employment, proper education, decent housing, and practical medical, free public transportation, with an efficient financial safety net to back it up and kick in to protecting their citizens in times of need. Because a social democratic system is fueled with higher paid taxes, which then the resources are allocated appropriately, since the cultural architect and the socioeconomic infrastructures are fundamentally rooted to efficiently benefit people. As the entire resources are invested in the public sector to maximize return by producing competent and knowledgeable citizens that are not worried and frightened to death to lose their jobs, which some even commit suicide and enact host of criminal activities when losing their vocation and suddenly become devoid of their subsistence. Marcus J. Borg, in The God We Never Knew: Beyond Dogmatic Religion to a More Authentic Contemporary Faith, wrote, "The point is not that Jesus was a good guy who accepted everybody, and thus we should do the same (though that would be good). Rather, his teachings and behavior reflect an alternative social vision. Jesus was not talking about how to be good and how to behave within the framework of a domination system. He was a critic of the domination system itself."

In contemporary societies, quality education is not a right, but a prestige for the few, where education is scaled through politics and not influenced by skilled educators, where students are molded into what to think, rather than how to think, which this of course boils down to how to protect and preserve the very corporate capitalist system, keeping many unaware of life-changing opportunities and a better future. They know that true education and literacy is the most potent force in existence, which can relinquish viable knowledge and information to shake the core of deceptive practices of a decayed system of learning that exploiters are standing on.

Practical alternatives are a socialist democrat system, not in the form traditionally advocated through violence and bloodied revolution leveraged by proletariat dictatorship, but via peaceful transition and evolutionary processes where the activities of a social democrat government for the common good replaces the activities done by private corporate capitalists for the benefit of the few. Or via co-op institutions, where political and economic structures are peacefully shifted into collective ownership of workers. They are then elected as a board of directors entitled to one share one vote in a democratically elected environment, where transfer of wealth and productive forces into the hands of workers becomes possible, making the new realms of co-op business activities gradually replace the status quo. Let's side track into a co-op institution and briefly explain how it manages to operate.

Co-ops are imbued with humanitarian concept of doing business; its ideology is based on democracy at work, requiring collective participation of each worker with one share and one vote, solidifying the overall policy of the system's philosophy for common good and not aimed at maximizing profit for the few. The workers are the actual owner of the means of production and are members of a board of directors, which will decide what to produce, how to produce, where and when to produce, and what to do with the profit and the surplus values the workers themselves created. Kofi Annan said, "Founded on the principles of private initiative, entrepreneurship and self-employment, underpinned by the values of democracy, equality and solidarity, the co-operative movement can help pave the way to a more just and inclusive economic order."

Kofi Annan further said, "In an age where community involvement and partnerships with civil society are increasingly being recognized as indispensable, there is clearly a growing potential for cooperative development and renewal worldwide."

The nucleus and decency of the co-op system lays in the fact the no one is allowed to make 150-200 times more than other workers, making people's lives unbearable and almost impossible to keep up with rapid pace of inflation and recessionary criteria, since their wages are stagnated and not raised accordingly, where top executives, the elites, CEOs, and giant corporate owners make so much money, which creates horrifying inequality, making life living hell for the majority of inhabitants. Martin Filler, in art, force, building, said, "Despite the persistent image of the architect as a heroic loner erecting monumental edifices through sheer force of will, the building art has always been a highly cooperative enterprise."

The point is clear when the board of directors, which are the workers, are the actual voters, which must live with the decision they make; they will not vote to produce toxic products or pollute the water and the environment for worse since their family and loved ones also will bear the consequences of their dire decisions. They will not commend and practice outsourcing and transferring the company to foreign lands to minimize their cost and hence practically destroying the locals and communities for the sake of making more money for the few greedy individuals. Because the corporate capitalists know no boundaries, understand no limit, it is estranged to equity, does not believe in common good, but in maximizing profit. They believe in collective teamwork only to collect others' fruits of labor, and throwing them bones for subsistence, and to keep them barely alive to produce more for the boss's lavish lifestyle.

They devour and exploit nature and humanity to the point of exhaustion until collapsed with no remorse. In co-op, workers are self-administered and will make sure to implement democracy at work where the hallmark of the entire system is there are no major shareholders who can override good decisions made on behalf of the community. People at the bottom would be in charge of their own destiny and institutionalize the power of production and enjoy the surplus values, which is a fresh way of organizing our life for the better and in reaching dynamic and progressive goals.

Kent Conrad, States, Large, Land, said that: "There are large cooperatives all across this country. Land O'Lakes is a $12 billion club functioning all across America. There are rural electric co-ops in 47 states. Ace Hardware is a cooperative." With many taxi cab companies and bakeries across the land giving hope and future prosperity for all. Arthur Potts Dawson Food, Create, Growing, said, "We are stronger as a group than an individual. Think in a cooperative and communal way, set up local food hubs and create growing communities."

Boutros Boutros-Ghali said, "Co-operative enterprises provide the organizational means whereby a significant proportion of humanity is able to take into its own hands the tasks of creating productive employment, overcoming poverty and achieving social integration."

Workers owning their own companies at municipal institutions and co-ops, at credit unions, and so forth, with one share and one vote, a true democracy at work should happen peacefully from the local to state to national level. The evolutionary structure would gradually move from a system that is in decay, stagnated and in a state of deadlock to a genuine productive system of co-ops, which could actually save people and direct them to control their destiny. And to make sure progressive movements do not get caught in traditional socialist system or get deeper entangled in traditional capitalist system or even a communist system. But where a democratic economy run by workers for improvement of the communities can take place addressing the well-being of the very people and community producing the goods and services, since the surplus value and all the profit is to be prioritized and allocated for the common good and not spent privately by mob-like characters in a casino-like economy and wasted on no good deeds.

This historical exchange should occur with no violence and through civil actions and by peaceful means. Because innocent lives must not be wasted since corporate cultural of policing and repressive fascism can be instrumental with murdering, assassinations, torture, and imprisonment manifesting a totalitarian state of existence. This overhaul and constructive paradigm shift should occur from the local to state to federal level, where social and economic stagnation and deadlocks are able to change into dynamic productions and a new way of life to preserve humanity and what is right.

And because history has taught us when people are forced into deplorable living conditions by stalemated regimes and systems in decay, where the rights of citizens are trampled. They will learn their way out of their conundrum position and into a new social order, which unfortunately contemporary corporate capitalists are facing stagnation and chaos and turning into a mundane system of corporate oligarchy. But one should rest assured, ties will not positively turn unless aggressive legal and organized actions are taken, and for everyone to stand up for what is right and to reclaim the belief already ingrained into sociocultural ways of our life, seeking justice.

The new system should shed light on education, economy, employment, population control, decent housing, free public transportation, good public health system, clean environment, stop global warming by activating renewable energy and going solar, look into a zero carbon economy and to stop fossil fuel usage, to lower greenhouse effect, clean water, quality emigration laws, stopping all activities on atomic, chemical, bacterial wars, and halt cyber, and drone attacks, and to make other inhumane weaponries obsolete, stopping wars of aggression, unanimously acting in concert with the rest of the world to stop terrorism, halt police brutality, look into marriage and family laws, and to stop instigating and commoditizing females for profit, and eliminate sex industries and prostitution, where child sexual abuse and pedophilia is going rampant. And further investigates religious fanaticism, stop prejudice against minorities and women, and look into gun control.

We ought to know how damaging a decentralized free market economy and corporate capitalist enterprise system can be, if the role of multinational corporations and corporate oligopoly, which have put an end to fair competitive market and made the death of the so-called laissez-faire possible. The new system should goad into pluralism, social and cultural freedom, to uphold public sector responsibilities and to push for social democratic alliance and to leverage the economic system of co-ops. To mean and prioritize the right to live, liberty, and the pursuit of happiness for all, to insure human rights.

To challenge dictatorial regimes and terrorism, and to help and aim at unfolding perplex questions and concerns about God and divinity. Humanity needs to connect with their maker and for many to become liberated from the clutches of ignorance and incredulity (cynicism, attitude of habitual disbelief), grasping enlightenment and to enter into the realm of spirituality. It should remind us of Kant's argument in idealism, critical (Kant), refers to Kant's theory of knowledge. The essence of critical idealism is Kant's sharp distinction between what is given to us in our experience (sense impressionist) and the structures (forms of intuition and the categories) the mind uses to arrange, interpret, and evaluate that which is given.

Hence, our senses can enslave and exploit us with worldly pleasures and make us addicted to money, power, and influence, where we burn with desires to unleash ruthless behaviors in serving lower-selves and sometimes at the cost of destroying millions of people with no remorse. We ought to be reminded that every time we serve power and prestige and overlook inhumane self-conduct or ignore the tyranny of the system imposed on the innocents because of self-interest and what we also hold at stake. We disempower justice and cover up the truth against the fundamental rights of the republic, which sanctions so many from having to live the bare minimum, denying them a decent life and leaving them with no choice but to vigorously fight back. And rightly so, since the right to live and liberty for all is a stranglehold and has turned into just empty rhetoric and an opprobrious (derogatory, demeaning, insulting) slogan for billions, which are living a daily gradual death.

The fabric of diversity living and getting along in the name of compassion and humanity are insanely discouraged and fading away, where seeing each other as rivals is embarked on with a demonic portrait of black, white, brown, red, yellow, and so forth. These are exercised and accepted as the norms, perhaps not knowing it is the system that feeds and irrigates these cancerous diseases and toxic environment into good-natured people, mutating them into monsters against each other making many desolated from acting human. These expert psychologists, prominent social and political strategists, design dubious programs and intricate media controversies, where the technology of spreading news and information are broadcast and communicated in very subtle ways beyond the psyche of the common man to grasp many of the complex and troublesome programs and vicious outlets that are causing menacing and ugly attributes among people.

The mega corporate media have recidivism (falling back into bad behaviors), stifling the truth and manipulating the upper echelon of society into myopia and turning them into habitual fiction readers, rather that confronting and getting the populace to fight for so many tumultuous and covert matters created by the privileged class, entrapping us all into horrendous situations where decisive social discourse is ignored by making us actually believe politics is dirty, and it is best to stay away from politics, so just let's forget about it and go fishing and play golf. The plutocrat and their lackey corporate media place us exactly where they want us to be by keeping so many and especially the influenced people silent against their insidious and criminal activities.

We ought to know that we have reached an era where global consciousness is fertile enough to plant eye-opening seeds of enlightenment and realize that we have the potential to constructively cultivate and identify with each other from the perspective of humanity. And not through civil law violations and superiority complex and from looking at the world through narrow-mindedness and deliberately damnable (wicked) socioeconomic factors and cultural prejudices with entrenched racism. Since religious competition and many other manufactured ill agendas and troublesome issues, like ethnicity, sex, and class differences has forced masses of people into isolation and a caste system. Because corporately induced democracy is too ambiguous (doubtful, equivocal, inexplicable) and amply ambivalent (uncertain, self-questioning), which has created an atmosphere where the state has become a sole servant to private institutions, since even creating the public goods like free public education, health care, housing, decent employment, public transportation, clean air and water act, safe foods, paid vacation, and so forth are influenced by corporate elites for the worse. And the solution cannot be sought from the mainframe of a capitalist system, as no private enterprise is to created public goods or any goods at all without making maximum profit. But people are relentlessly persuaded by mega corporate media into believing that the only system efficiently feasible is the capitalist system, like it is ordained by God. It is a social economic system that can survive fake patriotism, class differences, militarism, and concentration of wealth, catastrophic wars, and the threat of nuclear biological war, divide and conquer, global warming catastrophe. Corporate oligopoly insists on individualism through ideological domination and conditioning, where everything and everyone is treated as objects to be exploited for making money. The solution to our problems is not more capitalism, because no abusive relationship is ever possible from a capitalist system, other than solely being taken advantage of and becoming commoditized to nourish the sociopathic behaviors the capitalist regime enacts to objectify making more money, no matter at what cost. We must also realize we evolve collectively by nature in dynamic ways, rather than operating separately and alone to bring quality social, economic changes. The good news is that people become receptive and resonant with what benefits them, mentally, spiritually, emotionally, and financially, rather than belittling them and turning them into producing machines through "division of labor" and assembly lines alienating them from their very beings and turning so many into robots specialized in producing a specific product and discarding them at the employer's prerogative.

The alternative in having a communist system is just too good to be true, which at this stage of our lives can only seem a utopia. Since our ideological belief system to rationalize such grave expectations have not yet matured enough to accept what Marx said about communism, he stated that communism comes after socialism and in this society, and there is full equality. That means there is no more state and no more money. Everything is run communally and owned by everyone, and there is no more scarcity. He also said each according to his ability and contribution and to take according to his need. We are also going to face proletariat dictatorship, which must implement its role, as Stalin did in Russia, and Mao did in China, and Pol Pot did in Cambodia, and Fidel Castro did in Cuba, and so forth, since they literally performed evil and inhumane actions to make the transition from socialist era possible to communism, because any kind of dictatorship and despotic behavior is certainly going to encounter an impasse and a very stiff resistance from freedom-loving people across the world.

To overcome what now seems a utopian state and in making these highly ambitious goals possible, is for humankind to take a giant leap toward self-denial and utterly believing in humanitarian agendas and productive communal work, rather than acting in self-interest alone. Then the state also needs to be eliminated since no government is needed to enforce contracts and property rights; neither military nor police force is necessary, basically expecting the masses to act flawlessly making a piece of heaven possible. I attest without transcending into a higher realm of consciousness and quality education impacted with dynamic and progressive cultural revolution, which can carry society into the premises of ideological enlightenment and welfare; no social reform of that magnitude can possibly take place. Because the average intelligent and advanced rational mind has not yet matured to accept such gigantic task.

I am saying we need to first reach a state of mindfulness, where we are lucky enough to utilize 15%-20% of our brain capacity from 100% potential, which is likely to happen gradually with time since time and persisting to acquire knowledge and correct information is the essence and the key in unlocking the troubles facing humanity. If it is possible for dolphins to use 20% of their brain making them so intelligent and playful since they utilize and maneuver by the most sophisticated sonar system and echolocation, then why not human progress into a state where they could also run their affairs with so much intelligence, using more percentage of their brain to accept communism without bloodshed, but not able to do so now, since we can witness Russia and China and Cuba and so on failing socialism and communism. This should make us focus and emphatically insist on making more sense of things and adapt to acquire more knowledge, information, and ascent into ever more rational minds, exploring meta intelligence and mindfulness to enjoy the fruits of utter enlightenment and understanding, which sure can bridge a safe way to human prosperity—then you can name it what you like.

Hence to make change possible, we need intelligent and awakened minds compounded with proper timing when the system in question is faced with a systematic crisis and unable to advance because it is stagnated and entangled into a web of uncertainties and begins to deteriorate from within. Other utopian thoughts like anarchism also manifest progressive agendas, which again are not practical unless revolutionary ideas can make a paradigm shift into raising the overall mentality of the people and their intelligence, and adamant enough for not accepting exploitation of any kind.

Alexander Berkman, in *The ABC of Anarchism* (1929) originally asked, "What is communist anarchism?"

The more enlightened man will become, the less he will employ compulsion and coercion. The really civilized man will divest himself of all fear and authority. He will rise from the dust and stand erect. He will bow to no tsar either in heaven or on earth. He will become fully human when he will scorn to rule and refuse to be ruled. He will be truly free only when there shall be no more masters.

Anarchism is the ideal of such a condition, of a society without force and compulsion, where all men shall be equals and live in freedom, peace, and harmony. The word anarchy comes from the Greek, meaning without force, without violence or government, because government is the very fountainhead of violence, constraint, and coercion. Anarchy therefore does not mean disorder and chaos, as you thought before. On the contrary, it is the very reverse of it; it means no government, which is freedom and liberty. Disorder is the child of authority and compulsion. Liberty is the mother of order.

Alexander Berkman, in *The ABC of Anarchism* (1929), wrote:

"Anarchism ... rests upon the doctrine that no man has a right to control by force That is to say, that there should be no war, no violence used by one set of men against another, no ... So anarchists generally believe that, whether as groups or individuals, no man who believes in force and violence is an Anarchist."

It is not to say reaching such ambitious goals to truly free humankind from the yoke of oppressive powers is not possible; in contrary, they are very much practical. But not before reaching enlightenment and collectively realizing the true devilish nature of systems that are despotic and inhumane in their very structure and fundamental beliefs. We ought to understand it is our mind and our mental state of accepting something as true or not, which is diagnosed in enslaving us or freeing us. Because there is no power ever created than the power of collective uprising and tsunami of masses resurrection, when fueled with adequate knowledge and information against that which is perceived as destroying humanity.

Historically speaking, the reason "slavery" and "feudalism" existed was because the overall mentality accepted such an abusive system, and slaves and serfs were not conscious and enlightened enough to realize the collective power they held to overpower the tyranny of either one of the oppressive systems that was imposed on slaves by their masters and on serfs by landowners. According to the dictionary, feudalism was a system of political organization prevailing in Europe from 9th to about 15th centuries, having as its basis the relationship of lord to vassal (a person under the protection of a feudal lord to whom he has vowed homage, obligation and fealty, a feudal tenant, one in a subservient or subordinate position) with all land held in a fee as chief characteristics homage, the service of tenants under arms and in court, warship, and forfeiture, and with any of various political or social systems similar to medieval feudalism. Once a system is overhauled, all the institutions supporting, promoting, and encouraging it are bound to destruction, since the new system will bear and materialize its own progressive culture of thinking and its values system, which will be aggressively pursued until they sink in and are accepted as the norm.

For instance, to promote capitalism, people like Walter Lippmann and Edward Bernays used the "Freudian theory" to deal with the public's conception of communism; he believed that we should not be easing the public's fear of communism, but rather promote that fear and play with the public's emotions of it. This theory was so powerful that it became a weapon of its own during the Cold War. They utterly believed people are not moved by rationality and the power of inference, but they should be manipulated by the power of emotion seducing them to call for their own exploitation, which they manifested through mass propaganda to foster fear and anxiety. By keeping people in a limbo state of mind and under psychosis of permanent war where they are leashed with agendas and culture of thinking, which best serves their corporate bosses and to keep the corporate oligopoly system intact by selling defective products to the masses of people to feed corporate profit. We ought to recognize that advanced socioeconomic techniques and socio-psychoanalysis are literally factored in to make us susceptible and influence with operating outside of our conscious ability and awareness. We need to know that many filthy rich capitalists play deadly games, where "free cheese is always in the mousetrap."

Noam Chomsky said that, "Bernays wrote a book called *Propaganda* around 1925, and it starts off by saying he is applying the lessons of the First World War. The propaganda system of the first World War and this commission that he was part of showed, he says, it is possible to 'regiment the public mind every bit as much as an army regiments their bodies.' These new techniques of regimentation of minds, he said, had to be used by the intelligent minorities in order to make sure that the slobs stay on the right course. We can do it now because we have these new techniques. This is the main manual of the public relations industry. Bernays is kind of the guru. He was an authentic Roosevelt/Kennedy liberal. He also engineered the public relations effort behind the U.S.-backed coup which overthrew the democratic government of Guatemala. His major coup, the one that really propelled him into fame in the late 1920s, was getting women to smoke. Women didn't smoke in those days, and he ran huge campaigns for Chesterfield. You know all the techniques—models and movie stars with cigarettes coming out of their mouths and that kind of thing. He got enormous praise for that. So he became a leading figure of the industry, and his book was the real manual."

In the era of capitalism and so-called modernity, millionaire and billionaire clubs are infested with hierarchical corruption which is going rampant. Mob-like organized crimes act against the powerless by killing, maiming, torturing, and imprisonment of the innocents, and against whoever is not complying with brutal and inhumane ways of treating the poor. The only crime of the helpless is their outcry for justice and wanting to live in peace. Because, as profit is accrued at the top, miseries and squalid living conditions are built up at the bottom and the money made is meant to serve the ruling class and the powerful, where laws are purposely made to keep people apart and hostile toward each other to preserve the status quo. They have titled so-called friendly nations, which should belong to international communities and those which should not belong or into alliance nation, and those which should universally be isolated, as if the citizens of the undesirable countries have anything to do with politics, which should resonate with any callow-minded individual (deficient in wisdom, credulous) that so many so-called unfriendly nations are under huge dictatorial rule in which they have no authentic voting power to make any difference other than what the totalitarian governments decide to do. And to make matters worse, the advocates of human rights and democracy push to slap innocent people, which they brag want to make free with unbearable sanctions and stark punishment, bombing them, and count so many dead and maimed with millions, leaving their homes migrating to unwelcome places, from their birthplace, which has now become the slaughterhouse, but then are counted as collateral damage. Someone please tell me what is the reasoning in that—by the way, this is occurring in those nations that encourage civility of mind and manner and rational behavior, and of course in God's name; above all, they do have the voting power to change the course of history against so many tyrants of the world since many fascist regimes and religious extremists are either covertly or openly supported and armed to their teeth countering their citizens and the indigenous people in many parts of the globe. These traumatic events materialize because we are entering into a radically odd position in our human history; the systems of governing are starting to decay and we are confronting a global economic system that is stagnant and stalemated. These systemic characteristics are forcing people to push for a fanatical change, which of course are confronting dictatorial behavior and fear by the ruling elites, which in turn are trying to find an answer for their traumatic and austere (stern, harsh, inexorable) situation. This, in turn, calls for a power change since so many are experiencing pain and suffering as deepening crises are becoming unbearable for billions of people globally, which reminds the ruling class of what Micaville said: "It is better to fear you than to love you." He also said: "The end justifies the means," which is turning many so-called democratic governments into hyenas acting monstrously in opposition to their own nations, treating them with inhumane response, since political dissidents are executed, unequivocally imprisoned, tortured, and where civil rights are nothing shorter than mockery. The history shows no regime change of any kind is the answer and with no offense, but in many cases accompanied with violent and bloodied revolution since the average intelligence and education is below standard and not ripe enough to handle the complexities of political and socioeconomic crises in modern time. And unless people are truly invested in becoming more educated and trained to understand the real political and socioeconomic dilemmas facing them, it is going to be business as usual, which should remind them of the word insanity, which Einstein puts this way: "Doing the same thing over and over again and expecting different results." In many backward places, planned market economy and collective ownership of the means of production to fairly distribute goods and services and to democratize the wealth of the nation and productive forces is the answer, where a few cruxes would not privatize what belongs to people. They do not have to wait until nations become absolutely industrialized and for technology to reach its peak and mature, which we should then expect ripened status for a bloodied revolution as income inequality and living standards becomes stark against the poor and the working class. The capitalist system runs its course, and the rich and the poor line up to clash to bring about radical changes of any kind through violent revolution. What Marx and others forgot was that we are not in the business of selling delicatessen; the working class cannot just spell some kind of voodoo on the capitalist system and poof, they vanish. We should think about so many innocent lives being slaughtered and at least show sensitivity to what is to become of a nation before rolling up our sleeves for making a positive change. And yes pain will end abusive behavior and violence, as moral depravity and corruption, extreme inequality in income, poverty and remaining indigence because of unemployment where public welfare are satirical, meant to humiliate the victims of poverty and gorgonizing (stupefying) them with so little relief that is for sure nothing shorter than humiliating the needy with rampant crime and violence—we sure need a positive change. But it is so vital to literally have sensible and wise plans to efficiently execute them, to gradually shatter the foundation of a tattered system. But then if we are talking about gradual positive changes as technology progresses and advances, modernization also materializes and pushes nations to be more educated and literate, because gaining knowledge and information is the key to deal with the intricacies of new technology and innovations that congruently bring about modernization and have environmentally positive criteria conducive for mental and behavioral growth where referendum and voting power could manifest great evolutionary changes beyond violence and murder. Again, to stop bloodshed, there are several can-do alternatives; for one, we should break up monopolized industries and "too big to fail" corporations to allow realistically fair and just competition, where a free enterprise system can truly flourish and be watched over by a competent central government. Unless the invisible hand of the market can become vividly visible where government does actively participate in the mechanism of supply and demand and strategize for the allocation of resources, people will get the finger. People need to debunk the idea of liberalism and free market economy, which has been unleashed and has gone too far in making people's lives so miserable and way below the poverty lines, but the rich get richer since they live with abundant prosperity at the indignant people's cost. Ideas that undermines the role of the governments and say that government is not the answer to our problem—government is the problem. They manipulate our minds, as we are an illusion into an unrealistic world. We must realize that the government is not evil as Milton Friedman and his very rich followers believe, so that they could further foster exploitation and enslave us. In reality the government's hand needs to replace the invisible hand of the market to mitigate meritocracy and correct the widest income inequality in today's world between the rich and the poor and to avoid violence, where a big clash between the haves and the have-nots can promulgate practical hell, and to avoid violence because of so much disparities, where so many cannot survive anymore. And by the way, stop these inhumane tactics by making few targeted individuals as successful symbols, and then go haywire in your propaganda and profess that everyone can become Bill Gates, the Walton family, Oprah, Steve Jobs, or President Obama. And conclude it is billions of people's fault they are at the bottom and have the audacity to count and call them just lazy people and choose to forget about prevalent injustice and the "implicit bias" against the deprived and the destitute, which you have designed and laid the ground work for. Or the ownership should take over the private power structure that has caused so much ill. And permit the system of co-ops to gradually take over and dominate the mechanism of the market economy or let the West European social-democratic economy system Scandinavian countries are operating under be manifested in North America as well and in other parts of the globe. Perhaps then the entire world could benefit from international economic alliance under the same practical system of a collective co-op system. Brilliant ideas and significant strategies can stem from a common sense solution, if no fear and true freedom of thought and action is allowed. Economic liberty, ingenuity, compelling thought, provoking plans, and superb innovation, skillful and knowledgeable maneuverability, a very positive paradigm shift with a cultural revolution in work ethic and solidarity can substantiate a very fruitful economic system where collective bargaining will involve everyone for the best outcome, which can replace the system already in decay. It is then expected from the powerful socially oriented economy explained above not to push for national interest, but also to act humane toward other less fortunate nations internationally, where predatory economics will not create hateful backlash from other nations. In the meanwhile, we should respect the communist system which in all honesty denies the almighty God openly; at least the atheists wield their dagger from the front, where it can be seen, giving one a chance to defend oneself. They are decent enough not to act hypocritical. The real fear stems with those charlatans who stab god-fearing people from behind and ironically say they believe in God, but do not mind God at all, and act so incredulous and phony. Also what Marx and others like him did not indicate is when we are supposed to know technology has reached its pinnacle and is time for the revolution, since technology is changing at a very high rate where digitally automated machines and robotics are taking over. Which, by the way, helps to expedite communication as fast as the speed of light through the internet (Facebook, Google, Yahoo, Skype, Twitter, YouTube, Instagram, Wikipedia, and so on) via cellphones, fax machines, satellites, TVs, and other means of information and communication. if there is going to be a revolution, and I so much hope not a bloodied one, it is going to travel very fast to other neighboring countries, perhaps even the entire globe causing a domino effect of radical change in many parts of the world. It is very difficult to stop people from learning about the news and becoming influenced to fight for their rights, making it hard to accomplish decisive covert operations, to hide or camouflage the truth.

When countries have to deal with systematic crises, there are no other choices but to invent and innovate ways that are entirely different from doing the same thing, which has proven futile. In many cases, institutional changes are necessary to democratize wealth and to change the ownership that will ban exploitive and despotic behavior of the few with Napoleon syndrome.

In the meanwhile, hopes are lost and the entire allocation of resources is unjustly distributed, and wealth is hugely polarized between the haves and the have-nots, where thousands are forced to lose their lives for one reason or another. Because they are not facilitated with the very basic standard of living and for billions to live in sub-human conditions so that a handful few can live an unimaginable life of fortune and extravagance, where the super-rich hallucinate that it is God who abundantly and so generously gives them money at the cost of horrific standards living for the poor. The super-rich waste millions and billions of dollars on their lavish lifestyle.

But these moguls of fortune are not intelligent enough to realize that life on Earth is seriously threatened and in need of immediate respond and positive remedy. The system of plutocracy and corporate oligopoly refuses to see they are living at the people's devastating expense, where thousands perish every day as the super- rich are literally enjoying a life of plenty and magnificent luxury utterly acting indifferent to the sordid condition of humankind and a destructive world facing its inhabitants.

How would you make changes applicable to a system that used to do well, in comparison to a feudal system or slavery where dark ages were upon us and people were basically treated like animals? But then when the old system had their runs and faced predicaments and intricacies that generated irresolvable contradictions and rendered antagonistic behaviors toward the very productive forces that gave birth to them— then, it was time to go. And yes, it took aggressive force and violence to get rid of them, and I am afraid sometimes for the loss of millions of innocent lives because of bloodied upheavals and ugly encounters.

Many are pumped up and refer to history where revolutionary changes can only take place through violence, and they insist on no other viable, peaceful solutions to make dynamic transitions possible. To them, moral imperative dictates that masses of people should overthrow the system, acting like barbarians. As if everything is supposed to progress and improve through evolutionary process, except the power of our wit and reasoning, despite enormous findings and accomplishments in every important scientific field and even putting human robots on the moon. We just need not to act so backwardly to resolve our social and economic differences and the system of our governing by killing and through bloodshed and by lawlessness and savagery like when slavery transitioned into feudalism via bloodshed and violence, as did feudalism transitioned into capitalism. We should realize we live in an age of consciousness equipped with enough intelligence to know better. If not, then we should all wonder if our mindfulness and the power of our reasoning has ever grown at all because our acting civil should stewardship us amidst turmoil and instability. But the fact is, despite what we want to believe, human intelligence and collective knowledge and understanding has appreciated, so has our overall consciousness, and that is the truth. We witness when soldiers are sent to unjustified wars to kill and maim innocent lives, the very same soldiers that "under false premises" were sent to take innocent lives and count them as collateral damage, commits suicide when they return from the war of aggression. That is why we should have an inkling of intelligence to know that so many human beings do have a conscience and possess heavenly emotion, very sensitive in not wanting to do wrong, to not play with these caring souls, to not misinform and violate their right to know the facts, to stop feeding good people's mind and thought, body and soul with poison for your own gains—it is utterly wrong. On the other hand, the terrorists do capitalize on this stupefied behavior and hostile decisions made and access the victim's family's sons and daughters, brothers and sisters and other family members and citizenries to recruit them to war for their own gains. They too send so many to act inhumane and take innocent lives "under false premises," promising the manufactured terrorist a key to heaven where they will be rewarded with plenty of goodies, where Allah will favor them over others. How infinitely ignorant that is. It makes one really puzzle why would the merciful and the compassioned God of Ibrahim, Moses, Jesus, Mohammed, and 124,000 other sacred profits of God and the proprietor of the Earth and heaven above be so pleased to see innocent lives taken and enjoy God's children to suffer as such? Go figure.

We should not be delinquent and deliberate in ignoring the unlocking of our cognitive ability, which literally takes place by gradually freeing more percentage of our brain cells—in which it ascends and delivers humanity to realms beyond our imagination, when it does. And it already has propelled us forward from the caveman mentality to what we experience as modern life, where the goal is to conquer other planets and perhaps harness them for the benefit of humankind. And in getting closer to fulfill the eternal purpose in objectifying our human destiny, where reaching God and the higher power becomes so well-known and clearly manifested and even the dumbest of us all can witness and resurrect against the stupidity and our clumsiness of truly claiming our creator.

Stop acting like beasts by mandating a global holocaust where hell is to wait us and start to pay attention to our evolutionary miracle-like brain and conscious, which has relentlessly endeavored and meandered in accelerating its celestial task to save us from the clutches of ignorance and in moving toward its goal to arrive us into the promised land, despite treacherous behaviors of the few, and their deviously ironclad-like conduct to obstruct what is just. This often impedes but never is powerful enough to halt the virtue of higher powers of heaven. The contemporary challenges that are holding back societies are the fusion of state and corporate power, which has reached the pinnacle of plundering, looting, and pillaging, where it seems the more powerful and privileged the ruling class becomes, the more deluded they are with the business industrial complex backed up with the military industrial complex against the forces that are keeping the system intact.

This myopia (a lack of foresight or discernment) of acting in secret tribunals to restlessly conspire against people is not aligned with God's work and the time promised to capture the essence and the very reason we are here. This calls for the helpless to unanimously speak the undeniable truth to the powerful and make them understand these despicable conditions which so many are stuck with, and it should call for an amicable solution to humanity's problem. And there are potential dangers facing the entire system if no quality and plausible solution is expected soon. The super-rich should be warned and come to terms in grasping that human beings are a wholesome entity that must not be broken to pieces, and if so, the wrath of God will be upon us, boomeranging everyone. We already possess very destructible weaponry to instantly annihilate what we know as human life. And hence, we must remind ourselves that no violence is an answer, as good breeds good and evil breeds evil, and the gambling bet is on innocent human lives. And any system change must occur peacefully to resolutely remedy our differences and the mess we have created; above all we must prove our non-hypocritical claim of believing in God we trust.

Why not live and honor in what we actually claim and build a humanitarian superpower rather than a military industrial complex where trillions of dollars are rampantly spent on unjustified military and logistics, looking for an improvised enemy to justify the infinite numbers of armaments accumulated to force others into do or die situations, which has counterintuitively threatened people and stifled the very foundation of virtues and what we stand for as a civilized nation.

Civility should be demanded by actively participating in restoring goods, as Ralph Nader says: "There are two kinds of people one which believe everything, and the other which believe nothing, and both lack thinking." Just remember it is a republican state where our forefathers and so many good souls lost their lives to restore, and not a corporate state where greed and irresponsibility has shackled people with unbearable living conditions, testing their limits into acting desperate and suicidal. This should call upon consciously awakened people to feel accountable and get out of their comfort zone to make things right, where life would not happen to be so damn hard for billions and so ridiculously luxurious for just a handful of menacing souls.

We ought to know the era of awakening and responsibility, the era of consciousness and accountability, and the time parameter where so many are alerted and care to understand the structure of power and the world that surrounds them is here. The truth is that at slavery time or at the feudal era, the victims knew who was slashing them and murdering and raping them and making them work harder than animals. But then the system of corporate capitalism became much more elaborate in doing wrong against its victims, as Sheldon Wolin discussed in an interview with TruthDig columnist Chris Hedges.

In his book *Democracy Incorporated*, inverted totalitarianism is different from classical forms of totalitarianism. It does not find its expression in a demagogue or charismatic leader but in the faceless anonymity of the corporate state. Our inverted totalitarianism pays outward fealty to the facade of electoral politics, the Constitution, civil liberties, freedom of the press, the independence of the judiciary, and the iconography, traditions, and language of American patriotism, but it has effectively seized all the mechanisms of power to render the citizens impotent.

Throughout his scholarship Wolin charted the devolution of American democracy, and in *Democracy Incorporated*, he details our peculiar form of corporate totalitarianism. "One cannot point to any national institution[s] that can accurately be described as democratic, surely not in the highly managed, money-saturated elections, the lobby-infested Congress, the imperial presidency, the class biased judicial and penal system, or, least of all, the media." Wolin continues: "Unlike the Nazis, who made life uncertain for the wealthy and privileged while providing social programs for the working class and poor, inverted totalitarianism exploits the poor, reducing or weakening health programs and social services, regimenting mass education for an insecure workforce threatened by the importation of low-wage workers."

Wolin writes: "Employment in a high-tech, volatile, and globalized economy is normally as precarious as during an old-fashioned depression. The result is that citizenship, or what remains of it, is practiced amidst a continuing state of worry. Hobbes had it right: when citizens are insecure and at the same time driven by competitive aspirations, they yearn for political stability rather than civic engagement, protection rather than political involvement. "If the main purpose of elections is to serve up pliant legislators for lobbyists to shape, such a system deserves to be called 'misrepresentative or client government.' It is, at one and the same time, a powerful contributing factor to the de-politicization of the citizenry, as well as reason for characterizing the system as one of anti-democracy."

The result, he writes, is that the public is "denied the use of state power." Wolin deplores the trivialization of political discourse, a tactic used to leave the public fragmented, antagonistic, and emotionally charged, while leaving corporate power and empire unchallenged.

"Cultural wars might seem an indication of strong political involvements," Wolin writes. "Actually they are a substitute. The notoriety they receive from the media and from politicians eager to take firm stands on no substantive issues serves to distract attention and contribute to politics of the inconsequential. In classical totalitarian regimes, such as those of Nazi fascism or Soviet communism, economics was subordinate to politics. But under inverted totalitarianism the reverse is true. Economics dominates politics—and with that domination comes different forms of ruthlessness."

With all of that, it is the time to hope for the change, but you must be the change and should stop taking the tranquilized medicine of non-activity, hoping others to do what everyone needs to do, without you lifting a finger. It is not an exaggeration to say we are sequestered into accepting illusions as reality and normal, and sometimes we are not humble enough to admit many issues that are killing us and wrong, which need to be confronted with reason.

We need to condemn our divisiveness, corporate greed, and bailing out the super-rich by taxpayers' money, GMO food, global warming and contaminating the sources of our food and water supply, polluting the air we breathe, trillions spent on military industrial complex bleeding us dry, outsourcing jobs, genocide and wars of aggression, police brutality, unlawful incarcerations, no due process of the law against the apprehension of intellectuals and the whistleblowers.

Gun control, mega media indoctrinating people with false reports and misleading information, defrauding billions from people's hard-earned money pushing them into foreclosures, no regulation for unleashed bankers and corporation, lack of balanced budget, deteriorating educational system, unemployment, no savvy and efficient medical system, no housing subsidies, no educational subsidies, horrendous infrastructure, not raising the minimum wage.

Horrible immigration policies, exploitive tax system, "too big to fail" entities, not to mention wrong ways of dealing with crime, where violence is going rampant and ever present, supporting autocratic regimes, prosecuting those at the top and not putting all the guilt on the little men with no executive power. Stifling all legislative activities by corporations and powerful lobbyists, stopping fraudulent insiders on Wall Street defrauding people out of billions, not using available and efficient alternative energy sources to implement and mandate more safe environmental policies, and regulative laws against big carbon monoxide-producing companies.

Halt masquerading and distorting those with progressive thoughts and agendas. Stop beleaguering (attack from all sides, harass) democracy and insist on people's Constitutional rights, and for the love of God, do not rewrite the Constitution to render the system futile. Stop marginalizing people and put an end to racial profiling where intrusive activities are misconstrued by mapping, acting uncivilized and without due process of the law and the misuse of power to illegally intimidate and apprehend minorities and ethnic groups. Why not stop spewing hatred and venom toward so many, sowing fear and discord among so many good souls who believe in our democracy system of government and sincerely try to become a productive member of society. Stop giant corporate conglomerates from shoving toxic and inhumane conditions in our throats and forcing us to digest them, generating so many problems, more than any nation deserves. Discourage paying fealty to electoral politics to create allegiance against what needs to be done to rescue people from this horrendous situation we call living.

If the government really cares to authenticate democracy and human rights and truly manifest the right to life and the pursuit of happiness for all and perhaps is adamant enough to save the system by peaceful means, then they should make dynamic changes that can resonate with the masses of people for financial security and for a life worth living. They should make sincere efforts to substantiate the emerging left-right alliance to dismantle the corporate state, stopping bureaucracies and getting rid of red tape. Stop bushwhacking (assaulting, ambushing) innocent citizens in the name of national security, through spying, insidious surveillance, and eavesdropping. After all, this is a place nations under autocratic regimes look up to for guidance referencing freedom, democracy, justice, and human rights.

The politicians need to collectively support a gradual change into a co-op system of economic and social endeavors, stop changing the nature of nature to maximize profit and stop burning food and burying cows, buffaloes, pigs, lambs, poultry, and so forth to raise the price of meat and fowl in a desperately hungry world. In the meanwhile, make the corporations pay their fair share of taxes, which most pay less than 2% of taxes, or find loopholes paying no taxes at all, while investing billions in places with no hardcore tax policies, since in many of them, authorities can be bribed and bought to turn a blind eye.

Why not decriminalize drugs for medical rehabilitation since many users have health problems? Stop suppressing addiction and start helping those through professional medical assistance and decisive therapy. Bring illegal drugs to the surface, and let's deal with it by educational means and taxing it higher, which will mitigate and perhaps get rid of drug trafficking and its peripheral troubles and the menace it causes for humanity. Put more women in higher posts and stop discriminating against women. And most of all, do not believe politicians who say the right things but are far from actuating them.

Criminalization is the mode of the government and the culture we practically live in. And unless economic justice prevails, decriminalization is not going to materialize, which should uproot the very foundation of society that is contemptuous and belittling toward those less fortunate and the deprived, since so many are forced to do wrong to survive. And a failed education system is proportional to the rise of incarceration of millions with no available opportunities as society's crime rates have statistically skyrocketed without any constructive and structural solution to the vast problem of crime. And if not intentionally planned to make repeated offenders, since many so-called felons have chronic mental sickness with no available medical therapy and professional help to rehabilitate and correct the situation that jailed them in the first place. This sure can help to make a safer neighborhood and society where they are to live in after being released. To make matters worse, the so-called felons are not clear and free from their insidious social and desperate economic status after they are released and have paid their dues to society because they are labeled as "felons" for the rest of their lives which condemns them to unemployment and denying so many from earning the bare minimum wage or any other income, leaving a good reason to become a repeated offender and hostile toward a system that has declared war on them. And since there are no incentives for either the legislative or the executive branch of government that are heavily influenced by the powerful lobbyists and private mega corporations, no resolute public good is ever instituted. And for humanity's sake, stop redefining and reconfiguring the Constitution to fit the oligarch behaviors of the elites, which strips people of their fundamental rights and dignity. And halt changing the nature of Mother Nature, stop suppressing the poor and the very productive forces of society, the workers, who are the main reason for your deep pockets and surplus value.

Do not push further austerity on so many people who are already burdened and enslaved with despicable and squalid lifestyles beyond human imagination. Stop producing your mega media propaganda machine as it is defective and the bewitched act as robots to consume more artificially desired stuff which you homogenize and push to pursue.

Capitalists' moral mission is to see individuals and self-interest as the only propriety and as the only accepted norm; we should accept altruism to be immoral and that is why so many problems have repercussions and are reflected to humanity in undeniably ill ways. To protect corporate oligopoly, we have amassed the most mass surveillance, which has turned democracy into a sham and the government of the people, by the people, for the people converted into an autocracy controlled by corporate elites.

I strongly believe in so many intellectual and frontline fighters who struggle for justice, equity, liberty, and human rights; they are compassionate enough to risk their lives in many parts of the world for a better living condition and to save humanity. But I also believe that we have reached an age of consciousness and intelligence and must resolve our differences by peaceful means. And I am sure no decent human being should ever ignore the loss of innocent lives through violence and criminal behaviors. And the moral imperative should call for reasoning and humanely dialogue, since any of us could act like the elites do, and perhaps even worse, were we in the position of power.

It is the 21st century, we should act like it, and not get stuck in a caveman mentality where the dark ages are upon us. And yes, history has proven that change has many times happened through violence and killing, but bear in mind, as many as those bloodied times, and many times over dynamic and authenticated changes has taken place by cooperation and peaceful means as well, rather than by killings, which we should gracefully cherish nonviolent behavior. That no violence should take over the power of wit and understanding when faced with complicated issues and to prove it, just take a survey by the civilized world and ask if violence should be the answer.

Marx believed that: "It is only possible to achieve real liberation in the real world … by employing real means … slavery cannot be abolished without the steam-engine and the mule and spinning-jenny, serfdom cannot be abolished without improved agriculture, and … in general, people cannot be liberated as long as they are unable to obtain food and drink, housing and clothing in adequate quality and quantity. 'Liberation' is a historical and not a mental act, and it is brought about by historical conditions, the development of industry, commerce, agriculture, and the conditions of intercourse, and so forth. Based on the theory of the productive forces and related perspectives, the economic systems of the former Eastern bloc and the present-day socialist states the state accumulated capital through forcible extraction of surpluses from the population for the purpose of rapidly modernizing and industrializing their countries, because these countries were not technologically advanced to a point where an actual socialist economy was technically possible,[1] or were a socialist state tried to reach the communist mode of production. The philosophical perspective behind the modernizing zeal of the Soviet Union and People's Republic of China was based on the desire to industrialize their countries."

The fact is unless the global productive forces and the masses' consciousness is pinnacled, contrary to what Marx and Lenin and others, with the exception of Trotsky, believed: True communism is possible in one country where the industrial and economic forces have matured and will domino effect to the rest of industrial world with advanced and progressive cultures; technology and human intelligence are mature enough and ripe, no economic and sociocultural with meaningful changes are to take place. Either way an emotional or demagogic call for revolution by hostile means is not a viable option, when the proper forces to make a smooth transition possible are not available yet. If history should be an indicator, then we need to question why Russia, China, Vietnam, Cuba, and Cambodia and alike did not succeed their discourse. They are still not rational enough to make sense of what they have started since vacillating between capitalism, socialism, acting revisionism are still very far away from adopting communism.

They failed their bloodied revolution, losing millions of lives with no avail, because the fundamentals of productive force and the superstructures of feudal Russia and China at the time of revolt were not ready, and neither was the world for such exorbitant (drastic) social and economic changes to internationally assume and truly take place. We need to harness the notion of emotional outrage, despite its justification and altruism, until the fundamentals of revolt have globally matured. No nation is an island anymore; we are all interactively connected, and it is time to realize no groups and no nation or any society should be isolated or left alone in their struggle against any sort of tyranny.

Furthermore, should we think that slavery and feudal changes or the renaissance for that matter would ever be possible if the productive forces and the culture of thoughts, the ideology and awareness would have not been ready to switch into the new system and to have reveled (celebrate) its outcome? But one thing is for sure, which is if the revolution was to take place in North America, then, it will manifest itself with a much better result than in Russia, China, and others alike, since the leverages for a dynamic and quality change are not cosmetic; we are not in a feudal state, but are living the era of a capital intense society which is the highest stages of capitalism known as imperialism rather than living in other primitive eras not suitable for reliable and progressive changes, which were doomed to failure.

Could our predecessors have expected for the slaves to bring about the social changes that capitalists have or could they have expected the feudal to place a man on the moon, and create the miracle-like inventions that capitalists have done in their time? Yes, our perceptions and incisive awareness and consciousness might be ready, which perhaps could overpower our momentary lapses of reason for a revolutionary idea to take place, but to be sure, we must have the fundamental forces of economic and social production available to induce such historical change. This should also awaken not only the masses of the poor, but the capitalists themselves to investigate the stalemated, stagnated, or matured system, which once was dynamically productive, to avoid bloodied upheavals, and to correct it if still room is left for more progress and believing in social order and prosperity for all. Or is it really time for the capitalist system to go?

Referencing history, the maturity of productive forces and the widening gap between the poor and the rich might have caused social uprising and turmoil. But also, any time the more powerful government like the Persian empire, Egyptian empire, Arabian empire, Mongolian empire, Chinese empire, Greek and Roman empire, Ottoman empire, British empire, and so many others, felt like they needed to expand since they might have noticed their economic demise or they just wanted to add territories to their empire.

They attacked and destroyed other weak nations, especially if the less powerful nations owned valuable resources. This should remind us of today's modern warfare and militarism taking place in many parts of the world where the corporate capitalists compete for the resources of developing countries by either unfair trade practices or through militarism.

Superpowers first stir troubles in many parts of the world, then talk about peace, democracy, and human rights, which is followed by sending trillions of dollars' worth of arms to dreadful and bloodied regimes of their choice to kill millions in the name of doing business and making money for the few. They are able to cause these inhumane atrocities because they are equipped with the technology that makes the world perceive what corporate mega media intend the world to comprehend as reality, but not the actual reality. This should remind us of fascist and autocratically orchestrated techniques that the few super-rich control and manifest, rather than democratic techniques and products which people should control. To avoid making freedom-loving people of the globe lost and not to brainwash them to stay on the wrong side of justice and what is right. To change the status quo and to bring about a more just economic system, where true democracy and socialized goods can equitably be allocated among masses of people, where the workers would be enjoying the fruits of their labor, where trillions of surplus value is not concentrated in the hands of the private enterprise, but is to make sure the basic necessities of living are prioritized, including proper employment, retirement security, free education, free health care, subsidized housing, free transportation, and more are socialized.

Marx and others predicted that true social revolution is only possible in advanced industrial nations that have reached economic maturity, and do not historically fit the criteria and neither fits today's world social economic and cultural agendas. The truth is Marx did not predict that billions, even trillions, of dollars could electronically be transferred in a couple of seconds, where outsourcing has become the norm in many industrial and powerful nations, since the multinational companies invest in countries with plenty of raw materials and dirt cheap natural resources and labor.

They also establish the puppet government of their choice, a neo-colonialist system of governing, which are exploiting the native resources and cheap labels, murdering and torturing and imprisonment of their own citizens, since they all work in concert as superior classes against the deprived and international working class, which has quelled most of the pressure in nations that have peaked industrially and managing to avoid socialist revolution. Marx did not predict the wars of aggression pursued by looting, plundering, and extortion, taking other's helpless nations' natural resources and raw material becoming the norm. He must not have expected the explosive power of the computer, the advent of the internet with amazingly quick communication technology, and the super advanced jet engines, the power of outsourcing and the global economic expansion and counter-trade (a form of international trade in which purchases made by an importing nation are linked to offsetting purchases made by the exporting nation) and the potential for nuclear, chemical, bacterial, cyber wars, and terrorism, which is shifting the national boundaries, making the entire world act like an entire village, where everything is immediately accessible by the international monetary system through trade and militarism.

Until the resources of the planet are depleted to the point of exhaustion and collapse, which we should already see its dire signs, then it is perhaps possible for the poor, the destitute, and the global working class to confront the murderous agents in decisive ways and make a worldly socioeconomic and cultural revolution compatible to the 21st century, being dynamic and progressive enough to carry humanity into the next couple of centuries, where the system can make a meaningful life and happiness relatively possible and not made to belittle God and trash humanity in the name of accumulating infinite wealth and power.

Our mental progressiveness and higher understanding of social and natural order can empower us to rationally conceptualize and induce dynamic intelligence; it is only possible in accordance to scientific breakthroughs.

And enabling society to perceive a culture of thinking interconnected with the advancement of technology and industrial mode of production grants us a paradigm shift into new consciousness and assembly of thoughts that leverages humanity to enter into a new notion of civilization, enabling societies to digest and comprehend the dynamics of historical events. For example, "division of labor" and mass production were only possible because of the invention of assembly lines, which industrial breakthroughs made possible.

The problem is the relationship of the production that is an imprecation (curse), since it distorts and exploits the nature and humanity and commoditizes everything and everyone in its path for profit and not for the sake of creating public goods compatible with the sustainability of the social and natural order. This private opulence at the cost of public misery needs to end since the poor are paying with their lives to feed a system that has become dull and acts indifferent to the suffering of so many bereft of basic necessities to sustain them. The system has turned fair competition and appropriate market functions into sociopathic individualistic nature.

The system has violated nature; it has disturbed class order to the extreme, where the middle class are becoming an endangered species and the working class cannot make a living anymore. It has turned into sociopathic politics fed by corporations and mad institutions to focus on wealth creation for the elites—and the hell with everyone else.

People are cast into dire positions where upper mobility is impossible since the masses of people are stuck in terrible financial situations; this personality disorder and antisocial conduct must stop by the power of reasoning and in the name of human virtue and not by murdering each other.

Marx believed: "It is only possible to achieve real liberation in the real world ... by employing real means ... slavery cannot be abolished without the steam-engine and the mule and spinning-jenny, serfdom cannot be abolished without improved agriculture, and ... in general, people cannot be liberated as long as they are unable to obtain food and drink, housing and clothing in adequate quality and quantity. 'Liberation' is a historical and not a mental act, and it is brought about by historical conditions, the development of industry, commerce, agriculture, and the conditions of intercourse, and so forth. Based on the theory of the productive forces and related perspectives, the economic systems of the former Eastern bloc and the present-day socialist states the state accumulated capital through forcible extraction of surpluses from the population for the purpose of rapidly modernizing and industrializing their countries, because these countries were not technologically advanced to a point where an actual socialist economy was technically possible,[1] or were a socialist state tried to reach the communist mode of production. The philosophical perspective behind the modernizing zeal of the Soviet Union and People's Republic of China was based on the desire to industrialize their countries."

If pressured enough, people can make the privileged elites open their eyes that are blinded with power and prestige. They should incessantly be reminded of them acting delusional, which can be corrected if enough push by the truth-teller is implemented to open the eyes of plutocracy and avoid a bloodied class war. If keen enough, we can clearly see that Mother Nature, the very reason to our existence, works gradually and is an evolutionist in its pursuit of giving life and making dynamic and decisive apparatus possible for humanity to enjoy. We are part of nature and should act like it. For some, it might be easy to say corporate tyranny must be overthrown, no matter at what cost, but it must not occur at the cost of millions of innocent lives to be murdered, which violence will surely bring.

Every time we are violent, we eviscerate (to take out, to make deprived of vital content or force) and insult the very intelligence and human mindfulness that has collectively enabled us to do the impossible. Resorting to force and barbarism will kill the civility of mind and manner and the power of compassion in all of us; it will breed more ills, demonic and horrific conduct as it has in the past if history is to remind us and is witnessed.

The mechanism of power that betrays those marginalized and the destitute, the powerless, and the poor can be shifted. But then, what guarantee does anyone have if we are not educated and wise enough to keep others intact? Those who are supposed to govern and rule us from doing the same or even worse. If we are not mentally competent and do not possess the dynamics and the technology of thought to manage our problems with this corporate state now and resolutely manage to communicate savviness and wisdom to them, then what should make us confident that we can make it happen with an alternative system, if any?

Discourage talks about sublime (exalted, elevated) madness and violent confrontation to deal with the system, where moments of extremities might call for revolt. The power of reasoning can unlock and speak the undeniable power of truth to the power and acclaim its sovereignty where no man should resist, unless wanting to act beastly and assume savage behavior.

We live in an era where our overall mentality bears enough intelligence to retaliate against the mechanism of powers that betray those whom they are supposed to rule and care for, but it must happen in a dignified and civilized way because we are in profound need of humanity and the daunting question should be "why not?" Why not activate the potentiality of our human brain which collectively has the literal power to rescue humankind from the clutches of ignorance and where kinship and meaningful perspective could sooth our pain and anguish and replace breathing and living devastation.

Why procrastinate until it is too late and why not get out of this entrenched madness and act humane to stay against the root causes of evil, which has caged and imprisoned our soul in the name of profit. Let our failure leverage and aim us at enlightenment where human spirit can kindle to do well and make peace and justice possible and to realize we are unbalanced and will extinguish faster if we resort to nuclear, biological, chemical, and many other vicious weaponry that can wipe us all, making Holocaust-like tragedies many time over, where no day will be left to call it a day.

Let's necessitate, rehabilitate, and resuscitate our love for each other and become one against all atrocious and inhumane behavior. We must become warned of our abysmal mistakes we are making and condemn the real perpetrators of crimes and misconduct. Let's be human. Because violence will end in revenge, and revenge is a very potent force that will travel the endless road of outrage and violence, which creates a vicious circle of beastly acts until millions of lives are senselessly taken. It should be obvious that criminal behaviors are odious no matter which side is causing them.

We need to know that either through a conscious decision or a momentary lapse of reason, any violent action should be counted as human failure and must not be challenged through the barrel of gun because humanism, tolerance, and patience along with constructive dialogue should always be the answer. And hence, an all-out effort must be directed at bulls'-eyeing, and to target the heart of raising the plural consciousness of the people and to equip them with correct information, higher education, and knowledge, so that they can truly digest and understand the complexity of the system which is rendering them helpless.

And to detect the anatomical structures of power and exploitation and replace it with a new manifesto to emancipate billions from the ironclad indecency and ruthless economic programs, as the financial despots and the Byzantines of today's world laugh at democracy and human rights, where they know their autocracy of corporate power rules. Truth diggers are incessant in their effort to stand against this hegemony of behavior, which is structured to put an end to inhumane living standards manufactured by the corporate power that is blinded with greed and cannot see. Trapping billions of people through forced economic hardship has created a vicious cycle of poverty and violence that is meticulously designed, where upper mobility is stopped, despite the due diligence of many desperate souls from getting out of their miserable situation, but they cannot, since they are confined within manipulative social and economic policies with devious intent, nimbly designed for corporate capitalists to reach their financial target.

Since This is not justifiable morally, socially, economically, and not by any other human standard. And all in the name of money by which corporations have replaced God. As Pope Francis says, "Money drenched with blood, and often innocent blood" has blinded the evildoers with no sign of receding from their criminal and bizarre activities against humanity and nature. Where corporate capitalists are concerned with profit as their bottom line, are taking innocent lives, and are also destroying nature, the only source of our subsistence. And unless honest education awakens humanity on exponential population growth, overconsumption, and diminishing natural resources, we will all be faced with tragedies beyond our means to correct. We must stop the traditional way of doing things and access a new compass to avert humanity from complete ruin and toward a safe haven into the future. Corporations' traditional way of getting rich with an unrestrained economy must change, since they plunder and exhaust nature and overexploit human resource, and all in the name of free economy.

These wealthy moguls have to reach their financial goal and monetary bottom line every time they venture. But nature does not have a bottom line; it goes in a circle, and when they profoundly disturb the cycle of spring, autumn, winter, and summer through global warming, then, everyone must pay a heavy price and sometimes their lives. It is not that corporations are not aware of our gradual and accelerated demise by producing so much carbon monoxide, causing unbearable pollution and floods, mudslides, tsunamis, earthquakes, tornados, famine, wiping out the rain forest, and with hundreds of other ill environmental results, which are destroying biodiversity, the ecosystem, and its biological derivatives. They are very well in tune with their relentless attack on everything humanity stands for, but are demonized by greed to do anything about it. The rich elites are well aware the reason people die in disasters is not because God has cursed them, but because the resources taken hostage by the rich are not relinquished to do disaster management and set forth catastrophe prevention programs in preparation for tragedy prevention before they strike. But the nightmare does not stop with loss of lives; the cataclysmic effects extend to the entire planet, since the adverse effects of global warming on many species is making them extinct because many lack the resiliency to survive under the traumatic conditions imposed on them. They are extremely vital to our existence.

Overexploitation of the world's resources, overpopulation, with an overly polluted environment, energy scarcity, with hundreds of other dire consequences facing us, is arrogantly taken by neoclassical economist as externalities. What is considered externalities for corporate capitalists, which they take for granted to do as they please, are the very continuation of life for billions of inhabitants of the planet, which we must have to survive.

They try to convince us the causes to injustice in the world are abstract and irresolvable, as they pacify any attempt from humanity to perhaps correct dilemmas with dire consequences, which the corporations have created, including them turning a blind eye to annihilation of the entire planet and its dwellers, which if serious and constructive attempts to fix this horrific situation are not viably done, and soon, there will be no hope of future generations or any survival at all.

Someone said, "We are in a race with education and catastrophes, and unless we wake up to education, we will all be terminated." This policy of no law, no rules, and no consequences must be stopped for the powerful, where the mighty rich can do as they please to the common wealth of a nation, boycotting people's hope, desolating their livelihood, and eliminating any prospect left for future generations to grasp and hold onto.

We need to wake up to this literal emergency soon, and unless we return to a world of cooperation and collectively attend to the immediate threat facing us all, we will soon be riddled with a cascade of disasters beyond our means to rescue humanity and nature. Where many believe this debt-based economy system of waste with unbridled consumption is not dynamically reformed, it will soon bring down an end to what we know as the industrial revolution.

The effect of giant corporate economy on the world has left a ruthless inefficiency on so many people who die every day because of food and water depravity and famine that has turned humanity into vast herds of prey and made the super-rich into a handful of predators hunting human beings; they artificially raise prices and manipulate the world market to maximize their profit as they insanely fight the natural and social order, amassing 80-90% of the wealth into the hands of 1%, leaving the 99% of the world's population to barely survive on 10%-15% of the entire global resources.

And since every lawful and legal entity is corporatized, proper and decisive responses need to occur outside of their realm of power by peaceful mass demonstration, organized civil disobedience, and steady reactionary movements directed at the enemies of humanity, in demanding fundamental changes rather than accepting no good incremental reforms, as they play as safety valves in prolonging the real causes to people's miseries and misfortune.

This madness must be stopped if there is going to be a slight chance left for humankind to survive corporate atrocities that have become a life and death situation for so many and an insurmountable challenge for the wise to overcome. It is time to realize that no nation or any society should be at the mercy of a power individual or influenced group because they will be victimized and will not fare well; no man can resist not abusing his power. We are social and self-interested beings; no one should prevail with one's self-interest agenda at the cost of common good and society, where social apparatus and the common goods should work well for the benefit of the entire society, with no one left behind. The bottom line is that in individualistic societies where individuals benefit at the cost of the group, war-like culture, including racism, social injustice, prejudice against women and children, prejudice against the poor and the weak, against minorities, infinite wrong against nature itself, religious resentment encouraged by the sectarian charlatans in making superficial difference. Even God is not immune to their perils and toxic lectures to make money and so forth happen because no one is safe to the atrocities of human greed, which must be controlled. And because authenticated altruism and much better humans are the products of a social and cooperative system, they are delivered in a less hostile and negatively competing environment, where common goods are truly recognized and prioritized.

Someone wise once said, "Don't ask God to guide your footsteps if you're not willing to pick up your feet." Take steps toward nullifying and dismantling the relentless efforts of the corporate capitalist system that has become numb to causing the destruction of the entire planet. Outlaw them for maximizing wealth in the name of taking lives, take their social license away, and inactivate their murderous behaviors; let's be delighted that we are not part of doing so much ill to humanity. Let's make sure to be congenial (to get along) and belong to the right side of history, as we must repeatedly remind ourselves that we are here for a short time and will return to where we came from one way or another.

Let's carry the dignified truth with us when it is time to transcend to a higher realm of existence, to stand erect with a chip on our shoulder and keep our head up to answer with no hesitancy and say, No. I did not murder, I did not rape, or cause any irreparable harm to humankind," when we are investigated by the authorities of heaven. Socrates said "it is better to suffer wrong than to do wrong." We ought to know it is not the application of common sense that is lost, but greed and self-interest agendas have gone haywire, and the premises encouraging its reckless behavior is about to make humanity an endangered species if not wisely corrected or entirely stopped.

It is imperative for any progressive system to direct its goals and activities at a global scale where the greater good is to benefit everyone, to avoid acting small and narrow-mindedly, and not to become restrained in doing justice because of social, cultural, nationality, race, ethnicity, sectarianism, color, gender, religious, economic classification, or any discriminatory factor.

Otherwise, it will lessen or sanction its overall objectives deemed at helping the entire humanity from reaching its full potential, as the system should transcend beyond concocting nebulous (vague) and petty differences that are traditionally made to keep us apart.

If human potential for advancement is fully realized and prevails, "No can manifesto" will be a thing of the past, where seeing God the almighty should become explicitly clear and closer to one than one's jugular vein, where the mind of God will lead to acquaint the mind of man in expediting amazing discoveries to capture wondrous and captivating realms within human existence.

Henry "Fritz" Schaefer, five time Nobel Prize nominee, Graham Perdue Professor of Chemistry and director of the Center for Computational Quantum Chemistry at the University of Georgia, as cited in *What Your Atheist Professor Doesn't Know (But Should)* by Stephen Williams: "It is evident that an acquaintance with natural laws means no less than an acquaintance with the mind of God therein expressed."

I strongly believe we will overcome our malignant social and financial roles and will reach the mountain top of human consciousness and become enlightened to unanimously vote for the common goods of the entire planet and its inhabitants. I also believe we have the means to substantiate quality changes that can empower us to expedite global social solidarity where a better system can play a huge positive role and be a catalyst in opening plural brain might and collectively materialize a dynamic educational culture to direct billions to the end of the tunnel, where there is light and away from darkness and predatory practices, with no beastly behaviors.

Humanity must move toward justice, peace, and sustainability, where equity, compassion, love, and dignity become the norm so that everyone can live with no fear and is able to have their deepest wishes and desire answered to furnish a good cause and bring about happiness and true affinity for all. Believe in divinity and in asking God for a piece of heaven on Earth and hope for personal serenity of mind, body, spirit, and for social and global tranquility. It is noteworthy that humanity has entered into a very complex period that certainly calls for brightness of mind and vigilant character, since we are attacked from many angles and in various ways, occasionally without even noticing many subtle onslaughts; we must maneuver and act alert to ward off their hazardous impacts.

Of course terrorism, war of aggression, fear of atomic and nuclear war, global warming, and presence of fascist and despotic governments, fear for economic depression, and other nasty stuff are well alive and should worry humanity. But unless the root cause to so many cultural, spiritual, social, and economic ailments are diagnosed and meticulously attended to, they will bring the end of time. The real problem is with the gradual fading away of the essence of humanity, which we meditate on in private domain and public pursuits to strengthen and rejuvenate our lives.

In our everyday quest for advanced technology and further automation endeavors, it slips our mind that humanity is losing ground to robotic progression. We are engaged with evermore industrialization and soulless technology is becoming part of our thinking process and living pattern, which inevitably wipes out the hallmarks of being human.

Historical facts dictate as tools, instruments, and machineries progress, more shift and displacement of humans originates, where gradual disconnection and divergence of dwellers pinnacles at present age. As science advances and revolutionizes technology, it gives birth to societies that characterize the individualistic state of mind, which since befitted capitalist mentality extremely well and played an ace into the financially elites' hands, and they exacerbated the traumatic effects of individualism by further isolating humanity.

It is not a secret that because of technology we have remarkably transcended to a dynamic human realm and have magically masterminded the influx and the outflow of information, but industrialization and technology have also rubbed humanity from its sense of belonging and interconnectedness, disconnecting so many from nature and turning billions into rat race societies.

The irony is that capitalists are obsessed with teamwork, collective activities, and co-ops; they adore mass production, assembly lines, and division of labor, which maximizes commodities. The fruits of collective efforts, all the profits and values created by communal work must go to private ownership of the means of production, the capitalists, which in return, the workers have to put up with starving wages in order to survive.

It should make sense to have prognosis of troubles facing us and not saunter to compromise our precious human qualities, or jeopardize celestial human feelings and emotions, not to ignore our sense of justice, morality, and sacrifice, kinship and laughter, devotion, or our sense of feeling alive, which without sharing it does not mean much—acting compassionate, humanity's wonder for beauty and love of nature, our passion for art and music. Not to lose sight of our beliefs in God and the heavens above and to hail creativity, to cherish human imagination, to capitalize on our human intuition, and a host of other meaningful and valuable human attributes, which we cannot do without.

Let's not be forced into self-denial and become purged from who we really are; let's not act zombie-like and be possessed only with our own affairs, and let's stray from behaving stoically toward others' pain and suffering, which should be alerting, since we slowly but surely are giving into becoming robot parallel, in acting cold and mechanical toward what should matter. We ought to accredit our human qualities and value our sense of reasoning power, our prudency, because we are conscious beings who can deliver miracles through evolutionary thoughts and in making the right choices. Humanity must deprecate (harsh disapproval) violence no matter who, or which side, is to blame; it is true that we can become enslaved by our greed and insensible desires.

The bottom line is about behaving decent, since it does not matter what sort of economic system needs to prevail; what certainly matters is the politics behind the financial and governing entities that manipulate the entire social and financial agendas.

If fraudulent and dishonest people are to manage funds, the allocation of resources, and to control the incomings and outflows of the markets for their own interest, then even God-sent monetary policies and miracle-like socioeconomic plans and strategies won't help because the crooks will find loopholes and undignified ways to disenfranchise people from their legal and natural rights. Their heinous actions make dying easy for millions and living very difficult for so many innocent souls.

Therefore, we must pay attention to who is who in the world of politics and not employ insidious characters who often buy their way up to hold high positions and abuse their power for self-interest and their own ambition. They pay fealty to make citizens defenseless and influence policies where it befits them, which instead, citizens ought to engage candidates with integrity and elect those agents truly committed to working for the people, rather than abusing their might to fill their deep pockets and extort what belongs to the republic.

What differentiates us from the rest of the beasts is that we are astute, can be amiable (convivial, sociable); we have the will to choose and to communicate with awakened conscious. We can potentiate our mind power to one day conquer the entire cosmos, to become part of heaven above and kneel to God.

But in order to fulfill our objectives, we must first live and let live in peace and respect others' sovereignty. We need to behave righteously before employing any other business; we should appreciate and respect creation since God is the proprietor of all there is. God is omni-temporal, omnipresent, omnipotent, omniscient, and omni-benevolence, in which we should trust and be reminded that no one has the right to punish others or ought to be allowed to take anyone's life.

The cosmic energy from the source circulates in everything and everyone in trillions of forms and shapes, which must be respected. It substantiates varieties in existence since in turn "the life-force itself" is the effect of an infinitely potent and greater cause that is beyond the human nervous system and senses to discern, but we certainly are able to see the majestic intent and the sublime work of God, as infinite creatures are the recipients of God's delightful work.

It is crucial to distinguish hocus pocus claims in proving God and to reject charlatanism and baseless advocacies of the almighty, but rather fathom the majestic effects of God's intention, to believe in our maker through faith. Absorbing philosophical theories and compelling scientific notions have acknowledged a higher power beyond what we can experience and are fascinated with the intricacies and wonders of the forces of universe. Common sense is challenged and flares rational thinking to believe in God.

Without accepting God, humankind will lose enormous ground in moral behavior and righteous actions, as no mortal should be trusted with absolute morality and utter virtuosity. All beings, other than God, are relative, impermanent, and bound to destruction that should not be assumed as absolute, but only God. It is true that modernism and the age of reason plays and upholds decisive outcomes in our lives, which need to be reckoned with; otherwise how would morality would be probable, if depleted of intelligence and in lacking wisdom. Further it does not matter how advanced and modernized humanity becomes; we must appreciate the absolute power of the universe, which has favored humankind to keenly adopt and yet acknowledge our effort to identify with nature, to converge and fulfill human destiny.

"I believe that a full understanding of this remarkable human capacity for scientific discovery ultimately requires the insight that our power in this respect is the gift of the universe's creator, who in that ancient and powerful phrase, has made humanity in the image of God (Genesis I: 26-27). Through the exercise of this gift, those working in fundamental physics are able to discern a world of deep and beautiful order—a universe shot through with signs of mind. I believe that it is indeed the mind of that world's creator that is perceived in this way. Science is possible because the universe is a divine creation." — former Cambridge University professor of mathematical physics John Polkinghorne, as quoted in his book *Quantum Physics and Theology: An Unexpected Kinship*

Under premises of bad faith, Sartre mentions self-deception, particularly the act of not accepting that one has freedom of choices, and hence evading responsibilities, and avoiding the anxiety of decision making, where lack of self-acceptance, especially the act of not admitting or fooling oneself about what is true about oneself and lack of self-assurance or self-esteem that denies one from acting upon existence and provides the condition for operating as a thing in existence.

This should awaken one to know oneself and grasp knowledge of one's environment and natural phenomenon inducting inference and the power of reasoning, to test hypotheses by means of observation and experimentation, where cultivating human and natural resources can benefit humankind, which should solidify this undeniable fact that the more we learn and are intelligently updated and attuned with the wonders of the universe, the more enthralled we should become with the awesome power of God. All our choices and decision makings ought to be positively productive, as God intends them to be, and align with constructive endeavors and not struggle in vain, but with having a purpose.

Let's be reminded that man is not all-knowing God and when people act with good intentions and behave within moral context, it can significantly improve relationships among the inhabitants, but it can also produce unintended repercussions or undesirable consequences. What is considered morality for some might not be so moral for others that can be of double standards and perhaps create ambiguities in different societies. When certain ethically oriented concepts are admissible only because they are inextricably associated with that act, it should raise a delicate question of morality to whose standard. Because moral dilemmas can occur in mutually exclusive ethical actions, or moral choices are equally binding, often leading to puzzling situations.

This should call for seeking knowledge and adapting to more learning, to march toward reaching the epoch of humanism, and to conquer advanced fields in science, philosophy, and cultural dynamism, in which people can be enlightened to become the ultra-beneficiaries of what life has to offer. Higher conscious can allow more equitable societies, since humanity is so far away from behaving just, in which so many are struggling every day to make ends meet, as they are literally treated as they should be condemned to do hard time, even if death beholds them—what is all the fuss about?

We live in a world where our abysmal ignorance has hampered our awareness of the reality, making millions unable to detect the demonic forces living among us, as the predators are hiding behind closed doors; they are immune to any legal persecution or any other justifiable punishment. It seems power and influence have blinded the violators, where they utterly have forgotten God, as if the culprit's sadistic financial rituals are hardwired into their brain with one-track-mindedness to worship money replacing God.

We are relative beings and ready to mix emotions; our feelings change with time, and we vacillate and can be compromised. We should not be relied on as absolute beings; we will have our flaws and are vulnerable to imperfection; our dark side can cause colossal moral depravity and may unleash abhorrent ill results beyond imagination, as known in so many genocides and exercised in other beastly deeds through the course of human history.

We are permeable to the forces of evil and assailable from baggage of greed, hatred, resentment, intolerance, prejudice, egotistical behaviors, cynicism, and other ugly conduct, but the good news is that we have the potential to overcome darkness, no matter how prone we are to sinful and dreadful maneuvers. Otherwise, humanity would definitely not be capable to carry on for billions of years and still be standing. It is precisely because the power of goodness and virtues is much more potent than wickedness in humankind, which has surely managed to win, and in outdoing the vile stuff. Hence, making it necessary to deny obsession for the material world and reject what tempts us to do wrong and to understand it is what we do not see that decisively controls what we do not see.

Newton's theory of cause and effect is applicable to the visible world, which without, it would have perplexed science, knowing that it is the "unseen world" that rules what is perceived and known to us, which has puzzled the most prominent scientists, not knowing the motives and why things are the way they are in the subatomic world of particles and in quantum life. The irony is that the more science digs into the unknown and unravels mindboggling phenomena, the more curious and interested scientists become in finding out about the awesome power of an intelligent designer behind the majestic universe.

The birth of science as we know it arguably began with Isaac Newton's formulation of the laws of gravitation and motion.

It is no exaggeration to say that physics was reborn in the early 20th century with the twin revolutions of quantum mechanics and the theory of relativity, said Paul Davis.

"Science is incompetent to reason upon the creation of matter itself out of nothing. We have reached the utmost limit of our thinking faculties when we have admitted that because matter cannot be eternal and self-existent it must have been created." — physicist and mathematician James Clerk Maxwell, who is credited with formulating classical electromagnetic theory and whose contributions to science are considered the same magnitude as those of Einstein and Newton.

The reality brings us much closer to the vicinity of idealism, absolutism, the theory that absolute is defined by the dictionary as regarded as "a mind, ego, self, spirit, soul is the fundamental, undermined reality in the universe upon which all things depend for their existence but which depends on nothing else for its existence, further, all things can be rationally deduced, from which all finite things flow in a progressive development of its thoughts, and in which all things exist as a thought." In idealism, Plato puts it this way: "the true, absolute reality is the realm of the perfect, independently existing, unchanging, timeless form (ideas), and the true object of all knowledge."

It perhaps sounded preposterous when Berkeley's idealism, sometimes mentalism, or immaterialism was first introduced, which concluded that, "1-The theory that the universe is an embodiment of a mind. 2-Reality is dependent for its existence up on a mind and its activities. 3-all reality is mental, spiritual, and psychical, matter the physical, and does not exist. 4-No knowledge is possible except of mental states and processes and that is all that exists. Reality is explained in terms of such psychic phenomena as minds, selves, spirits, ideas, and absolute thought, rather than in terms of matter. 5-Only mind type activities and their idea type content exist. The external world is not physical.

The above assessment could have perhaps been an exaggeration, portraying Berkeley as an irrational idealist. And it would have been perhaps normal to think that Berkeley did not make much sense because only atoms were retroactively known to scientists then, but later on appeared sub-atomic particles known as quarks, and quantum mechanics revolutionized our perception of the so-called reality, which modern science is grappling with as we speak, trying to understand the unseen world. Many scholars and philosophers of the past insisted on this. "To be is to be perceived"; according to Berkeley, the physical world exists only while it is being perceived.

The discovery of new subatomic particles has shed light on fundamental forces of nature, where the indivisible world of "quark" is the building blocks of all that is observed, including humans, trees, cars, buildings, the birds and the bees, stars and the entire galaxies, and everything else, where for so long the question was, did matter (our brain) first make thoughts possible or was a soulful mind and spirit and a thought responsible for giving birth to material beings?

Berkeley had two overriding philosophical concerns. The first was to deal with skeptical worries about the material world. How can we know that such a world exists? The second was to counter what Berkeley saw as the growing tendency of the scientists and philosophers of his day to push God to the periphery in their thinking about the world. Scientists were beginning to adopt an increasingly mechanistic view of how the universe worked, with God required, at best, merely to crank the starting handle on the great world machine, after which his presence was no longer required. Berkeley wanted to bring God back to center stage, and rightly so, since discording cosmic conscious from what is human is just not possible, where human spirit is undeniably fed by the sacred energy of the universe.

We often look for what is already driving us, where we search for purpose to satisfy the dynamics that control our lives and in search for meaning. We intuitively (unlearned) look for answers as we meditate on questioning: Who am I? How did we get here? Where did we come from? Why are we here? How did it all begin? Where are we going? What does it all mean? Is there any purpose? Who is behind this remarkable cosmic discipline? What is driving our astonishing and orderly universe? What is consciousness? Can we locate consciousness in our brain? And so on. It does really not matter if one has made up one's mind to play existentialist or deny our creator, since searching for meaning is etched into our soul. It is in our DNA to subconsciously look for a cause and to perceive God, since the effects and the complexity of the entire cosmos is way beyond our human mind to assess. What is obvious is did we not appear out of nowhere, just by chance, and without an infinitely smart creator?

"I have concluded that we are in a world made by rules created by an intelligence. Believe me, everything that we call chance today won't make sense anymore. To me it is clear that we exist in a plan which is governed by rules that were created, shaped by a universal intelligence and not by chance." — Michio Kaku, theoretical physicist and string theory pioneer.

What is clear is that there are basically two schools of thought. "Atheists" also called nonbelievers, or the skeptics, which they are under the impression that some non-intelligent, non-instinctive matter accidently "poof" started it all. Then we have "theists," or believers in God who accept that an idea, a thought, a spirit, some sort of energy, a soulful source initiated life from the very beginning.

"People take it for granted that the physical world is both ordered and intelligible. The underlying order in nature-the laws of physics-are simply accepted as given, as brute facts. Nobody asks where they came from; at least they do not do so in polite company. However, even the most atheistic scientist accepts as an act of faith that the universe is not absurd, that there is a rational basis to physical existence manifested as law-like order in nature that is at least partly comprehensible to us. So science can proceed only if the scientist adopts an essentially theological worldview." — physicist Paul Davies, winner of the 2001 Kelvin Medal issued by the Institute of Physics and the winner of the 2002 Faraday Prize issued by the Royal Society (amongst other awards), as cited in his book *God and the New Physics*.

But eventually the science atheists upheld proudly to grandiose the empirical world, where everything is logically assessed and experimentally tested with precise results, and definite outcomes proved otherwise. As science and technology also validated there are no matters, they tore into subatomic particles and the world of quantum physics and string theory, a theory in physics that says "all elementary particles are manifestation of the vibration of one-dimensional strings." They testified even the hardest of matters are in the realm of subatomic world and comprised of "quarks," or known as "antiparticles," which are with no doubt energy driven, leaving no ambiguity that our universe is idea driven and fueled with sacred energy emanating from an intelligent source beyond human grasp. Where the cosmic energy is the source, the cause that is circulating in everything and everyone in billions of forms, if not trillions to substantiate varieties in existence, which we are the effects, since in turn the life force itself is the effect to a cause that is beyond our nervous system and human senses to discern.

"I'm not an atheist, and I don't think I can call myself a pantheist. We are in the position of a little child entering a huge library filled with books in many languages. The child knows someone must have written those books. It does not know how. It does not understand the languages in which they are written. The child dimly suspects a mysterious order in the books but doesn't know what it is. That, it seems to me, is the attitude of even the most intelligent human being toward God." — Albert Einstein

Clearly, cause and effect is the essence of Newton's world, which is only applicable to what is seen. Without it, science will be perplexed in the visible world, but reason forces us to accordingly believe in what seems unreal, such as thoughts, memories, emotions, feelings, numbers, the maneuverability of our senses and how they communicate with the external world, and send messages back and forth to our nervous system, and our brain, as our bodies obey the commands to execute a task or the quantum world, the world of string theory and our faith in God, which ironically, humanity cannot survive without. I believe it is the world of the unseen that rules what is perceived and known to us, as we are only able to visualize and detect the effects of what is not seen, which has puzzled the most prominent scientists not knowing why things are the way they are in the subatomic world of particles and in quantum life.

"The more I study science, the more I believe in God." — Albert Einstein

According to the representational theory of perception adopted by many of the leading thinkers of Berkeley's day, we do not perceive the world directly. Rather, our perception of the world is intervened (mediated) by reliable mental entities called ideas. What makes it interesting is the more scientists explore and dig into the unknown, the closer they come to the so-called mumbo jumbo (abracadabras) of Berkeley and his colleagues. It seems the world of matter is just an illusion or should appear different without our sensory intervention. Berkeley believed there are no material substances, only mental substances.

Suppose, they say, for example, when you look at an apple, what you are immediately aware of is not the apple itself, but convincing sensory appearances that exhibit, as it were, before your mind's eye. What you experience directly are changing ideas of shape, color, and so on, moving across your internal, subjective cinema screen. The apple itself lies behind these sensory semblances (appearances) as their cause.

Chiefly a 20th century philosophical movement embracing diverse doctrines but focusing on analyses of individual existence in an unfathomable universe and the plight of individuals who must assume the ultimate responsibility for acts of free will without any certain knowledge of what is right or wrong or good or bad should be redefined. Because contemporary philosophers, prominent scientists, physicists, scholars, and thinkers have unlocked many puzzling matters via technology and through power of reasoning and deductions, where inquisitive characters and sound-minded researchers unanimously believe in intelligent design, where definite roles of a divine intelligence could not be overlooked in grandly impressive creation.

And unless we earnestly believe in our almighty creator and having a dependable moral compass, so many can turn loose to do the unthinkable, including wrongdoings in a bloodied revolution, or in any other turn of event, which does not make any sense "to do wrong for making it right" and sure be afraid of the fact that "what comes around, goes around," where sooner or later, the punishment or the reward catches on.

And yes, we also are relatively the product of our environment, since of course, the rich elites are no exception and to believe otherwise defies logic, which must indicate a double standard of what reason should dictate since successive generations of affluence, their next and next propagations (descendants) are exposed and become disciplined to follow their predecessors footsteps and culture of thinking to identify with the cultural pretext and its creeds to mandate what their forefathers deemed necessary to keep the status quo, to facilitate and preserve the foundation of their prestige and power.

I challenge those who can be put in the atmosphere of wealth and power, and if they could be positioned in similar social and economic class as the rich elites, it will be very difficult to believe they would do otherwise.

What I am saying is, when people are not exercising the mechanism of influence and power and are not holding and are devoid of managing too much wealth or do not hold highly authoritative command, it makes it easy for them to be judgmental.

And they are not practically engaged with the actual situations and phenomena and not able to experience what is truly taking place. It makes them irrelevant to the actual mechanism of what is taking place and unfamiliar with circumstances, making it very difficult to facilitate thorough and correct judiciousness. We need to understand we can be vulnerable to sell out and become tempted with the goodies of life, as it is so difficult to challenge the toxic environment, and alluring (seductive) circumstances that people evolve with 24/7, definitely matters in their overall decision makings, as it can often manifest character flaws, and misconduct.

Unless the very cultural fabrics and thought processes of any dysfunctional society are fundamentally changed, it will be business as usual, in which without a grassroots cultural revolution in socioeconomic agendas, it will perhaps be a temporary fix, but most definitely not innovatively reliable and not progressively sustainable in the long term.

It is not rational and does not make any sense to call for savagery and resort to violence in resurrecting against the system and showing vengeance to overthrow the plutocratic governments, which of course are going to be fueled with chaos, looting, rape, murder, loss of innocent lives, and other unthinkable tragedies; there are many peaceful means and practical alternatives to get rid of unduly corrupt systems. In the meanwhile, any sound mind should ask when in a capitalist system. Often money means life especially for the poor and the disadvantaged, since without a doubt billions live below the line of poverty, then who is really asking for war, when 62 individuals own more wealth than half of the world's population. When so many people are dying because of hunger and lack of nutrition, lack of medical care, and without proper hygiene, but 90% of the profit and world resources goes to 1% of the globe's filthy rich, which since has placed people between a rock and a hard place, then who is really at fault? And I wonder if God has anything to do with it.

I believe that the imperial elites and the filthy rich are testing people's boiling point, petrifying the helpless. They are so immersed in their game plans and do not realize you must leave people some practical option to survive; if billions of deprived and helpless souls could do metempsychosis (reincarnate) themselves into a better situation, they would have done so, if they could get out of financial cul-de-sac of living, they would have done so. Obviously the international capitalist system cannot drain the gridlocks of the social and economic swamp, and as incompetent as the system is, they sure look for a way out through wars and violence, where discarding lives and fear of punishment is the key for their survival.

But despite the brutal behavior of the rich elites, the objective should be to stop violence and to save people regardless of their faith, race, gender, nationality, and social and financial status. If so, then why should any future system resort to outrage, inhumane punishment, or barbarism, since it will defeat the intention to institute a more civilized and orderly government. And unless we earnestly believe in our almighty creator, so many can turn loose to do the unthinkable—no matter what are the turn of events, including a bloodied revolution, and be afraid of the fact that "what comes around, goes around," perhaps with a little delay, but certainly the wickedness of one's action catches on.

Where the cosmic energy is the source, the cause circulating in everything and everyone in billions of forms, if not trillions to substantiate varieties in existence, which we are the effects, since in turn the life force itself is the effect to a cause that is beyond our nervous system and human senses to discern. What is clear, the cause and effect is the essence of Newton's world, which is only applicable to what is seen, since without it science will be perplexed in the visible world, but reason forces us to accordingly believe in what seems unreal, as thoughts, memories, emotions, feelings, numbers, the maneuverability of our senses, the quantum world, and our faith in God, which ironically humanity cannot survive without.

The reason we identify with thoughts, ideas, feeling, emotions, and memories is because we are also energy driven; the fact that we discern through our senses and identify with our mind is because we are energy driven, are our senses, our minds and memories, which should make one wonder: What do nominal apathetic disbelievers think? But I honestly applaud atheists and agnostics, as they do not behave hypocritically and hide behind the veil of religion and God, as many prominent figures and the ruling elites do, to institute their ungodly plans against the innocent people for the sake of maximizing profit. Let's overcome this regiment of dehumanization and overwhelming travesties and not scoop so low to pride our lower selves, rather than acting pious to patent our higher selves because humanly conduct should call for the integrity of mind, body, and spirit to act efficaciously (virtuous, moral) and positively productive.

Since the overwhelming signs of cosmogony (the creation of the origin of the universe) finger point to an intelligent source infinitely greater than humankind, where compelling evidence is colossally stronger than you think in which for some reasons beyond human comprehension. It seems we are being tested, as divinity, orderly nature and living protocol should remind us of a deity and call forth decency in mind and manner against all odds and oppose the deprecation of (attack, berate) irrational bodily desires and toxically tempting environment, where clean living deems necessary, as if we must pass this phase to graduate, and ascend to higher realms.

We are destined to due diligence for becoming awakened and to reach an evolutionary enlightenment epoch to bring the best out of humanity and kneel to God and proudly utter we are worthy of your image. This need not leave any doubt that wrongdoings and cruelty in actions will fail, where ignorance can become one's worse enemy, leaving us with no choice but to relentlessly march toward gaining knowledge and information, to become educated, intelligent, and learn to be compos mentis, and as ethical as possible, to remote the evils of idiocy and filter out curses of dullness, but to adhere to significant living, improving the self and for helping others, so that we can live a life worth living and align to connect with the caravan of a purposeful universe. To proudly lift one's head up and honestly say "I did not live in vain. I fulfilled what I was sent here for, as I did not search for a 'hedonistic paradox,' which defines a person who constantly seeks pleasure for himself will not find it. Since my desires were not motivated by self-indulgence in physical gratification or rancorous (nasty, malevolent, spiteful) behaviors, despite a cultural view that elaborated on a hedonistic approach in life and found pleasure in humanism."

It is a bit of a smother to reach one's constructive goal here in America and materialize one's mission, that I believe is worth mentioning because we have gone so far away from the horrific days of slavery and prejudice that we ought to claim today's world as more civilized than before, as we should for now faithfully depend on the Constitution, that is the bread and butter of our American lifestyle. I am sure the Constitution has contributed plenty to the relative freedom people presently enjoy and are able to say what we deem necessary, write without persecution, to vote without discrimination, believe the faith we want, and assemble peacefully to denounce injustice. Because of democracy, we can better manifest the vibrating voice of God we call consciousness and impregnate living with the best of life's offerings.

Because of freedom and democracy people can test their shortcomings, their ignorance, and their positives and negatives, their success and failures, and not be afraid to talk about it or seek help, where any cultural, scientific, philosophical, social, political, economic, psychological, sexual, or any other subject for that matter can be examined in the laboratory of life, which can reflect us positively and bring us closer to the miracle of tutelage (enlightenment) and truth. Socrates believed that no one does evil of one's own free will; if one knew the good, one would not hesitate to do good. One commits evil only from ignorance of what the good is.

To further challenge our way to access the pinnacle of freedom and true democracy without fear, as many nations are not as lucky to experience. We should gravitate toward reaching an ideal society where one might presently say that is utopia talking, but then again, let's not deny human volcanic potential, which can build the impossible if fully cultivated and should prove the pessimists wrong.

We know that science is the most reliable way to understand the real world and what science indicates is true awareness, since within the sphere of conscious able nature and meticulously disciplined universe, our findings and experiences become possible. It is no longer an enigma that a formless, shapeless energy oriented, and unseen thought molds and controls what is formed.

The conscious is the universe. It is the reality in which we experience the physical world, and it is within the light of human awareness that we make the actual physical world possible. We see a subjective self and the outside objective world, in which we acquaint the substantive matter through our senses, where in reality this duality does not exist. The body and mind conceptualize through consciousness experiencing itself, body and mind are the experiences in the consciousness, in which consciousness is the universe, manifesting infinite possibilities, infinite imagination, infinite creativity, infinite intuition, infinite synchronization, infinite liberation, infinite insight, infinite love, infinite freedom, infinite aspiration, infinite beauty, for the mind of man to perform magic, that is a undeniable part of the wholeness of this miraculous event we call life.

With riveted might and destined to harness the neuroplasticity of man's brain where equanimity (balance) of mind is molded and made to collectively conquer what seems impossible, as we optimize and lay the fertile ground for the next stages of our evolutionary life process as possible.

Obviously man cannot hold on to what is impertinence. Once we realize the transcendent part of humanity is not constrained within life and death, we can let go of the fear of holding to what does not pertain; then we have discarded the fear of death. The truth will set us free; it will trigger self-awareness and potentiate one to discover self, which is interwoven with the might of universe.

And yes, we sometimes go through so much pain and suffering that can perhaps break us, but difficult times mold the bearer of agony into a sturdy and tough individual that often morphs and transcends one to discover a higher self, which can mature us because of fulfilling enormous tasks despite the dark seasons. It seems that the almighty mold can make us through darkness. As the caterpillar crawls and twists and turns, not realizing it is destined to become a beautiful species with wings, to elegantly fly, as butterflies play a critical role in our environment. Its purpose, other than being part of an evolutionary ecosystem, is just to allow the more conscious mind to enjoy its grace and colorful wings.

And with no doubt, enlightenment enables us to exit the cocoon of darkness since knowledge and information empowers man to bring out the best of technologies in sociocultural, socioeconomic, socio-industrial, and many other exciting fields, endorsing humanity with enchanted power to fly exquisitely and to serve our destiny well and in becoming as glorified as we can be, where no tyrannical system or any other ill-willed creature can stop what is just, where goodness is promised and prudence destined to be.

Our first priority should be to believe in an intelligent and orderly world, in which we are undeniably part of God's plan to purposefully carry the torch of living. To reach human destiny, to defy what is chaotically manifested, where humanity can bring balance and preserve equity, to deny the rich elites the might and stop inhumane powerful regimes from destroying the entire world, since many of them are blindly rushing to end it all. We must awaken to the offenders' wrongdoings since humanity must not give in to unintelligent and disorderly conduct before it is too late.

After all, countless scientists, scholarly minded physicists, and visionaries do not grapple with myth-driven ideas to chaotically present their findings. And in making scientific inquires based on an unorderly world and irresponsible settings, where they hope and often spend years and years of surgical research to methodically innovate new ideas for better living, where reason and disciplinary manifesto can be constituted based on an intelligent and resolute nature, which without constructive discoveries would never be possible.

"If you study science deep enough and long enough, it will force you to believe in God." — Lord William Kelvin, who was noted for his theoretical work on thermodynamics, the concept of absolute zero and the Kelvin temperature scale based upon it.

In cultivating reason, studying science, refining philosophy, or digging any other educational subject, an awakening ideology should result in "no logical paradox" where fallacies are defied and that logos (divine wisdom) pervade all things and all activities in the universe. As the foremost requirements are objectified in human beings in conscionable forms and intelligence, believing in divinity, in having faith, empathy, and hope, in sweet and bitter memories, in courage, intuitions, and in our senses and believing in self.

In good feelings and emotions, in reasoning power, in seeking freedom, honesty, truth, and justice, in making sacrifice, in our stewardship, in our fatefulness, in our curiosity and devotion, in our longing (craving) to belong where we know we matter, in safety, and in being immune from life's perils, in our collectiveness (groupie nature) in seeking kinship and happiness, knowledge, and information, and in asking why, in having will and responsibility, purpose, in our prayers, and in our wishing wells, in our compassion, generosity, in patience, and defying the odds, in resenting and challenging bad times, in our trust, dignity, respect, in our appreciation, in being grateful and considerate, in our responsibility, imagination and dreams, love and beauty, in virtuous conduct and feeling proud, in philanthropy and helping others, in behaving as human beings, as the infinite voice of God vibrates in good conscious, making incessant revelations to viable souls, granting humanity the worthiness of God's image. We must ascend to a realm where guns do not speak louder than words, not even for goodness and morality's sake, but because the push of a button can literally wipe out half the world, where pressing one more button can destroy the other half. What is promising: The overall global mentality seeks peace. It is thrilling to know new generations have surpassed excellence and are equipped with intelligence and potent reasoning ability beyond expectation, and since women are definitely enlightened to fully participate in challenging the road ahead.

No bigotry intended, but more women ought to compete for capturing higher posts. Since by nature they precede men in "emotional intelligence," they are attuned with multitasking, where they have to navigate between jobs and family responsibilities. Women are also as good as men, if not better, in having the ability to apply knowledge, to manipulate one's environment or to think abstractly as measured by objective criteria. In a competitive world, no nation can stand on one leg for too long and truly succeed by keeping the other half at a disadvantaged position.

"Too often the great decisions are originated and given form in bodies made up wholly of men, or so completely dominated by them that whatever of special value women have to offer is shunted aside without expression." — Eleanor Roosevelt

And lastly, let's not forget, in any democracy oriented society, we learn to moderately exercise our complexities. We can discard our inferiority complex and pick up a lesson or two to devoid a superiority complex. But we cannot openly defy inert or habitual indisposition of activities unless rectitude (goodness, righteousness, virtue) can stem out of democracy through awaking and by the power of induction, that is literally not possible in a dictatorial environment.

"Believe you can and you're halfway there." — Theodor Roosevelt

If a nation is not stubborn to advance in education and literacy and is reluctant to socioculturally persist on insightfulness, where gaining information and knowledge can decisively help to train and make us realize the significance of being free, then we most likely become disappointed with no avail. The edicts (order, instruction) of freedom can correctly be managed and mindfully digested through enlightenment and by reasoning might of societal do's and don'ts, to overcome unawareness, to behold important tasks, and to help humanity reach the pinnacle of success without extreme collateral damage.

Open-mindedness makes it possible to receptively acquaint with what is human and perhaps competent enough to trash vile behaviors in making a better world possible. Democracy can definitely serve as an arable (tillable-fertile) ground to plant healthy seeds for a new life; no better tool can alert us of the alarming state that we are globally engaged in, and the only way through which we need to correct our disparaging (insulting atmosphere) that is absolutely not befitting what should be human. Knowing if you do not stand for something constructively positive, you can fall for anything ruinous, and perhaps illusively (deceptive) destructive.

By deceptive, I mean one should question how any system, organization, any government, network, or any entity for that matter can get rid of poverty, extreme income inequality, economic collapse, hunger, corruption, terrorism, war of aggressions, forceful displacements of innocent people, or any other inhumane misdeed by purposely feeding into such malicious and disorderly conduct; mishaps as such are literally the cause of societal ailments. We cannot be in the business of normalizing violence and expect benevolence. It can only define insanity as "doing the same thing over and over again and expecting different results" — Albert Einstein

Because the system is not potentiated to truly educate the masses, does not have the means to correct its inherently flaws, and cannot constructively deal with its stern shortcomings, hence, refuges to force and violence as the only alternative to quell opposition, quite critics and frighten the people.

It is not exxaggerated to say that: global establishment has failed, private tyrannical institutions, and the oligarchical elites, they have replaced the state despotic power, what keeps it afloat is the military industrial complex, just like Roman Empire, Mongolian Empire that had suppressed people on the account of military aggression, and via exerting dictatorial rules. Mega corporations in cahoots with imperialist governments have managed to internationally create growing workers insecurity by design, risking the collapse of the whole capitalist system. Where contrary to the past eras, modern life style that the capitalist system desperately needs to export the so called freedom and democracy, to sell its ideas through affiliated media advertisings, Hollywood, Bollywood and alike, via news agencies, and by its propaganda machines, which has ironically become a blessing in disguise for the world consumers. It enables ideas to spread as fast as the speed of light, where thoughts, and war of notions can become wild fire compeer (equal), and quite damaging if conceits (concepts) are not dynamic and progressive in nature; since empty rhetoric and belligerency should undermine a nation's pride, and question its credibility as a herald (harbinger, forerunner) for freedom, human right and democracy. Making liberty and hope for the pursuit of happiness as futile and a farce, as bellowing into the bigger end of a horn.

Because of significant advances in media technology and revolutionized ways of communication through which spreading imperative agendas and decisive news has well evidenced the omission of occurrence (failure) of governmental institutions; as well as exalting people's awareness, denoting the leap manifesto and the impetus behind the paradigm shift which has consequence to the solidarity of the left transnational communities. The left is collaborating to defy inept leaders in many parts of the world, where billions are striving to cultivate transformational leadership rather than transactional charlatans.

People are adamant to grass Rooty castrate (change) the existing state of affairs, and are haughtily (high hat, proudly) determined to challenge the utopian state of mind to assert progressive socio-cultural, socio-political, and a pragmatically socio- economic system. It is greed and arrogance of the corporate elites and their goon's systematic abuse of power which has prompted division and hostility forming radical ideologies, often dangerous ones, as well as chaotic that can unnecessarily beget violence and mandate loss of thousands of lives, if not millions, so that a better system, a savior can be born.

"The corporate plutocracy somehow believes no better living is ever possible without their incredulous and incriminating ways of dealing with society in the name of a free market economy, which unleashes its predatory behavior repressing the middle class, the working class, and the poor, and exploiting what has already caused so much damage to the entire globe beyond repair."

History can reference that: no ruling system can for long survive by killing the human within the system, where they strive to operate through fear and govern by force, as the imperial elites, and the superbly affluent desolate caring and deny responsibility as power and pride blinds them evading fair play and bereft justice, since the culprits blatantly (vulgar, offensively, brazenly) promulgate (declare, proclaim) self- interest and encourage corruption. "It is imperative for any progressive system to direct its goals and activities at a global scale where the greater good is to benefit everyone, to avoid acting small and narrow-mindedly and not become restrained in doing justice because of social, cultural, nationality, race, ethnicity, sectarianism, color, gender, religious, economic classification, or any discriminatory factors."

Democratic governments should effectively serve the citizens who helped put them in power, rather than to mislead and become complicit in the afflictions of the mighty rich, dealing in connivance with misdeeds for the wealthy elites against the people.

God bless goodness, God bless freedom and democracy, God bless human rights, God bless justice, God bless global unity, God bless liberty and the pursuit of happiness, and God bless America.

— Patrick Henry's "Give me Liberty or Give Me Death"

Printed in the United States
By Bookmasters